LEAN
AND Lovin' It

To my wife, Susan,
for her limitless love and enduring support

Lean AND Lovin' It

*Exceptionally Delicious
Recipes for Low-Fat Living and
Permanent Weight Loss*

DON MAUER

ILLUSTRATIONS BY CATHIE BLECK

CHAPTERS PUBLISHING, LTD., SHELBURNE, VERMONT 05482

Published by Chapters Publishing Ltd., 2085 Shelburne Road, Shelburne, VT 05482

Library of Congress Cataloging-in-Publication Data
Mauer, Don.
    Lean and lovin' it: exceptionally delicious recipes for low-fat living
and permanent weight loss / Don Mauer; illustrations by Cathie Bleck
      p.   cm.
    Includes index.
    ISBN 1-881527-97-2 (softcover)
    1. Reducing diets—Recipes.   I. Title.
RM222.2.M3796 1996
641.5'63—dc20   95-53856

Printed and bound in Canada by Best Book Manufacturers, Inc.
Louiseville, Quebec

Designed by Susan McClellan

Don Mauer's "Sweet and Sour Cabbage" originally appeared in *Thin for Life: 10 Keys to Success from People
Who Have Lost Weight and Kept It Off* by Anne M. Fletcher, Chapters Publishing Ltd., 1994.

10 9 8 7 6 5

ACKNOWLEDGMENTS

To my wife, Susan. For your patience, unflinching conviction and intuitive sense about good ideas and great food.

To my Mom. For your love and support. For Christmas and birthday gifts over the years that provided me with much of my kitchen equipment, including my first food processor, and many wonderful cookbooks.

To Tarry Fadel. For your starting everything by writing a praise-filled letter about me to the *Chicago Sun-Times*. And for sharing many wonderful recipes and believing a new life could emerge from the wreckage of the past.

To Bev Bennett. For selecting my story for the "House Special" feature of the *Chicago Sun-Times*. Without your assistance and accurate advice, I would not have become a columnist or a cookbook author.

To Sharon Sanders. For being the first person to contact me about my low-fat recipes and lifestyle. Your original feature article about me would have shamed a shameless publicist for its continuous high praise.

To Olivia Wu. For believing I was able to write about food and taking a risk by allowing me to be a columnist. For your encouragement and for teaching me the essentials of column writing.

To Anne Fletcher. For introducing me to a national audience through your books and requests to appear on television and in newspaper articles. Without your assistance, I would not now be a published cookbook author.

To my brother Chef Thomas Mauer. For your keen insights, patient explanations, terrific ideas, tremendous recipes and love.

To my brother Robert. For your unerring belief in me, your spiritual strength and your confidence-building statement, "you're on your way," which continues to ring in my ears.

To Rux Martin. For your keen insights shared from the first time we spoke. For your excellent guidance and understanding.

To Dick Carter, Tim Ward, Raymond Shaheen, William Wurch, B.K. Siewerth, Barry Keefe, Joe Rozanski, Sherman Kaplan, Eric Harvey, Becky Cianci, Andy Lycke and the crew at Continental Cablevison, Barry Estabrook, Jane Bollinger, Donna Mason, Dee Hatch, Audrey Kates Bailey, Scott and Kristen Moore-Davis, Cindy Simoni and the wonderful crew and staff at UNC-Television, Renee McCoy and the terrific staff and crew at WRAL-TV, Chef John Draz, Iva Freeman, The Culinary School of Kendall College, Jackie Dulen, Georgene Pomplun, Greg and Heather Hakanen, Kathryn Ann Mauer, Darlene Bates, Victoria Bates, Kalon Sloan, Joanne Klappauf and Darlene Penrod, for without your assistance, guidance, generosity and belief I would not be here today.

Thank you all.

CONTENTS

Preface

I WROTE THIS BOOK to share my food and ideas with as many people as possible. I love good food, and you must, too, or you would not be holding my book in your hands.

I have always believed great-tasting food can also be healthy food. I always try to use the freshest ingredients I can locate, with the least amount of fat and oil possible. I season everything the way I like it, so that when it arrives at the table, no additional seasoning is required.

Most of my recipes get 20 percent or less of their calories from fat. By using this book, you can choose what you wish to prepare based on your palate. What sounds good? What tickles your fancy? The answers to those questions will always lead you in the perfect direction.

I hope you enjoy reading and cooking from my book. I loved writing it and throughout the process could barely wait for other people to make my recipes and try my food.

As has always been true since I started spreading the word about low-fat food, I'd like you, if you are so inclined, to write me. If you have a great-tasting low-fat recipe you'd like to share with me, write me. If you have a favorite recipe that you know is way too high in fat and want help in lowering it, send it to me. If this book touched your life in a positive way, share your thoughts with me at:

P.O. Box 1363
Cary, NC 27512-1363
or by e-mail at: leanwizard@aol.com

I can hardly wait to hear from you.

—Don Mauer

INTRODUCTION: MY STORY

Christmas Eve, 1989. I tipped the scales at 308 pounds.

August 1990. I weighed 205 pounds.

Today, I weigh 195 pounds.

Was I sick?

Yes. Sick and tired of being fat.

Am I healthy today? I've never been healthier. Here's my story.

I DIDN'T WAKE UP ON CHRISTMAS EVE, 1989, and discover that my weight had ballooned up 150 pounds from the night before. I'd been heavy since I was 10 years old. Those were the days when my mom dragged me to the "husky" section of a department store to buy me pants. When we arrived, there was always a group of chubby boys, all with their moms, and all staring down at their shoes as their moms held up pairs of pants and said, "Do you think these will fit?"

Ugh.

For the next 30 years, I went on every diet that came along. Did I always lose weight? You betcha. Did I ever keep the weight off? Never. Every time I stopped dieting, I gained back everything I had lost, plus a few pounds. Total frustration. At 40, I gave up on dieting, and to keep from being embarrassed, bought my "husky" clothes through the mail from a big guy's catalog.

When I was 41, friends and relatives suggested I begin making annual visits to my doctor for complete physical exams. They believed, and rightly so, that regular visits could extend my life. So I made an appointment and off I went. The nurse took what seemed to be massive amounts of blood for testing and then invited me to step on the office scale. I became nervous when she put the "big" weight on 300 and sent the little weight scurrying to 0. It took only a couple of nudges before I realized I weighed 302 pounds. Up till that moment, I had no idea I was over 300. How could that possibly be?

Simple: I didn't own a scale. If you think I wanted to fly out of my bed each morning, race to the bathroom and jump on it gleefully to "see what I weigh today," you'd be wrong. I didn't have a clue and didn't want one.

My doctor sat me down for our consultation and said I had two problems. First, my cholesterol. My tests indicated it was 240. Much too high. The doctor handed me a single sheet of paper with a list of low- and no-cholesterol foods on it. "Change your eating habits and replace the high-cholesterol foods with these," he counseled.

The second problem was weight. The doctor said: "You're gonna have to do something about the beef."

Misunderstanding, I said, "I have done something about it. I eat more chicken and turkey than ever before."

"That's not funny," he said. "I'm referring to the bay window hanging over your belt. At 302 pounds, you must lose weight." He suggested several hospital-run, doctor-monitored, liquid-diet programs. Since I'd never succeeded in keeping off weight that I lost, I rejected his suggestion. I thought about it for more than a year. On Christmas Eve, 1989, my sister-in-law took several photographs, including one of me. When her prints came back, I stared at my picture for a long time. Until that moment, I had never really seen myself.

Burn Your Britches and Don't Look Back

RIGHT THEN AND THERE, I decided I had to do something. I contacted a liquid-diet program, just as my doctor recommended. I resolved to lose 100 pounds, and 30 days later, enrolled in the program. My resolution was not made lightly. This was going to be the last time I tried to lose weight. If I didn't, I was never going to try again. If I succeeded, I vowed to keep it off forever. By the time I finally began my liquid diet, I weighed 308 pounds and my cholesterol was 260.

I also decided to burn my bridges. If you looked in my closet, you would have seen clothing that fit me at 308 . . . 280 . . . 250 . . . 230. Whatever I weighed, I always had something to wear. I got a huge cardboard box. I wrote "FAT BOX" in big, black letters on all four sides, and I parked the box next to my closet. As I lost weight and my clothing became baggy, I cleaned the clothes and placed them in my fat box. After I lost 70 pounds and my liquid-diet program was completed, my box was three-quarters full.

My program's dietitian tried to teach me the exchange-diet system. An exchange diet is one in which foods are grouped according to categories: bread, meat, milk, fruit, vegetables and fats. You are allowed so many "exchanges"—portion sizes—of each per day. That works fine with a basic meal: a slice of toast, a piece of fruit, a glass of milk. But figuring out how something like a fajita fit into the system and how many exchanges it involved was too confusing for me. I didn't understand the diet then and I still don't.

My Fat Busting Begins

I HEADED TO A BOOKSTORE in search of a solution. I discovered *The Choose to Lose Diet—A Food Lover's Guide to Permanent Weight Loss* by Dr. Ron and Nancy Goor (Houghton Mifflin, 1990). The Goors' book almost grabbed me by the shoulder and tossed itself into my hands. I returned home and consumed the book as voraciously as I had once consumed a slab of prime rib. What secret did the Goors share? Two words: *low fat*.

Following the Goors' concepts, I decided to create a food plan for myself that was based on 2,000 calories per day and derived 20 percent or less of calories from fat. I bought a few low-fat cookbooks and began. I was halted almost immediately. The food I was preparing based on the recipes from those books was bland, flavorless and sometimes oddly textured. There was no way I would maintain a lifetime commitment to eating this kind of food.

Instead, I decided to begin overhauling my personal, higher-than-high-fat recipe collection to fit my commitment. Ever since I was 15 years old, I have loved to cook, and I had two boxes loaded with my favorite recipes. I removed as much fat from them as I knew how.

What happened? I continued losing weight. By August of 1990, I was 205 pounds. Between the liquid diet and my new low-fat regimen, I lost 103 pounds in eight months. My cholesterol was at a doctor-pleasing 172.

Once I had begun to lose weight, I decided to reward my progress. It turned out that my secret to achieving and maintaining weight loss would be my new reward system. First, I resolved to stop using food as my payoff. No losing 10 pounds and celebrating with a hot fudge sundae. In January, I set reachable five-pound goals. As I achieved each goal, I presented myself with two gifts.

The first gift was music: Each time, I purchased a much-desired jazz or classical-music compact disc. As I got smaller, my music collection got bigger. By the time 113 pounds had melted away, I owned 22 new discs. Throughout the years since then, when I listen to those discs, I am instantly reminded of my healthy weight loss, and I smile and congratulate myself.

The second gift was clothing. I always loathed shopping in big men's stores. I thought pure cotton sweaters were really cool, but they hadn't looked so cool wrapped around my orcalike belly. Each time I lost 10 pounds, I bought a medium-size, bright and colorful sweater. Once I lost 103 pounds, my new sweaters fit perfectly and looked great. Today, each time I wear one, I remind myself why I own it.

Was I ever hungry eating in my new lean way? Nope. Did my food taste good? It tasted terrific and continued getting better. Was this deprivation dining? Hardly. I slowly continued to lose weight and finally stopped at 195.

Low-Fat Wizardry

IT IS NOW MORE THAN FIVE YEARS since I lost 103 pounds. Most important, I have continued learning how to make just about any recipe leaner, either through substituting one or several ingredients or by adapting it to lower-fat cooking techniques or a combination of both. I discovered hundreds of ways to remove the fat and maintain or increase the great flavor.

What are the two keys to my discoveries? The first key is curiosity. Every single time I retrace my steps through the process that led to a low-fat breakthrough, I find the phrase "I wonder if . . ." at the beginning. The second key is a willingness to fail. The chocolate cake that first came out tough and rubbery meant I was a step closer to one that would have a soft and delicate texture. A wimpy chili was just around the corner from the one that sang with flavorful depth.

The recipes you will find in this book bring together everything I have learned since Christmas Eve, 1989. They are more than just tested and tasted. They are what I serve for breakfast, lunch and dinner, week in and week out—my personal favorites. The great majority get only 20 percent or less of their calories from fat because I believe that is the healthiest balance in a food plan.

At the beginning of every recipe is a story, a technique, a solution or a thought about that dish. I have included nutritional information at the end of each so you will know exactly what the finished dish contains. That way, if you count calories, it'll be easy. If you count fat grams, it will be just as easy. If you are on a restricted-sodium diet, you'll know which recipes are appropriate as is and which ones need to have the salt adjusted. A few of the dessert recipes include variations for diabetics so that sugar can be eliminated. Most recipes also offer LeanTips, LeanSuggestions or LeanNotes. These give a wide variety of hints on how to cut more fat or add more flavor or vary the recipe.

In the following chapters, I explain how I feel about exercise. I cover the different ingredients I like to use. I tell how I removed the high-fat ingredients hiding out in my kitchen and what I keep on hand to prepare lean meals easily.

Some of these recipes go together in a flash, others are for special occasions and gatherings. They have two things in common: Each is truly lean, and each is exceptionally delicious.

USE IT TO LOSE IT

I LOVE TO EXERCISE. That's a statement I never believed I would ever make. Up until five years ago, I never exercised. At 308 pounds, I had one regular activity: opening and closing the refrigerator door. I exerted myself only when opening a particularly well-sealed bag of M&M's.

Through grade school, junior high and high school, I never went out for sports. I tried to duck every gym class I could. I hated track, wrestling, gymnastics and tennis.

After I enrolled in the liquid-diet program and lost 10 pounds, my wife, Susan, suggested I go to the grocery store, head for the produce section and locate the potatoes. She said, "Find the five-pound bags and put one in your left hand and the other in your right." She told me to walk around the store for a couple of minutes and see how it felt to have those 10 pounds back.

I did as she suggested. I probably looked pretty funny, waddling around the store—no grocery cart—with a sack of potatoes in each hand. After only a few short minutes, those bags got heavier and heavier. I broke a sweat and my shoulders began hurting. I headed straight back to produce and actually wheezed a little when I set them down. Hmmmm. Not only did I realize how significant my 10-pound weight loss was, I discovered I was out of shape.

The program that helped me lose my first 70 pounds told me that the majority of people who continue to exercise and maintain their food plan will keep off most of their weight for at least one year. Made sense. But everyone who stopped exercising regularly regained all the weight they lost in short order.

Ho boy!

Right then and there, I committed myself to a regular exercise program. I purchased the best stationary exercise bicycle I could afford. My wife was pleased I was exercising, but she was very unhappy that her comfortable living room had become Mauer's Gym.

After a while, riding the bike every day became more difficult. Soon, I was exercising less and less. I read about walking being one of the best forms of exercise. Off I went on a short walk. It felt great. I breathed in the fresh air with its many wonderful scents. I stopped to speak with a neighbor about her fantastic rose garden and she gave me a cutting. I became a walker. I sold my stationary bike and closed Mauer's Gym. Susan was thrilled to have her living room back.

During the next few years, I continued to walk for five out of every seven days. This was fine until I received a letter from a woman who had attended one of my seminars. She wrote, "I think it's incredible you lost 100 pounds. . . . Why didn't you adopt a more vigorous exercise program than walking?"

She went on. "I have recently lost 20 pounds and began a five-day-a-week exercise program combined with low-fat eating. I do 30-plus minutes of aerobic exercise for five days combined with weight training on three days. . . . My body fat dropped from 21 percent to 16 percent after just eight weeks. I'm thrilled!"

Her enthusiasm got me interested, so I gave her a call. "Are you still exercising?" I asked her.

"Absolutely," she said. "And I feel great." She indicated that if she skips a workout she really misses it, and she watches what she eats on those infrequent lapses.

"The most interesting thing happened since I changed my eating and exercise," she said. "Now, I eat six times a day. I have breakfast, lunch and dinner as well as some low-fat snacks in between meals when I'm hungry." That made sense to me. New studies seem to indicate that eating smaller amounts frequently throughout the day is the best way to lose weight and keep it off.

That letter and conversation altered my perspective on my own exercise program. When I looked at what I was doing, I noticed that my walking had slowly lost its aerobic impact because it had turned into more of a stroll. I began heading out first thing in the morning before breakfast and started what I called "soft" jogging at regular intervals throughout my walks. These jogs elevated my heart and breathing rates. The first couple of times, my calves and thighs ached some, but overall I felt better. When I got used to my heightened workout, I increased the length and speed to a true jog.

Shortly after this, I found myself falling just short of the mark. Weather, cramped schedules and random unalterable circumstances usually reduced my exercise routine to three days a week. I changed my goals. Instead of trying for every other day, I aimed for every day. That way, if once or twice a week I couldn't get out and exercise, I'd be closer to my goal than before. For the first month, I was out there like clockwork, five out of every seven days.

Once I was comfortable with the increased regularity of my exercise, I started doing push-ups, jumping jacks and other aerobic exercises at my local park. My energy levels for the remainder of each day actually increased. Instead of having less energy, I had more. I lost some weight and noticed the shape of my arms and legs and chest changing for the better. My clothes fit well generally, but as muscles replaced fat, some became a touch more snug.

Today, it has been more than six months since I changed my exercise program. Now, when I occasionally eat more than I plan, it doesn't ever show up on my scale. I look forward to exercising. Some mornings, when I wake up early to avoid the heat and it's dark, I think, "Naw, I won't go this morning." Five minutes later, my eyes pop open again and I go.

I get into my sweats and cross-training shoes and head for the woods. Fifty minutes later, I return dripping wet and feeling terrific. While exercising, I usually have at least one good idea, which I immediately write down and then head for the shower.

Best of all, I've seen no letup in my desire to exercise. I heartily recommend it.

CREATING A LEAN KITCHEN

ONCE I BEGAN TO CHANGE my recipes and ultimately my daily food plan from high-fat to low-fat, I noticed my kitchen was changing, too. Exorcised were all the high-fat ingredients that filled my pantry and refrigerator—no more butter, nuts by the pound or saved-up bacon grease. Either certain commodities were banished forever, or substitutions had taken their place.

Exorcising the Fat

■ Mayonnaise

I got rid of regular mayonnaise right away. It has 11 fat grams per tablespoon, just 2.5 grams short of being pure oil (fat). Five years ago, there was no such thing as a nonfat mayonnaise. Reduced-calorie mayonnaise had 5 fat grams per tablespoon, which was still too high. I lived without mayonnaise for almost two years, until the nonfat kind appeared on my supermarket shelves. At that time, nonfat mayonnaises weren't too tasty and had an odd texture. Today, they are decent in both respects and work well, replacing 11 fat grams with zero fat grams.

If you don't like nonfat mayonnaise, try the new low-fat mayonnaise now available, which uses water as a stand-in for oil. It has a single fat gram per tablespoon and is almost indistinguishable from the original version. I keep a jar in my refrigerator at all times and one in my pantry.

■ Sour Cream

I also booted sour cream out of my kitchen. One cup has almost 50 fat grams (almost 30 of them saturated). At first, I replaced it with light sour cream, until I realized it retained 60 percent of the fat. I finally substituted nonfat sour cream. At least two national brands are a close approximation of the real thing. They have a creamy texture and can stand the heat of a sauce without curdling.

Select those brands with the shortest ingredient list. The longer the list, the less the product tastes and acts like the real thing. Look for brands that use cornstarch (often listed as modified starch on the label). Finally, buy one or two that fit these criteria and taste them. You want a smooth texture. Avoid those that are slick and slippery on the tongue, with a flat taste.

■ Milk, Cream, Cottage Cheese and Yogurt

I also waved goodbye to whole milk, half-and-half, cream, full-fat cottage cheese and full-fat yogurt. I replaced the whole milk with skim milk. At one time, I thought skim milk looked like bad water. Today, I cannot drink whole milk. It is far too rich—like drinking whipping cream.

I know of only two national brands of nonfat cream cheese: Healthy Choice and Kraft. I prefer each for different reasons. When I need a baked product, such as a cheesecake, to come close to the high-fat version in texture and flavor, Kraft seems to work best. When it comes to a cream-cheese frosting sweetened with powdered sugar or brown sugar, I reach for Healthy Choice. Kraft's nonfat cream cheese becomes thinner when powdered or brown sugar is added and does not return to its previous consistency even when refrigerated.

Instead of half-and-half, I now use canned evaporated skim milk. It is found right next to the regular evaporated milk in all supermarkets. Evaporated milk has 10 fat grams per ½ cup, whereas evaporated skim milk has 0.3 grams. That's a big difference. Evaporated skim milk can be whipped, just as light cream can. It "sets" a low-fat pumpkin pie filling exactly as high-fat evaporated milk does. It adds body and a richer flavor to whipped potatoes, while adding almost no fat.

Full-fat cottage cheese (10 fat grams per cup) has given way to nonfat. The original may seem harmless enough since it only has 4 percent butterfat. It could be called 96 percent fat-free. Yet ½ cup has 5 fat grams. In contrast, 1 percent cottage cheese has only 0.3 fat grams per ½ cup. I look for the least amount of stabilizers and gums. I want my low-fat or fat-free cottage cheese to almost melt in my mouth and have a natural sweetness. I've had the best luck with local brands.

Toss out any cans of whipping cream or containers of nondairy whipped topping (yes, even the "lite" stuff). All these products are loaded with fat. Although nondairy toppings don't have any cholesterol, they are almost all uniformly loaded with highly saturated fat. When I need something similar, I make my own Lean n' Creamy Topping (see page 434).

For nonfat yogurt, I tasted and tested many brands and found that Alta Dena (from California) is the creamiest by far. Alta Dena's plain nonfat yogurt has a wonderful, almost sweet flavor; its nonfat fruit yogurts are sweetened with either honey or fruit juice, and the company doesn't use gelatin or other stabilizers to make the yogurt thick. This brand can be found in most health food stores. If you can't locate Alta Dena, there are other natural yogurts that are almost as good.

■ Cheese

I sent all my cheeses packing, except for real Parmesan. Since it is made from high-fat whole milk, cheese averages 9 fat grams per ounce, with over 60 percent of that saturated. Parmesan cheese is not much lower in fat—a single tablespoon has 1.5 fat grams—but that tablespoon is brimming over with the rich essence of cheese, so I don't need to use much. It melts beautifully and tastes wonderful. I keep imported Romano cheese on hand, too, for the same reason.

In place of regular mozzarella cheese, I ushered in a fat-reduced, part-skim-milk mozzarella with only 2 fat grams per ounce. It melts, tastes and acts just like its higher-fat relative. I also regularly rely on a reduced-fat sharp Cheddar. It has 5 fat grams per ounce and acts like the higher fat kinds. For topping a lean burger, I use nonfat American cheese food slices. Once I add mustard, relish, ketchup and an onion slice, I can't tell that my cheese has no fat.

■ Butter, Margarine and Shortening

I also rid my kitchen of butter, full-fat margarine, solid shortening in a can and lard. I almost never use butter or margarine. Instead, I substitute Promise Ultra Fat Free Nonfat Margarine, which is soft and spreadable. Its flavor is somewhat butterlike, and it looks and acts like butter-flavored gelatin. It cannot be cooked with, however, since it evaporates the moment it touches a hot skillet. But it helps keep a piece of toast, a bagel or pancakes from being dry, and thereby saves me many fat grams per week. It is found coast to coast in every supermarket in the butter and margarine section. Fleischmann's brand of squeezable fat-free margarine is located near Promise. I think it has a slightly better butter flavor, but it also cannot withstand heat.

My best supermarket discovery to date, which helps make up for the loss of butter flavor in everything from cookies to spaghetti sauce, is a product sold as either Butter Buds Butter Flavored Mix or Butter Buds Butter Flavored Sprinkles. The mix comes in a six-inch square yellow box and is found either in the diet section or the herb-and-spice section of every supermarket. The box contains eight packets. You whisk a packet into ½ cup hot water to make a pourable liquid, and allow it to stand for two to three minutes at room temperature until the mixture takes on the consistency of melted butter. A tablespoon has 6 calories and negligible fat. Made from salt, dried butter, guar gum (a thickener and stabilizer), baking soda and flavorings, it makes a fairly decent butter substitute.

I drizzle prepared Butter Buds over a baked potato, a piece of lean broiled fish or an ear of freshly cooked corn. I add a full packet of the dry mix to quick-bread batters to replace butter flavor. And I stir a packet into bottled nonfat spaghetti sauce simmering on the stove. Butter Buds also comes in a shaker bottle, and its contents can also be reconstituted by stirring together 1 teaspoon with 1 tablespoon of hot water.

■ Salad Dressing and Oils

Every bottle of full-fat salad dressing has hit the highway, too. Most regular commercial salad dressings contain from 6 to 8 fat grams per tablespoon. I pour at least 3 tablespoons on my salad, which would mean 18 to 24 fat grams. That's half my fat intake for the entire day. Now I keep a selection of my own nonfat or low-fat salad dressings in my refrigerator door. A small word of warning about commercial fat-free salad dressings: Not all of them are created equal. Read the list of ingredients (bring your reading glasses). Soybean oil is often found on the list of supposedly fat-free ingredients. The new labeling law allows food manufacturers to claim zero fat per serving if the dressing contains 0.5 grams of fat or less. I avoid those dressings, and make certain the ones I purchase are totally free of fat.

Pitch every bottle of vegetable oil except olive, canola or toasted sesame oil. I always have a small bottle of each available in my kitchen. Extra-virgin olive oil is from the first pressing, which makes it not only superior in taste to later pressings but smoother on the palate. Remember: All oils are 100 percent fat. Olive oil is no different. I use it in very small quantities, therefore it must contribute the largest flavor possible. A small bottle lasts for months.

I use canola oil whenever I don't want flavor to intrude. It has no cholesterol. It still has as much fat (13.5 grams per tablespoon), but it is the lowest in saturated fat of any oil. Since I use it in such small quantities, I spend a little extra money and use cold-pressed canola oil (Hain brand) from organically grown seeds. Again, a small bottle will do.

If you enjoy Asian cuisine, you have probably tasted toasted sesame oil as a seasoning. Toasting the seeds before pressing the oil from them increases the oil's nutty flavor by an astounding degree and also imparts a smoky aroma. I use this oil almost exclusively in Asian stir-fries, but in small quantities, with less than a tablespoon for four people, so each serving gets less than 4 fat grams. Because toasted sesame seed oil smokes at high cooking temperatures, I cook it over a lower heat than for other oils and add my ingredients the moment the oil starts to smoke.

Cooking sprays are also a very useful tool in the fat-fighting arsenal of a lean kitchen, allowing you to parcel out fat a gram at a time. I like the butter-flavored vegetable-oil cooking sprays for baking since they add big flavor. What I don't like are sprays that indicate on their label that they are fat-free when they are not. I know of no aerosol cooking spray that doesn't contain either all or primarily vegetable oil.

■ Eggs

I always have fresh eggs in my refrigerator. This seems contradictory, until you realize that I use them mostly for their whites, and an occasional whole one in a recipe for 12 or more people. That single yolk bestows a light texture and a rich flavor in proportion to the mere 0.4 fat grams that a serving contains.

Once in a while, I use nonfat egg substitute, such as Egg Beaters. This product seems to set a custard better, as in Luscious Fat-Free Rice Pudding (page 430). But I use it infrequently because it contains preservatives and costs 85 percent more than breaking my own eggs and separating out the white, which is what all nonfat egg substitutes are. I also make certain I buy the freshest eggs possible, because they seem to taste better. Not wishing to waste the yolks, I put them in a recyclable aluminum pie pan and leave them in the wild area of my backyard for any animals that mosey by.

■ High-Fat Meats

See any bacon, fat back, salt pork or sausage in your refrigerator? A bottle of bacon grease perhaps? To the trash. I usually use Canadian-style bacon instead of regular (2 fat grams per ounce vs. 16.3 fat grams) because bacon substitutes—whether beef, turkey or nonmeat— are still higher in fat than Canadian-style bacon. Most store-bought sausage is enormously fatty, with 80 percent of calories derived from fat. So far, no one makes a low-fat commercial Italian sausage, so I created my own (page 42). My sausage gets only 24 percent of calories from fat and has better flavor than any coming from a refrigerated grocery case because it uses fresh herbs and spices.

Are there any ordinary hot dogs (16 to 17 fat grams per link) out there in your kitchen? Toss 'em. If you have any turkey franks (8 fat grams per link) or chicken franks (8.8 fat grams per link), throw them out. I keep two national brands of low-fat (1 fat gram per link) or fat-free hot dogs in my refrigerator. I use sliced hot dogs as a topping for my pita pizza and once in a while I enjoy a beans-and-franks dinner.

■ Soups

Take a look in the pantry at the soups gathering dust on the shelf. Any regular cream-style soup should head straight for the food drive. Every other Sunday, I prepare a gallon of homemade broth (see pages 116 to 123). Whether chicken, beef or vegetable, broths are the cornerstone on which I build my low-fat and nonfat salad dressings, fat-free gravies and fat-free sauces. I sauté meats and vegetables in minimal amounts of broth instead of using oil. Having good homemade broths opens the door to flavorful and easy soups. If I have a bottle of homemade chicken broth in the refrigerator, I can have fat-free chicken noodle soup on my table in 15 minutes or less.

When time is short and I have no homemade broth on hand, I turn to good-quality canned broths. I highly recommend Campbell's Healthy Request Ready-to-Serve Chicken Broth. It has no MSG (monosodium glutamate) and is reasonably priced. If you can't locate it, try Swanson's Natural Goodness Clear Chicken Broth. It also has no MSG. Skim the fat from the surface, and it's ready to go.

■ Cereal

While you're in the pantry, take a look at your cereal boxes. If they indicate a higher fat content than 1 gram per 1 ounce serving, give them away. Check natural granola cereal, too. It can be some of the highest-fat cereal there is. I maintain a selection of five different cold cereals that have no added fat, salt or sugar.

■ Chocolate and Candy

Give all candy the boot. In the past, I often rewarded myself for reaching my weight-loss goal with a hot fudge sundae. Before I took to healthy food habits, I kept a 1-pound bag of plain M&M chocolate candies in my refrigerator and nibbled away a bag per night. Frozen chocolate-covered graham crackers and a quart of whole milk often called to me in the evening, and I consumed both down to the last crumb and drop.

If you keep chocolate goodies around and often take a pound of M&M's as a single serving, give them the heave-ho. Give away those chocolate chips, too, just waiting to sabotage your good intentions. Also, remove all sweetened chips. That means butterscotch, white chocolate, milk chocolate . . . all of them.

Some candy, such as gumdrops, is entirely fat-free. But all are sugar, with "empty" calories and no nutrients. An ounce has 100 calories and will make your blood-sugar levels rise. When they plunge, you'll feel hungry and head for more candy or something else.

Instead, when I want something sweet, I reach for dried fruit in the pantry: raisins, dried figs, dates, dried apricots, dried cherries, dried strawberries and dried fructose-sweetened cranberries. They have fewer calories per ounce than candy, and they contain natural vitamins, minerals, fiber and no fat. Since the sugar they all contain is fructose (fruit sugar) instead of sucrose (granulated sugar), my blood-sugar levels seem to rise and fall slowly, so I don't get cravings.

Stocking Up on the Good Stuff

EATING WELL IS NOT JUST A MATTER of throwing out the fat. That's the first step. The second, and equally important, mission is stocking the pantry and refrigerator with healthful ingredients.

Today, my refrigerator looks like a vegetable garden and fruit orchard on ice. Beautiful ruby leaf lettuce sits next to succulent asparagus spears and fresh basil leaves. Bright yellow Golden Delicious apples share shelf space with glossy seedless grapes and fuzzy kiwi. My pantry bins hold a variety of colorful onions and potatoes. Pantry shelves are lined with a variety of wholesome flours and an assortment of pastas, grains and beans.

I'd have to consume almost 30 medium apples or 24 pounds of asparagus or 91 tomatoes to reach the caloric peak of a pound of M&M's, which has 2,369 calories. And I'd have to eat 228 apples or 71 pounds of asparagus or 285 tomatoes to equal its 114 fat grams.

■ Grains and Beans

In moderation, pasta is an important part of my lean kitchen. I use domestic and imported pastas. If you don't have any rice, get some. I buy white and brown basmati aromatic rice. From the first time I inhaled the great aroma of basmati rice slowly simmering on my stove, I was hooked. Regular white rice is bland and has almost no taste, while basmati rice, whether brown or white, delivers terrific flavor, especially with a touch of minced fresh garlic or a teaspoon of curry in the cooking water. I also keep wild rice on hand for adding to mixed rice pilaf or wild rice soup (page 128). It costs a little more, but is worth it.

If you don't have canned beans—pinto, kidney and black—stock some. If you think you'll use dried beans, buy some of those as well. I always have organically grown beans, either canned or dried, ready for my use. I enjoy baked beans too and keep a couple cans of vegetarian nonfat beans on my pantry shelf.

■ Fruits and Vegetables

My refrigerator fruit drawer is filled with a selection of fresh and ripe fruit: grapes, apples, oranges and berries. Whenever my sweet tooth starts acting up, I quiet it with a piece of fruit instead of candy or a cookie.

Also, I stock several different kinds of lettuce (red leaf, Bibb and romaine), so I can make a salad whenever I want. I also make sure to have several fresh vegetables tucked in the refrigerated vegetable drawer.

■ Herbs and Spices

Dried herbs and spices play a pivotal role in creating flavor. If you can't remember when you bought some of the seasonings in your cabinet, toss them on your compost heap, save the bottle and replace the contents with the freshest herbs and spices you can buy. I get mine from a health food store that sells them in bulk. I buy small quantities to maintain the highest level of freshness possible.

I prefer sea salt. If I can get it, I choose sea salt that is sun-dried (rather than kiln-dried), so that all the minerals are preserved. I use a salt mill on my dining table and grind my own salt. It's probably a psychological trick, but it seems to taste better. Plus, it contains no additives.

I also buy my black and white peppercorns whole and grind them fresh when I need them.

■ Arrowroot and Cornstarch

Add cornstarch and arrowroot flour to your larder. Soups, sauces and gravies are normally thickened with a mixture of flour and fat or cream, both of which are high in fat. Cornstarch, a fat-free thickener, is readily available in the baking section of every supermarket.

Arrowroot (also called arrowroot flour) is the preferred thickener of professional chefs. Neutral in flavor, it lets other ingredients in a sauce shine through and imparts a satiny sheen. Arrowroot is located in the herb-and-spice racks of supermarkets. It is higher priced than cornstarch, so if you like it, locate a source that sells it in bulk.

■ Vinegars, Soy Sauce, Hot Sauce

While you're shopping, pick up a bottle of sodium-reduced soy sauce. Also, purchase a selection of vinegars for your new kitchen: balsamic, white and red wine vinegars and rice vinegar.

I maintain a collection of hot sauces. Some are relatively tame; others could remove the chrome from a faucet.

■ Sugar and Honey

Most brands of granulated sugar taste the same. However, all brown sugars are not created equal. Some have a definite molasses note; others do not. Sample different ones until you find the one you like.

I love honey, which can be used to round out the flavor of a dish. It's almost impossible to exchange honey for sugar in a cake or brownie, so you won't see it used that way in my recipes. All honeys have a flavor, some more distinct and stronger than others. I keep a variety in my pantry.

■ Vanilla and Cocoa

Artificial vanilla is less expensive than real vanilla extract, but it doesn't have its round, full flavor. The bouquet drifting from my teaspoon as I add it to a cake or pudding is both unbeatable and fat-free. I use the best I can afford. I find Nielsen-Massey in specialty shops and spend the extra few dollars for it.

Low-fat unsweetened cocoa powder is the major flavor provider in almost every chocolate dessert I create in my lean kitchen. There are several manufacturers of cocoa powder, and each of their products has a different taste. There are low-fat, medium-fat and high-fat cocoa powders available. Therefore, I read the label to make certain that whatever cocoa powder I am considering fits into my food plan. Dutch-process cocoa powder, sometimes referred to as Dutched cocoa, has a deeper color and more intense flavor than regular cocoa powder. Hershey's European style and Droste Dutch Cocoa are two excellent brands and are located in the baking sections of major supermarkets.

■ Water

I keep several bottles of spring water in my pantry. Generally, there is nothing wrong with tap water. However, many cities have tap water that doesn't taste very good. If you don't think it makes a difference, get up on a Sunday morning and make two pots of coffee. The first pot should be made with tap water, just like always. The other should be made with bottled spring water. Pour yourself a cup of each and see if there is a difference in the flavor. If not, stick with tap water. If so, consider having a service deliver large bottles of spring water to your home at regular intervals. That way, there's always a supply and you won't have to haul it from the store.

Tools and Equipment

MY LEAN KITCHEN WOULD NOT BE COMPLETE without a selection of nonstick pots and pans. Nonstick cookware allows me to brown and cook all foods with either a small amount of oil or none at all. My cookware is heavy-bottomed, which helps distribute the heat evenly from edge to edge.

A good kitchen scale is a blessing in my lean kitchen; I couldn't function without it. It gives me total and accurate control over portions. I use my scale to weigh cake batter if I am splitting it among pans so that each pan bakes exactly the same. With my scale, I can substitute cake flour by weight for all-purpose flour. Measuring out 3 ounces of 95 percent lean hamburger is a breeze. An ounce of breakfast cereal is a serving size, but how much is that? Put the cereal bowl on the scale and find out.

Last-Minute Takeout

In my fat kitchen, I used to maintain a selection of menus for places that delivered food. If you have any, throw them away. Chances are, not one of them prepares the kind and quality of cuisine you'll be dining on. If you don't have the time to make a couple dinners during the week, make a couple of things up on Sunday (broiled chicken breasts, soup broths, a casserole) and refrigerate them. Those can be your new fast foods.

Welcome to your new lean kitchen. Now you can begin to explore the recipes in this book with confidence.

Breakfasts

IN 1987, two years before I realized I weighed over 300 pounds, I smoked three packs of cigarettes a day. During that time, breakfast for me was what it is for most smokers—a cigarette and a cup of coffee. I never ate breakfast unless it was almost lunchtime on a special Saturday or Sunday. Then I'd go crazy with side dishes, juices and coffee. Followed by that cigarette.

Even after I quit smoking in 1988, I still didn't eat breakfast. I'd guzzle a 16-ounce bottle of Diet Coke and start my day.

The liquid-diet program that helped me to lose the first 70 pounds also started me down the three-meals-a-day road. "You gotta eat breakfast," the program leaders would say. So I did. What they didn't tell me was that my metabolic engine didn't start until I ate. The earlier in the day I eat breakfast, the sooner my metabolism begins to roar.

I get up at six in the morning, head out for my exercise, come back and jump into a cool shower. Then I head for the kitchen and make breakfast. If fresh local fruit isn't available, I pour out 2 ounces of no-fat-added cold breakfast cereal. My selection includes corn flakes with no sugar or sodium, oat bran flakes, puffed rice or amaranth flakes. Then I slice up half a banana, or strawberries or blueberries or peaches or whatever is in season. I don't need to add sugar or any other sweetener since I began using a fat-free nondairy product called rice milk. Rice milk, which is made from filtered water (sometimes spring water), brown rice and a touch of sea salt, is naturally sweet. It looks just like skim milk and can be purchased in 32-ounce containers from health food stores. Sometimes, if I am particularly hungry, I'll make toast and top it with some special jelly or jam purchased from my local farmer's market. Once in a while, I'll have fresh-squeezed orange juice or grapefruit juice. I now look forward to enjoying my nonfat breakfast every morning.

The following recipes are what I make for a Saturday or Sunday morning, when I've got more time and the inclination to prepare something fancier than cold cereal.

RECIPES

Country-Style Breakfast Potatoes

SERVES 4

WHEN IT WAS PAST MIDNIGHT, I used to love going to an all-night, breakfast-only restaurant and ordering a huge meal. I'd get pancakes, eggs, grilled ham, hash-brown potatoes, a large orange juice and large glass of whole milk. I loved the crispy-fried, onion-sweetened hash-browns the best. Since most restaurants still haven't figured out how to make lower-fat versions, I had to create my own at home.

My leaner breakfast potatoes are easy to make because I start with potatoes already baked and chilled. I don't have to use huge amounts of oil to fry with, since I am actually just heating them through. (When you're baking potatoes for dinner, toss in a couple extras. Once they are baked, cool them to room temperature, put them in a plastic bag and refrigerate them till needed.)

2   baked potatoes (8-9 ounces each), chilled
½   cup finely chopped sweet onion
    Salt
    Fresh-ground black pepper

1. Do not peel the potatoes. Cut them into ⅜-inch cubes. Set aside.
2. Spray the interior of a large nonstick skillet with vegetable oil and place over medium-high heat. Add the onion to the skillet. When the onion begins to sizzle, add the diced potatoes, stirring them around so they are in a single layer. Cook for 3 to 4 minutes. Lightly spray the potatoes with vegetable oil. Section by section, flip the potatoes over and cook for 3 to 4 minutes more. Flip and stir the potatoes for 2 minutes more, or until nicely browned. Add salt and pepper to taste. Serve immediately.

NUTRITIONAL INFORMATION PER SERVING (NOT INCLUDING SALT): 121 CALORIES, 0.4 G FAT, 2.5 G PROTEIN, 27 G CARBOHYDRATE, 0 CHOLESTEROL, 8 MG SODIUM.

"Good Morning" Griddle Cakes

MAKES 6 GRIDDLE CAKES, SERVES 3

WHITMORE THOMAS HAYNES (a.k.a. Bompa) was my maternal grandfather. Bompa liked nothing better than to get up early on Sunday morning and make a monster breakfast for everyone. Bompa always made himself a griddle-cake sandwich. He took a huge griddle cake and placed it on his plate. He'd butter it up and then place two fried eggs and four strips of cooked bacon on top. Another griddle cake would cover everything and be spread with additional butter. Finally, he'd pour on pure maple syrup. I can still see his enormous smile and the sparkle in his eyes as he thoroughly enjoyed his Sunday morning specialty.

One of Bompa's griddle-cake secrets was melted butter added to the batter. I banished it, since butter contains so much saturated fat and cholesterol. I replaced it with vanilla extract to make up for the flavor loss.

Instead of high-fat whole milk, I substituted skim milk. I left the whole egg in to add some flavor. However, I switched from granulated sugar to dark brown sugar to enhance the flavor.

Today, once my griddle cakes are nice and brown, I don't top them with butter. Fat-free margarine helps me wave goodbye to the 11.5 grams of fat every tablespoon of butter contains. I do top my griddle cakes with pure maple syrup. I don't miss the fat at all, and my smile is just as big as Bompa's.

1   cup all-purpose flour (not self-rising)
½   cup whole wheat flour
2   teaspoons baking powder
1¼   cups skim milk
1   large whole egg
2   tablespoons dark brown sugar
1   teaspoon vanilla extract
     Nonfat margarine and real maple syrup

1. Sift the flours and baking powder into a medium bowl. Set aside.

2. In another medium bowl, whisk together the milk, egg, brown sugar and vanilla until blended. Add the flour mixture and stir together until the dry ingredients are just moistened (they will appear slightly lumpy).

3. Preheat the oven to 200 degrees F. Place 3 serving plates on the top oven rack.

4. Heat a large nonstick griddle over medium heat. From time to time, drip a drop or two of water on the surface. When a drop slides, dances and evaporates, the griddle has reached the proper temperature. Spray the griddle lightly with vegetable oil and ladle on ½ cup of the batter for each griddle cake. Cook until the top is covered with bubbles and slightly dry around the edge, 2 to 3 minutes. Flip the griddle cake and cook until the bottom is golden, about 2 minutes.

5. Transfer the completed griddle cake to a baking sheet, cover and keep warm in the oven. Repeat with the remaining batter.

6. Using a hot pad, remove the plates and the griddle cakes from the oven. Equally divide the griddle cakes among the plates. Serve, passing nonfat margarine and maple syrup.

NUTRITIONAL INFORMATION PER GRIDDLE CAKE: 153 CALORIES, 1.3 G FAT, 6 G PROTEIN, 29.2 G CARBOHYDRATE, 36 MG CHOLESTEROL, 201 MG SODIUM.

LeanTip: If the griddle cakes are too thick, thin the batter with additional skim milk. I like to warm maple syrup in my microwave oven in a microwave-safe serving cup before bringing it to the table.

BUTTERMILK FRENCH TOAST WITH BLUEBERRY HONEY

SERVES 3

FOR YEARS, I have loved French toast for special Sunday morning breakfasts. The aroma of the cooking gets my mouth watering, and I can barely wait for the toast to reach golden-brown perfection.

After losing more than 100 pounds, however, I learned that French toast can be very high in fat. The batter in which the bread is dipped is really an egg custard, and the French toast is then fried in butter and drizzled with more butter when served.

Since I didn't want French toast to disappear from my breakfast table, I made some changes. Out went all the whole eggs except one. In went fat-free egg whites. Out went the whole milk, in went nonfat buttermilk. I bought a loaf of the best French bread I could find that contained no fat whatsoever, and I let it get stale so that the bread's natural moisture would be replaced by my flavorful batter.

Blueberry honey is the perfect sweet topping, since it has no fat and tons of flavor, and it counters the tangy buttermilk in the batter.

1	large whole egg
4	large egg whites
1	cup nonfat buttermilk*
1	tablespoon granulated sugar
½	teaspoon vanilla extract
½	teaspoon all-purpose flour
6	pieces day-old French bread, cut into ½-inch-thick slices
1½	teaspoons canola oil

1. In a large mixing bowl, whisk together the whole egg, egg whites, buttermilk, sugar, vanilla extract and flour until frothy.

2. Place the bread slices in the egg mixture and turn so that they are coated on all sides. Squeeze each slice under the liquid and let go, as with a sponge, so the liquid is absorbed inside.

3. Place a large heavy-bottomed nonstick skillet over medium heat and add the oil. Swirl the oil around the pan and when the oil is hot, add the bread slices. Cook for 1 to 2 minutes, until golden brown. Turn and continue cooking, about 2 minutes more. Turn only once or the French toast will toughen. Serve with Blueberry Honey.

NUTRITIONAL INFORMATION PER SERVING: 257 CALORIES, 6.2 G FAT, 14 G PROTEIN, 35 G CARBOHYDRATE, 74 MG CHOLESTEROL, 484 MG SODIUM.

If you cannot locate nonfat buttermilk, substitute low-fat (1.5%) buttermilk. It will raise the fat content by 0.7 grams.

BLUEBERRY HONEY

MAKES ABOUT 2 CUPS

1   cup clover honey
1   cup fresh blueberries, washed and picked over

Over medium heat, bring the honey to a boil in a small heavy-bottomed saucepan. Add the blueberries, reduce the heat to low and cook for 2 minutes. Remove the saucepan from the heat and spoon the honey over the prepared French toast.

NUTRITIONAL INFORMATION PER 2 TABLESPOONS: 67 CALORIES, 0 FAT, TRACE PROTEIN, 18 G CARBOHYDRATE, 0 CHOLESTEROL, TRACE SODIUM.

OVEN-BAKED FRENCH TOAST

SERVES 6

My friend Kalon Sloan from Asheville, North Carolina, challenged me to take her favorite rich, easy brunch dish and make it into one without as much fat. Her original contained a total of more than 100 grams of fat. No wonder she was concerned.

Those fat grams in Kalon's original recipe came from the whole milk (16 fat grams), light cream (46 grams) and whole eggs (40 grams). By substituting skim for the whole milk, evaporated skim for the cream and nonfat egg substitute for six of the eight eggs, I banished over 80 fat grams.

When my French toast comes out of my oven, it looks like a bread pudding baked in a velvety, vanilla-flavored custard. It's hard to believe how superb the flavor is with only 3.2 fat grams per serving.

1   loaf (8 ounces) French bread, cut into 1-inch-thick slices
2   cups skim milk
1   cup evaporated skim milk
1½   cups nonfat egg substitute, such as Egg Beaters
      (or 12 large egg whites)
2   large whole eggs
4   teaspoons granulated sugar
1   tablespoon vanilla extract
2   teaspoons Butter Buds, mixed with 2 tablespoons hot water
      Pure maple syrup

1. Lightly spray the bottom and sides of a 13-by-9-inch baking dish with vegetable oil. Fill the bottom of the dish with the bread slices, placing them close together. Build a second layer on top of the first. Continue layering until all the bread is used. The dish will be completely covered with bread and filled to the top.

2. In a large mixing bowl, whisk together the milk, evaporated milk, egg substitute or egg whites, whole eggs, sugar, vanilla and Butter Buds mixture until well combined. Pour the mixture over the bread. Cover with foil and refrigerate overnight.

3. Preheat the oven to 350 degrees F.

4. Remove the baking dish from the refrigerator and uncover. (It is not necessary to bring the dish to room temperature.) Bake, uncovered, until puffed and golden, 45 to 50 minutes. Remove from the oven and let stand for 5 minutes before serving with maple syrup.

NUTRITIONAL INFORMATION PER SERVING (WITHOUT SYRUP): 225 CALORIES, 3.2 G FAT, 17 G PROTEIN, 31 G CARBOHYDRATE, 73 MG CHOLESTEROL, 449 MG SODIUM.

Italian Vegetable Frittata

SERVES 2

SEVERAL YEARS AGO, I had my first frittata in an Italian restaurant. It was like an omelet, except less puffy and more substantial. It had sausage inside and cheese on top. Since no Italian restaurant I knew of prepared a frittata with egg whites and reduced-fat or nonfat ingredients, I turned to my lean kitchen for a solution. Oregano was a given, but I used fresh oregano from my herb garden. I traded whole eggs for nonfat egg substitute. I replaced the sausage with colorful, sweet vegetables. Finally, I topped the frittata with a sharp nonfat cheese. It is guiltlessly divine.

1	cup nonfat egg substitute, such as Egg Beaters, or 8 large egg whites
1	tablespoon skim milk
¼	teaspoon dried oregano leaves, crumbled (or ¾ teaspoon chopped fresh)
	Several grinds black pepper
¼	cup chopped red bell pepper
¼	cup chopped green bell pepper
¼	cup broccoli florets
½	garlic clove, minced
¼	cup sliced white button mushrooms
2	ounces nonfat Cheddar cheese, shredded (½ cup)

1. In a small bowl, whisk together the egg substitute, skim milk, oregano and black pepper until well combined.

2. Lightly spray a medium nonstick skillet with olive-oil spray. Over medium heat, cook the red and green peppers, broccoli and garlic for 2 to 3 minutes. Remove from the skillet and set aside.

3. Reduce the heat to low and add the egg mixture to the skillet; cook, tipping and swirling from time to time, until set. The frittata will be slightly wet on top. Do not stir. Top with the cooked vegetable mixture and the mushrooms. Remove the skillet from the heat, sprinkle the frittata with the shredded cheese, cover, and let stand for 3 minutes, or until the cheese melts. Serve immediately.

NUTRITIONAL INFORMATION PER SERVING: 121 CALORIES, 0.7 G FAT, 19.5 G PROTEIN, 7.8 G CARBOHYDRATE, TRACE CHOLESTEROL, 581 MG SODIUM.

LeanSuggestions

Since the frittata is so much like its cousin, the omelet, consider these variations:

■ Add lean homemade sausage or bits of Canadian-style bacon.

■ Use a variety of mushrooms, like shiitake or cremini, in place of the vegetables.

■ Use vegetables like chopped asparagus, chopped water-packed artichoke bottoms, or julienned carrots and zucchini. Add a tablespoon of chopped black Kalamata olives and a dusting of Parmesan cheese at the end.

■ Add bean sprouts, green onions, water chestnuts and a dash of sodium-reduced soy sauce for an Asian spinoff.

■ Omit the oregano and add chili powder or cumin and some chopped jalapeño pepper for a Tex-Mex version.

■ Cook some spinach leaves briefly and squeeze dry and add nonfat or reduced-fat Swiss cheese to the frittata.

Lean Breakfast Sausage

MAKES 2¾ POUNDS

EVEN THOUGH some new grocery store products brag about their "lower-in-fat" versions of breakfast sausage, they are still too fatty for me. All store-bought breakfast sausage, reduced-fat or not, has fat ground with the meat. I decided that pork tenderloin, because it is naturally lean (1.3 grams per ounce), would make the ideal foundation for my breakfast sausage.

It isn't the fat that makes breakfast sausage flavorful, but the seasonings. I like sausage with a slight bite, so in went fresh-ground black pepper. I also added some crumbled sage leaves, as sage has always been the seasoning of choice for breakfast sausage. After perusing several old country cookbooks, I discovered that marjoram, thyme and mace, in the proper balance, give breakfast sausage its distinctive flavor notes. My first batch was good, but I tinkered with the spice ratios, increasing the pepper and tweaking down the marjoram until it was perfect.

On Sundays, I cook up a couple of patties, scramble some nonfat egg substitute and load up two pieces of unbuttered toast with some farmer's-market strawberry preserves.

2½	pounds trimmed pork tenderloin, ground twice, for sausage
1	cup fine fresh white bread crumbs
2	teaspoons kosher salt
1½	teaspoons fresh-ground black pepper
1	teaspoon crumbled dried sage
¾	teaspoon crumbled dried marjoram
¾	teaspoon crumbled dried thyme
½	teaspoon ground mace
½	cup cold water

1. Place all of the ingredients in a large glass or ceramic bowl. With clean hands, gently knead the mixture until it is well combined; do not overhandle.

2. Cover and chill for 30 minutes. Form into 3-inch patties or stuff into a natural-sausage casing and tie into 3-inch links. Cook over medium heat in a nonstick skillet, turning once, for 4 to 5 minutes per side, or until browned.

NUTRITIONAL INFORMATION PER 2-OUNCE PATTY OR 3-INCH LINK: 67 CALORIES, 1.8 G FAT, 10.6 G PROTEIN, 1.5 G CARBOHYDRATE, 32 MG CHOLESTEROL, 225 MG SODIUM.

LeanTip: Refrigerate the sausage for up to 2 days. Or pack in 8-ounce portions in freezer bags and freeze for up to 6 months. To defrost, remove from the freezer and place in the refrigerator for 12 hours.

McMmmmm's Breakfast Sandwich

SERVES 2

My cousin Kathy Mauer solved her weekday breakfast dilemma magnificently. She told me that on rushed mornings, she used to head for the restaurant with the golden arches for its egg sandwich. Then she learned it had almost 16 fat grams. Her solution was to make her own on the weekend with low-fat ingredients.

By using nonfat margarine, nonfat cheese slices and very lean ham, she created a breakfast sandwich we dubbed McMmmm's. It honored the originator of the high-fat version and tastes mmmm . . . good.

To beat the morning rush, Kathy makes six of these sandwiches on Sunday afternoon and refrigerates them in separate recloseable bags. Then she grabs one in the morning on her way out the door. When she arrives at her office, she pops it in the microwave oven. Fast breakfast food with less than 3 grams of fat? Now that's a great way to start a day.

4	teaspoons nonfat margarine
2	English muffins, split and toasted
4	slices nonfat Cheddar cheese
4	thin slices 98% lean baked ham
½	cup nonfat egg substitute, such as Egg Beaters
	Fresh-ground black pepper to taste

1. Spread 1 teaspoon margarine on each English muffin half. Place a slice of the Cheddar cheese and a slice of the ham on each muffin half. Set aside.

2. Lightly spray a small nonstick skillet with vegetable oil and place over medium heat. Add ¼ cup of the nonfat egg substitute to the pan and let cook until almost set, about 2 minutes. Turn and cook the other side for 1 minute. Grind some black pepper on the egg. With a spatula, lift the egg from the pan and place it on a clean cutting board. Carefully fold the cooked egg into quarters and place on the bottom half of one of the prepared muffins. Place the top half of the muffin over the egg. Repeat, cooking the remaining nonfat egg substitute and placing it on the remaining muffin.

3. Microwave the sandwich on high power for 10 to 15 seconds, or until the cheese melts. Serve immediately.

NUTRITIONAL INFORMATION PER SERVING: 270 CALORIES, 2.7 G FAT, 26.5 G PROTEIN, 32 G CARBOHYDRATE, 13 MG CHOLESTEROL, 1,232 MG SODIUM.

LeanTip: Make 6 or 8 of these at one time. Allow them to cool completely. Insert each one into a small resealable plastic bag, seal and chill.

LeanNote: The high sodium content comes from the cheese and ham. If you are concerned about sodium in your diet, substitute low-fat, low-sodium versions, or use less cheese and ham.

Chips, Dips and Other Snacks

W HEN I LIVED IN ILLINOIS AND WEIGHED OVER 300 POUNDS, I loved Jay's potato chips. They were fried in corn oil and tasted wonderful, and I ate at least ½ pound of chips as a single serving. My first homemade dip was the one that uses a pint of real sour cream (almost 100 highly saturated fat grams) mixed with a packet of onion soup mix. When I ate a pound of regular potato chips and a pint of onion–sour cream dip, I consumed almost 260 grams of fat, the equivalent of almost 1¼ cups of vegetable oil—more fat than I now get in an entire week.

Today, I still love to snack on chips, but I no longer eat the fried kind. Instead, I make my own baked chips. I have also created low-fat dips to complement them, taking many dips that have been in my family for decades and reducing the fat to almost zero. My salsas have fire and flavor but practically no fat.

How can you take the fat out of your favorite dip? First, look at the components. Does it have any vegetable oil? Omit it or reduce it. Does it have regular sour cream or cream cheese? Switch to nonfat. Does it have mayonnaise? Replace it with low-fat or nonfat mayonnaise. Does it have cheese? Instead, use reduced-fat or nonfat cheeses. Are nuts called for? Reduce the quantity or substitute a nut-flavor extract.

Those alterations will turn a high-fat dip into an almost nonfat one, while maintaining all the flavor you expect.

RECIPES

Baked Corn Tortilla Chips

MAKES 54 CHIPS

SEVERAL COMPANIES now make baked tortilla chips. However, fresh-baked chips taste much better than commercial ones, especially when served warm from the oven.

1   9-ounce package corn tortillas
     Popcorn salt*

1. Preheat the oven to 400 degrees F.

2. Remove all the tortillas from the package. With a sharp knife, cut the tortilla stack into 6 pie-shaped wedges. Separate the wedges and place them in a single layer on a nonstick baking pan. Sprinkle with the salt. (Do this in batches.) Bake until the chips are lightly golden, 6 to 7 minutes.

3. Spread the baked chips on wire racks to cool or serve immediately. Repeat with the remaining tortillas. Serve with a favorite dip.

NUTRITIONAL INFORMATION PER CHIP: 16.7 CALORIES, 0.17 G FAT, 0.3 G PROTEIN, 3.5 G CARBOHYDRATE, 0 CHOLESTEROL, SODIUM VARIES.

LeanSuggestions

■ When sprinkling with salt, also sprinkle approximately 1 teaspoon cumin over all the tortilla wedges.

■ Generously dust the tortilla wedges with chili powder or a touch of cayenne pepper before baking.

LeanTip: If not serving them immediately, store the completely cooled chips in an airtight plastic bag.

Popcorn salt is ground finer than table salt and can be purchased at regular supermarkets. It is usually found in the salt section or with the popping corn.

BAKED POTATO CHIPS

I AM STILL NOT WILD about the fat-free potato chips on the market, so I experimented in making my own baked chips. These are the result. A food processor with a sharp blade is very important for slicing these chips evenly; a slice that is thicker on one end and thinner on the other will burn on the thin end before the thick end is baked. Sweet potatoes can also be baked in this manner.

>   2   large red or white potatoes
>   Popcorn salt (see page 49)
>   Chili powder (optional)
>   Cayenne pepper (optional)

1. Preheat the oven to 400 degrees F.

2. Wash and peel the potatoes. Slice them crosswise as thin as possible, using the 1-millimeter blade of a food processor, making certain all the slices are cut to the same thickness.

3. Place the slices in a medium glass or ceramic bowl and cover with cold water. Change the water twice to rinse off the starch. Drain and lay the slices out flat on a clean kitchen towel. Pat dry. Place them as close together as possible, but not touching, on a nonstick jelly-roll pan or pans. Sprinkle with salt, the optional chili powder and the optional cayenne pepper.

4. Bake for approximately 12 minutes, or until the potatoes begin to brown. Remove from the oven and spread on a wire cooling rack. Serve as soon as the slices are cooled. Or store the cooled chips in an airtight bag to maintain crispness.

NUTRITIONAL INFORMATION PER OUNCE: 92 CALORIES, 0.1 G FAT, 2 G PROTEIN, 23 G CARBOHYDRATE, 0 CHOLESTEROL, SODIUM VARIES.

PITA CRISPS

MAKES 72 CRISPS

SNACKING WAS ONE OF MY MOST INSIDIOUS HABITS. Crunching on 4 ounces of regular potato chips can swiftly add up to 40 grams of fat, now my limit for one day. Pita (pocket) bread is at the opposite end of the spectrum from potato chips. A round of pita bread has only 1 fat gram. Pita is also very versatile. It can be warmed and used to dip into LeanHummus (page 62); split in half and opened for a pocket sandwich; used as the crust for Pita Pizza (page 65); or cut into wedges, seasoned and baked, becoming crispy and tasty, as in this recipe.

6   pita pocket breads (7 inches in diameter), split and
        cut into 6 pie-shaped wedges and separated
1   teaspoon popcorn salt (see page 49)

1. Preheat the oven to 375 degrees F.

2. Arrange the pita wedges close together, rough sides up, on 2 nonstick jelly-roll pans. Sprinkle the salt evenly over the wedges.

3. Bake the crisps for 12 minutes, or until golden. Remove the pans from the oven and place the crisps on wire cooling racks.

4. Store the cooled crisps in an airtight container.

NUTRITIONAL INFORMATION PER CRISP: 12.5 CALORIES, 0.05 G FAT, 0.8 G PROTEIN, 2.5 G CARBOHYDRATE, 0 CHOLESTEROL, 47 MG SODIUM.

LeanSuggestions

■ Herbed pita crisps: Combine 1 teaspoon dried crumbled sage, 1 teaspoon dried crumbled thyme and ½ teaspoon fresh-ground black pepper with the salt. Sprinkle over the wedges before baking.

(continued)

■ Mexican-style crisps: Combine 1 tablespoon chili powder with the salt. Sprinkle over the pita wedges before baking.

■ Cheese crisps: Scatter 1½ cups of shredded nonfat Cheddar cheese over the pitas before baking and increase the baking time to 15 minutes. Serve immediately.

BAGEL CRISPS

MAKES 32 CRISPS

THIS IS A FINE WAY to make delicious bagels into a low-fat snack. Use your imagination with these. For example, you can prepare raisin bagel crisps (omitting the salt) and make a dipping sauce by adding a little honey and cinnamon to nonfat sour cream.

4   bagels (approximately 1 pound), cut into very thin slices
      with a serrated bread knife
1   teaspoon popcorn salt (see page 49)

1. Preheat the oven to 350 degrees F.

2. Arrange the bagel slices in a single layer on 2 nonstick jelly-roll pans. Sprinkle the slices with the salt. Bake for 15 minutes, or until the crisps are golden. Remove from the oven and place on a wire cooling rack. When the crisps are completely cool, store in an airtight container.

NUTRITIONAL INFORMATION PER CRISP: 19 CALORIES, 0.13 G FAT, 0.8 G PROTEIN, 3.8 G CARBOHYDRATE, 0 CHOLESTEROL, 73 MG SODIUM.

CHIPPED BEEF DIP

MAKES 5 CUPS

THE ORIGINAL VERSION of this tasty dip used to have more than 260 grams of fat—equal to the amount in 1¼ cups of vegetable oil. I removed almost all that fat by using nonfat cream cheese, nonfat sour cream and black walnut flavoring instead of walnuts. My new lean version has only 5.5 percent fat calories.

2　8-ounce packages nonfat cream cheese, at room temperature
1　16-ounce container nonfat sour cream
¼　cup skim milk
6　ounces chipped beef, torn into small pieces
¼　cup finely chopped onion
¼　cup finely chopped green bell pepper
¼　teaspoon black walnut flavoring*

1. Preheat the oven to 350 degrees F.

2. In a large bowl, with an electric mixer, combine the cream cheese, sour cream and skim milk. On medium speed, beat until smooth. Stir in the chipped beef, onion, green pepper and walnut flavoring.

3. Lightly spray the bottom and sides of an 8-by-8-inch baking dish with vegetable oil. Pour the chipped beef mixture into the dish and bake for 15 minutes, or until hot.

NUTRITIONAL INFORMATION PER TABLESPOON: 16.5 CALORIES, 0.2 G FAT, 1.8 G PROTEIN, 0.2 G CARBOHYDRATE, 1.8 MG CHOLESTEROL, 72 MG SODIUM.

LeanTip: Try this with baked nonfat potato chips or tortilla chips or use as a fresh vegetable dip.

Black walnut flavoring (called Black Walnut Flavor) is found with the vanilla extract in supermarkets.

Spicy Black Bean Dip

MAKES 3½ CUPS

To me, commercial black bean dips have always tasted flat, when they should be lively and luxuriant. Black beans have a naturally earthy flavor that blooms when they are heated. The flavors of sweet bell peppers, onions and cumin smooth the strong edge of these beans. Every time I bring out this dip, everyone eagerly grabs a baked tortilla chip and starts enthusiastically dipping. It's not long before it's all gone.

1	teaspoon extra-virgin olive oil
1	large green bell pepper, chopped (reserve 1 teaspoon for garnish)
1	small red onion, finely chopped (reserve 1 teaspoon for garnish)
2	15-ounce cans black beans, drained (reserve ¼ cup bean liquid)
1½	teaspoons ground cumin
½	teaspoon salt
2	tablespoons cider vinegar
½	teaspoon hot red pepper sauce

1. Pour the olive oil into a large nonstick skillet and place over medium heat. When hot, add the bell pepper and red onion; cook, stirring, until softened, about 5 minutes. Reserve ½ cup of the black beans and place the remainder, with the reserved bean liquid, into the skillet. Simmer, covered, over low heat for 10 to 15 minutes, or until hot.

2. Place the bean-pepper mixture, cumin, salt, vinegar and hot sauce in a food processor fitted with the steel blade. Pulse until the mixture is well combined but not smooth. Transfer the dip to a serving bowl and stir in the ½ cup of reserved beans. Garnish with the reserved chopped bell pepper and onion, and serve.

NUTRITIONAL INFORMATION PER TABLESPOON: 14.4 CALORIES, 0.15 G FAT, 0.9 G PROTEIN, 2.5 G CARBOHYDRATE, 0 CHOLESTEROL, 41 MG SODIUM.

LeanSuggestion: Warm-from-the-oven baked corn tortilla chips are the perfect accompaniment to this dip.

LAYERED TACO DIP

MAKES 9 CUPS

DARLENE BATES, MY SISTER-IN-LAW, brought the high-fat version of this tasty dip to a family party. Served warm, it features layers of refried beans, sour cream, olives and zingy taco sauce.

For me to continue enjoying this dip, I had to make it leaner. Nonfat cream cheese and nonfat sour cream helped vanquish almost 130 fat grams. No-fat-added refried beans replaced the lard-laden original beans. I slashed the quantity of olives by 50 percent and topped my new dip with nonfat Cheddar cheese. This is the truly excellent result.

Serve it in a clear dish to show off its colorful components. Leftovers make a light lunch with additional baked tortilla chips.

1	8-ounce package nonfat cream cheese, at room temperature
1	8-ounce container nonfat sour cream
1	16-ounce can no-fat-added refried beans
1	16-ounce bottle mild, medium or hot taco sauce
10	pitted large black olives, finely chopped
1	medium onion, finely chopped
1	small head lettuce, shredded
½	pound nonfat sharp Cheddar cheese, shredded

1. In a medium bowl, with an electric mixer, mix the cream cheese and sour cream until smooth. Set aside.

2. In a large microwave-safe serving dish, put a layer of each ingredient, in the following order: refried beans, cream cheese and sour cream mixture, taco sauce, olives, onion, lettuce and cheese.

3. Place in the center of a microwave oven and cook for 2 minutes on the high setting. Rotate the dish 90 degrees and microwave on high for an additional 2 minutes. Serve hot with baked tortilla chips.

NUTRITIONAL INFORMATION PER TABLESPOON: 14 CALORIES, TRACE FAT, 1 G PROTEIN, 1.9 G CARBOHYDRATE, 0.5 MG CHOLESTEROL, 107 MG SODIUM.

Sizzlin' Salsa

MAKES 4½ CUPS

I LOVE SALSAS for their fire and because they have no added fat. Fresh tomatoes make all the difference with this salsa. In summer, I use tomatoes and jalapeño peppers picked from my own plants. This is superb served with warm baked corn tortilla chips.

3½	cups peeled, seeded, chopped ripe plum tomatoes
1	medium-size sweet onion, chopped
½	cup finely diced yellow bell pepper
½	cup finely diced green bell pepper
1	jalapeño pepper, minced
2	large garlic cloves, minced
1	teaspoon salt
1	tablespoon distilled white vinegar
1	cup chopped fresh cilantro

1. Place all of the ingredients in a medium glass or ceramic mixing bowl. Stir together until well combined.
2. Cover and let sit at room temperature for 1 to 2 hours before serving.

NUTRITIONAL INFORMATION PER TABLESPOON: 3 CALORIES, TRACE FAT, TRACE PROTEIN, 0.7 G CARBOHYDRATE, 0 CHOLESTEROL, 31 MG SODIUM.

LeanSuggestions

■ A 28-ounce can of whole plum tomatoes can be substituted for the fresh, reserving the juice for another purpose. (Since canned tomatoes contain salt, taste before adding salt to the salsa.)
■ For more heat, add a second jalapeño pepper.
■ When this salsa sits, it can become watery. If this is undesirable, drain before serving.

EXTRAORDINARY ONION SALSA

MAKES ABOUT 2¾ CUPS

SAUTÉING RELEASES THE NATURAL SWEETNESS of the onions, leeks and shallots in this versatile salsa. Serve with warm-from-the-oven Pita Crisps (page 51).

1	teaspoon extra-virgin olive oil
2	leeks (white and pale green parts only), quartered lengthwise, washed and sliced
1½	cups chopped red onions
½	cup chopped shallots
2	tablespoons minced garlic
2	teaspoons chopped fresh thyme (or ¾ teaspoon crumbled dried thyme)
½	teaspoon salt
½	teaspoon fresh-ground black pepper
¼	cup nonfat mayonnaise
2	tablespoons chopped fresh chives (or green onion tops)

1. Heat the oil in a large nonstick skillet over medium heat. Add the leeks, onions, shallots, garlic, thyme, salt and pepper. Cook until the ingredients are not quite softened, about 5 minutes; do not allow to wilt completely. Transfer to a medium bowl and cool.

2. Stir in the mayonnaise and chives. Taste and season with additional salt and pepper, if necessary, and serve warm or at room temperature.

NUTRITIONAL INFORMATION PER TABLESPOON: 8 CALORIES, 0.1 G FAT, TRACE PROTEIN, 1.6 G CARBOHYDRATE, 0 CHOLESTEROL, 43 MG SODIUM.

LeanSuggestions

■ This salsa is incredible served with slices of French bread that have been grilled over a charcoal fire. Cut the slices crosswise, about ¾ inch thick. This allows the bread to become toasted on the outside while maintaining a slightly soft interior.

■ Try this salsa as a topping for Pita Pizza (page 65) with nonfat or reduced-fat cheese.

■ Garnish with a sprig or two of fresh thyme.

VEGETABLE DIP

MAKES ABOUT 2½ CUPS

Cottage cheese and yogurt combine in a sweet, smooth dip studded with bright chunks of ripe tomato and bits of green onion and parsley. Horseradish adds a bite. This dip is terrific for nonfat tortilla chips and homemade pita chips. Fresh vegetables, prepared for finger food, taste wonderful dragged through it. Serve this on a hot-out-of-the-oven baked potato instead of high-fat sour cream.

1½	cups nonfat or 1% cottage cheese
½	cup nonfat plain yogurt
2	ripe plum tomatoes, seeded and finely chopped
¼	cup thinly sliced green onions, including green parts
2	tablespoons chopped fresh parsley
2	teaspoons prepared horseradish (or more)
½	teaspoon salt

1. Place the cottage cheese and yogurt in a blender and blend until smooth, scraping down the sides once or twice, about 2 minutes.

2. Pour the mixture into a medium glass or ceramic bowl and stir in the tomatoes, green onions, parsley, horseradish and salt. Cover and chill for at least 1 hour to blend the flavors, and serve.

NUTRITIONAL INFORMATION PER TABLESPOON: 10 CALORIES, TRACE FAT, 1.7 G PROTEIN, 0.6 G CARBOHYDRATE, 0.7 MG CHOLESTEROL, 33 MG SODIUM.

LeanSuggestion: If you love garlic as much as I do, enhance this dip by adding a clove or two that has been pushed through a garlic press.

LeanHummus

MAKES 2½ CUPS

THE MORE TIMES I HAVE HUMMUS, the better I like it. It's a luxurious concoction of garbanzo beans (also called chick-peas), tahini (a fancy name for sesame seed paste), olive oil, lemon juice and garlic. It originates in the Middle East and is at its best when coating a warm triangle of pita bread. A good hummus has a rich, almost nutty flavor.

The problem with most regular hummus is the fat content. It comes not from the garbanzo beans, since they are normally very low in fat (1 gram per half-cup), but from the tahini (often called sesame butter) and the olive oil.

I added a touch of flavorful oil from Asia (toasted sesame oil) and waved goodbye to the olive oil and its fat calories. I also reduced the tahini and added some yogurt.

1	large garlic clove, peeled
1	15-ounce can garbanzo beans (chick-peas), drained (reserve some of the liquid)
2	tablespoons fresh-squeezed lemon juice
3	tablespoons tahini*
2	teaspoons toasted sesame oil*
2	tablespoons nonfat plain yogurt, plus more if necessary
½	teaspoon ground cumin
1	teaspoon salt

1. Drop the garlic clove through the feed tube of a food processor fitted with the steel blade. When it is finely chopped, stop the processor and add the garbanzo beans. Process for 30 seconds.

2. With the processor running, add the lemon juice, tahini, sesame oil, yogurt, cumin and salt through the feed tube. Process the mixture, stopping from time to time to scrape down the sides of the processor bowl, until the mixture is absolutely smooth. If the hummus is too thick or dry, thin with some of the reserved garbanzo bean liquid or additional yogurt. Taste and adjust salt. Serve at room temperature.

NUTRITIONAL INFORMATION PER TABLESPOON: 21 CALORIES, 0.9 G FAT, 1.2 G PROTEIN, 2.7 G CARBOHYDRATE, TRACE CHOLESTEROL, 76 MG SODIUM.

LeanSuggestions
■ Try LeanHummus (1.8 fat grams per 2 tablespoons) instead of peanut butter (16 fat grams per 2 tablespoons) with jelly on a sandwich: Omit the garlic and cumin, reduce the lemon juice to 2 tablespoons and add 2 tablespoons of the bean liquid.
■ Spread LeanHummus (0.9 fat grams per tablespoon) on a turkey breast sandwich instead of high-fat mayonnaise (11 fat grams per tablespoon).
■ Toss some LeanHummus with warm pasta and sprinkle on some finely chopped fresh parsley for a lean main dish.

Toasted sesame oil (labeled "sesame oil") can be found in almost all large supermarkets in the Oriental foods section. It can also be purchased in most health food and natural food stores as well as in Asian markets. Tahini can be found in many supermarkets and in health food stores.

SPINACH DIP

MAKES 4 CUPS

THE ORIGINAL VERSION of this dip came from the side of a dry vegetable soup packet. In its original form, an entire batch contained over 250 fat grams—more fat than in 1 cup of vegetable oil. By making two simple substitutions, I turned this from fatty to nonfat without altering the flavor and texture. Serve with dark rye cocktail bread slices toasted in the oven until crisp.

1½	cups nonfat sour cream
1	cup nonfat mayonnaise
1	1.4-ounce package dry vegetable soup mix
1	8-ounce can water chestnuts, drained and chopped
3	green onions (white and green parts), chopped
1	10-ounce package frozen chopped spinach, thawed and squeezed dry

Place the sour cream, mayonnaise, vegetable soup mix, water chestnuts, green onions and spinach in a medium mixing bowl. Stir to combine. Cover and chill for 2 hours before serving.

NUTRITIONAL INFORMATION PER TABLESPOON: 13.8 CALORIES, TRACE FAT, 0.4 G PROTEIN, 1.9 G CARBOHYDRATE, TRACE CHOLESTEROL, 106 MG SODIUM.

LeanTips
■ Check the sides of dry soup packages sold in supermarkets. Many contain a dip recipe. If the recipe calls for regular sour cream, substitute nonfat sour cream and kiss 2.5 grams of fat per tablespoon goodbye.
■ If the soup mix recipe calls for regular mayonnaise, substitute nonfat mayonnaise and lose 11 fat grams per tablespoon. Nonfat cream cheese works as well as high-fat.

PITA PIZZA

**SERVES 10 TO 12 AS AN APPETIZER OR
3 TO 4 AS DINNER, WITH A GREEN SALAD**

ALMOST FIVE YEARS AGO, as a guest at a small dinner party, I was served baked wedges of pita bread smeared with tomato sauce and sprinkled with cheese. The next day in my kitchen, I began experimenting. After several tries, I created these.

I shared this recipe with Joan Lunden on ABC TV's "Good Morning America." She could not believe how easy it was to prepare and how great it tasted. Once you give these a try, you'll never call Domino's or Pizza Hut again.

What's the difference? Fat—in large amounts. Most commercial pizza dough contains some oil (close to a tablespoon—13.5 grams) to make it tender. In contrast, each pita bread has only a single gram of fat. A half-cup of pizza sauce can contain up to 12 grams of fat, whereas nonfat spaghetti sauce has none. Finally, mozzarella cheese, even when made partly from skim milk, still has 5 fat grams per ounce, but fat-reduced mozzarella slices off more than half the fat.

6	medium pita breads
6	tablespoons nonfat spaghetti or pizza sauce
	Dried basil
	Dried oregano
6	white button mushrooms, cleaned and thinly sliced
1	medium green bell pepper, seeds and stem removed, coarsely chopped
3	green onions (white and green parts), chopped
¾	pound reduced-fat (2 fat grams per ounce) mozzarella cheese, shredded

1. Divide the oven into thirds with 2 racks. Preheat the oven to 425 degrees F.

2. Divide the pita breads between 2 nonstick jelly-roll pans. Spread 1 tablespoon pizza sauce over the surface of each pita, almost to the edge. Sprinkle the basil and oregano to taste on each. Divide the mushrooms, pepper and green onions among the pitas. Sprinkle ½ cup mozzarella cheese over each pita.

3. Bake for 12 minutes, or until the cheese melts and bubbles. Remove and cut into triangles. Serve immediately.

NUTRITIONAL INFORMATION PER SERVING: 296 CALORIES, 5 G FAT, 29.2 G PROTEIN, 37.3 G CARBOHYDRATE, 6 MG CHOLESTEROL, 729 MG SODIUM.

LeanSuggestions

■ For a Mexican-style pizza, omit the basil and oregano and sprinkle 1 tablespoon chopped fresh cilantro on each pita. Using disposable rubber gloves, seed and slice 1 jalapeño pepper and distribute over the sauce. Proceed as before.

■ Put this topping on corn tortillas instead of pita bread and the fat content will remain the same. I like to purchase tortillas made from stone-ground corn, because they seem to have more flavor. I toast my corn tortillas first, so they don't end up a soggy mess. Here's how: Separate the tortillas, distribute them on the oven rack for 4 minutes in a 425-degree oven, remove with tongs (they'll be hot) and proceed as directed above.

■ Is a pizza not a pizza if it doesn't have sausage on it? No problem. See Lean Italian Sausage (page 170). Add 8 ounces of the sausage to a small nonstick skillet and cook over medium heat, breaking it up with the edge of a plastic spoon or spatula. Once it has lost its pink color, remove from the heat, and cool before using as a topping. My sausage pizzas get fewer than 18 percent of their calories from fat.

■ Don't limit your toppings to those listed in the recipe. Consider a few chopped black or green olives or sliced chunks of water-packed artichoke bottoms. Fat-free hot dogs, sliced into thin rounds, make a great topping. Try different types of mushrooms, like shiitake, oyster or cremini. Layer on a few lean strips of grilled chicken breast. Strips of lean baked ham and drained crushed pineapple are super. Or try chopped cooked shrimp or sea scallops. Defrost a package of chopped spinach, wring it out so it is very dry and top the pizza with some, then top the spinach with fat-reduced Swiss cheese mixed with some mozzarella.

■ See Exceptional Onion Salsa on page 59 for another great topping idea.

Garlic Toasts with Fresh Tomatoes and Basil

SERVES 16

W HEN MY PARENTS came back from spending 1½ years in Rome, they brought with them remembrances of a terrific Italian appetizer called *bruschette*. The recipe my Mom had contained way too much fat, so I removed most of it. Since I was using a reduced amount of olive oil, I made certain to use extra-virgin, because it has a richer and more robust flavor. I didn't miss the fat, and neither will you.

1	pound fresh plum tomatoes, peeled, seeded and minced
½	cup packed fresh basil, minced
2	teaspoons minced fresh oregano (or ½ teaspoon crumbled dried oregano)
1	tablespoon extra-virgin olive oil
2	medium garlic cloves, minced, plus 1 large garlic clove, sliced in half crosswise
1	teaspoon salt
¼	teaspoon fresh-ground black pepper
1	16-ounce loaf crusty country-style Italian bread, sliced ½ inch thick

1. Preheat the broiler.

2. In a small bowl, stir together the tomatoes, basil, oregano, olive oil, minced garlic, salt and pepper. Set aside.

3. Broil the bread slices on a baking sheet about 4 inches from the heat, turning them once, until both sides are golden, about 2 minutes.

4. Lightly spray one side of each slice with olive-oil spray, then rub with the reserved garlic halves. Top each slice with about 1 tablespoon of the tomato mixture and serve.

NUTRITIONAL INFORMATION PER SERVING: 94 CALORIES, 2.1 G FAT, 2.3 G PROTEIN, 16.2 G CARBOHYDRATE, 0 CHOLESTEROL, 302 MG SODIUM.

ROASTED GARLIC BREAD

MAKES 18 SLICES; SERVES 8 TO 10

In MY FAT DAYS, I never began an Italian meal without garlic bread. I used to melt a stick of butter and then add 6 to 8 minced garlic cloves and let them soften slightly. My garlic bread had over 90 fat grams and more than 800 calories from the butter.

I had heard how wonderful roasted garlic was, but every recipe I saw began by slicing off the top of a garlic head and drizzling on a tablespoon or two of olive oil. Not exactly a low-fat concept. But I discovered that roasting the garlic makes a clove almost buttery in texture yet rich in garlic flavor, making extra olive oil unnecessary.

> 2-3   **large heads of garlic, impeccably fresh and firm**
>
> 1   **large loaf Italian bread**

1. Preheat the oven to 400 degrees F, with a rack in the middle.

2. Cut a piece of aluminum foil into an 18-by-12-inch rectangle. Trim the top of each garlic head with sharp scissors, without cutting into the cloves. With a sharp knife, cut each head of garlic crosswise in half and turn the cut sides up. Place the garlic in the center of the aluminum foil and lightly spray the cut side of each halve with olive-oil spray. Bring the edges of the foil together and seal. Place the packet in the oven and bake for 45 minutes, or until the garlic is very soft.

3. Slice the bread crosswise into 1-inch slices, without cutting all the way through to the bottom. Wrap the loaf in foil and seal completely. About 8 minutes before the garlic is done, place the bread in the oven.

4. Take the garlic packet from the oven, and remove the roasted garlic from the foil packet with a spatula. Place the roasted garlic on a small plate. Take the bread from the oven, and remove the foil. Place the bread on a platter or a large serving plate. To eat, use a small knife to pop out 1 or 2 cloves of the garlic and spread on each piece of the bread.

NUTRITIONAL INFORMATION PER SLICE: 71 CALORIES, 1 G FAT, 3 G PROTEIN, 13.4 G CARBOHYDRATE, 0 CHOLESTEROL, 161 MG SODIUM.

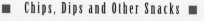

■ Chips, Dips and Other Snacks ■

SALADS

WHEN I WEIGHED 308 POUNDS, I made few salads, and those were extraordinarily high in fat. My egg salad, tuna salad, chicken and pasta salad, potato salad and cabbage slaw all used real mayonnaise. Since mayonnaise has 11 grams of fat per level tablespoon and gets 99 percent of its calories from fat, you can imagine how much fat was in my favorite salads.

When nonfat mayonnaise was introduced, I was probably the first in line to buy some. Did my new salads taste exactly as they once did? No. But they were close. I reincarnated other salads by using some of the new products that had almost no calories from fat.

On Sunday evenings, I often assemble a large tossed salad in a big stainless-steel bowl. I make certain the greens are spun as dry as possible, and then cover the bowl and keep it chilled. For the following nights, I can reach into my big bowl and have a beautiful salad in seconds. I add fresh tomato wedges at the last moment so they don't lose their flavor or their juice.

Pasta salads, made ahead, can easily serve as a brown-bag lunch for a couple days during the week, and a good low-fat tuna, egg or chicken salad can be stuffed into a pita pocket or put on regular bread. I've even recreated classic holiday salads so that everyone can enjoy them guiltlessly.

Recipes

■ Salads ■

BASMATI RICE AND FRESH CORN SALAD

SERVES 8

ORN-ON-THE-COB, with butter running in rivulets through the valleys between each kernel, means that it must be late July. I don't use butter anymore, but my heart still races during this time of year. Local corn comes in a rush and then stops. Creating different uses for
fresh sweet corn takes top priority so I can enjoy it as much as possible during its short run.

This cold salad combines aromatic basmati rice, golden corn kernels, tomato, peppers and
bits of nonfat Cheddar cheese, tossed together with a cumin-scented Italian dressing.

5	tablespoons fat-free bottled Italian dressing
½	teaspoon ground cumin
2	cups cooked basmati rice
4	ounces shredded nonfat Cheddar cheese
	(if unavailable, substitute fat-reduced Cheddar cheese)
1	cup cooked sweet corn kernels
1	fresh tomato, seeded and finely diced
4	green onions (white and green parts), thinly sliced
1	small zucchini, finely diced
1	medium red bell pepper, finely diced
1	jalapeño pepper, minced
	(for a milder salad, remove the seeds)
½	cup chopped fresh cilantro
	Bibb lettuce leaves, washed and chilled

1. In a large glass or ceramic bowl, whisk together the Italian dressing and the cumin.

2. Add the remaining ingredients, except the lettuce, and with a rubber spatula, stir and toss until the salad is well combined. Cover and refrigerate for 1 hour, or as long as overnight. Mound servings on the lettuce leaves and serve.

NUTRITIONAL INFORMATION PER SERVING: 105 CALORIES, 0.4 G FAT, 6 G PROTEIN, 19.8 G CARBOHYDRATE, 0 CHOLESTEROL, 339 MG SODIUM.

NOT-TABOO TABBOULEH

SERVES 6

TABBOULEH (TA-BOO-leh): What a seemingly odd name for an absolutely magnificent salad of bulgur wheat scented with mint and seasoned with olive oil. My friend Eddie, who is Lebanese, brought me my first tabbouleh. I slipped a fork in and tasted it. The blend of flavors and textures was superb.

Eddie generously shared his recipe with me, and then I tweaked it a little by using red onion and tomato for color and adding shredded carrot for sweetness.

My tabbouleh brims with health. I use organically grown bulgur wheat with organically grown parsley, cucumbers and tomato. It still has some olive oil—it wouldn't be tabbouleh without it. However, a serving gets only 18 percent of its calories from less than 3 grams of fat. This makes a wonderful lunch salad. Or stuff some inside whole wheat pita bread and top with alfalfa sprouts.

⅔	cup bulgur wheat
2	cups water
⅔	cup minced red onion
1	garlic clove, minced
1	teaspoon sea salt
½	teaspoon ground allspice
¼	teaspoon fresh-ground black pepper
1	tablespoon crumbled dried mint
2½	cups finely chopped fresh parsley (about 2 large bunches)
1	large carrot, peeled and finely shredded
½	cup finely chopped green onions, white and green parts
¼	cup fresh-squeezed lemon juice (about 1 large lemon)
1	tablespoon extra-virgin olive oil
1½	cups finely diced seeded cucumber (about 1 large)

1   medium vine-ripened tomato, seeded and finely chopped

1. Place the bulgur in a heatproof bowl. Bring the water to a boil and pour over the bulgur; let stand for 1 hour, just until the bulgur has softened.

2. Meanwhile, in a large bowl, stir together the onion, garlic, salt, allspice, pepper and mint and let stand for 30 minutes—no longer.

3. Drain the bulgur in a sieve, pressing hard to extract as much water as possible, and add to the onion mixture along with the parsley, carrot, green onions, lemon juice, olive oil, cucumber and tomato. Toss the salad well. Taste and adjust the seasonings. Cover and refrigerate. Serve cold.

NUTRITIONAL INFORMATION PER SERVING: 132 CALORIES, 2.7 G FAT, 3.2 G PROTEIN, 25 G CARBOHYDRATE, 0 CHOLESTEROL, 378 MG SODIUM.

LeanSuggestion: If you grow mint in your yard, here's how to use it in this salad. Omit the dried mint and add ½ cup finely chopped fresh mint when tossing everything together at the end.

Caesar Salad with Sliced Chicken Breast

SERVES 4

WHEN DINING OUT, I frequently ask for a Caesar salad. I have them leave off the high-fat croutons and bring the dressing and Parmesan cheese on the side. That way, I control the fat content.

Many restaurants have added a new twist to Caesar salad, broiling or lightly grilling a skinless, boneless chicken breast, slicing it and topping the salad with it.

I do the same at home, with my own fat-free dressing and a broiled chicken breast seasoned just the way I want it. With a few slices of warm French bread, my salad makes a low-fat and satisfying meal.

DRESSING

½   cup nonfat mayonnaise
¼   cup skim milk
½   teaspoon anchovy paste*
1   teaspoon fresh-squeezed lemon juice
1   teaspoon balsamic vinegar
1   teaspoon Dijon-style mustard
½   teaspoon Worcestershire sauce
1   garlic clove
2   tablespoons fresh-grated Parmesan cheese
¼   teaspoon fresh-ground black pepper

SALAD

4   skinless, boneless chicken breasts, lightly seasoned with
    Mauery's Seasoned Salt (page 248)

1   large head romaine lettuce, rinsed, cut into wide strips
      and spun dry (about 7 cups)
1   cup toasted bread cubes (from any bag of poultry-stuffing bread cubes)
2   tablespoons fresh-grated Parmesan cheese

1. Dressing: Place all of the dressing ingredients in a food processor or blender. Process or blend until smooth. Transfer to a small bowl or jar and chill the dressing, covered, for at least 1 hour, to allow the flavors to blend and mellow.

2. Salad: Set the broiler rack 6 inches from the heat. Preheat the broiler. Lightly spray the broiler pan with vegetable oil. Place the chicken breasts on the pan and place the pan under the broiler. Broil for 6 minutes, turn and broil for 5 minutes more.

3. Meanwhile, divide the lettuce among 4 chilled salad bowls and drizzle the dressing over each salad. Sprinkle each salad with ¼ cup of the bread cubes and ½ tablespoon of the Parmesan.

4. Remove the chicken breasts to a cutting board and slice each crosswise, divide among the salads and serve.

NUTRITIONAL INFORMATION PER SERVING: 251 CALORIES, 5.1 G FAT, 31 G PROTEIN, 17.2 G CARBOHYDRATE, 77 MG CHOLESTEROL, 962 MG SODIUM.

LeanTip: Leftover chicken breast, shredded or sliced, can be a quick and easy substitution for the broiled chicken breast.

Anchovy paste gives the classic Caesar salad flavor. It comes in a squeeze tube, much like toothpaste, and can be purchased in most supermarkets and specialty food stores. If it is difficult to locate, or if it is a flavor you do not like, omit it.

Cold Chicken and Pasta Salad

SERVES 6

WHILE WADDLING AROUND at a scale-busting 308 pounds, I got on a kick of dark-meat chicken salad lunches. I used to make up enormous batches and haul a quart to work with me. I'd also pack a stack of saltine crackers. I believed I was doing myself a big, healthy favor. I'm glad I didn't bet on it, because my chicken salad contained a whopping 118 grams of fat. Jumpin' chicken gizzards.

During my high-fat salad days, I asked my wife to stop washing my all-cotton jeans in hot water, so they wouldn't shrink so much. She chuckled and informed me that she had always washed them in cold water.

Where was the fat coming from in my original salad? The major culprit was mayonnaise. There was at least ½ cup, which added up to 88 fat grams.

Next, I took a look at those toothsome chicken thighs I had so nonchalantly tossed in. What makes thigh meat so delectable is its fat content—almost three times as much as breast meat.

Today, for a special Saturday lunch, I prepare the best chicken salad imaginable. It's loaded with pasta (an excellent complex carbohydrate), white-meat chicken, fat-free mayonnaise, red grapes and peas (for color and flavor with no added fat). It tastes rich, yet it has less than 3 fat grams—a meager 11 percent of its calories come from fat.

Now, I won't be cryin' fowl to my wife when I slip on my favorite jeans.

3	cups defatted low-sodium chicken broth
3	skinless, boneless chicken breast halves
2½	cups (5 ounces) shell-shaped pasta
1	cup nonfat mayonnaise
½	teaspoon celery salt
¼	teaspoon fresh-ground black pepper
½	teaspoon Dijon-style mustard

2   celery stalks, strings removed and cut crosswise into ⅛-inch slices
1   cup baby peas, cooked briefly, drained and cooled
1   cup seedless red grapes, washed, dried and sliced in half

1. Place the chicken broth in a medium saucepan. Bring the broth to a low boil over medium-high heat. Add the chicken breasts, turn the heat to low and gently simmer for 20 minutes, or until they are white and firm when pressed. Remove the pan from the heat and allow to cool. Remove the breasts, drain and chill. Save the broth for another use.

2. Cook the pasta in a large pot of boiling water according to package directions, about 10 minutes. Drain and rinse under cold water. Set aside.

3. In a medium mixing bowl, whisk together the mayonnaise, celery salt, pepper and mustard. Cut the chicken breasts into bite-size pieces and add to the mixing bowl along with the pasta, celery, peas and grapes. Stir and toss to combine. Cover and refrigerate for at least 1 hour before serving.

NUTRITIONAL INFORMATION PER SERVING: 227 CALORIES, 2.8 G FAT, 20 G PROTEIN, 32.4 G CARBOHYDRATE, 42.5 MG CHOLESTEROL, 569 MG SODIUM.

LeanTip: To improve this salad's flavor without adding fat, use the chicken broth in which the breasts were simmered to cook the pasta. Add enough water to the broth to bring the volume to 1 quart, bring to a boil and cook the shells. Proceed as directed.

Apricot Chicken Salad

SERVES 4

WHEN WE FIRST MOVED TO NORTH CAROLINA, a new friend there served her special chicken salad with apricot dressing. I was skeptical, but it turned out to be absolutely delicious. The only thing I do differently is substitute nonfat mayonnaise.

3	cups shredded cooked skinless, boneless chicken breast
¾	cup finely chopped sweet onion, such as Vidalia
¾	cup finely chopped celery (strings removed before chopping)
¾	cup canned apricots in heavy syrup, drained and pitted
1	tablespoon Major Grey's mango chutney
¾	cup nonfat mayonnaise
1½	teaspoons fresh-squeezed lemon juice
¾	teaspoon sodium-reduced soy sauce
¼	teaspoon fresh-ground black pepper
8	Bibb lettuce leaves, washed, spun dry and chilled
2	tablespoons finely chopped pecans, toasted*

1. In a medium mixing bowl, combine the chicken, onion and celery. Set aside.

2. In a food processor or blender, puree the apricots with the chutney. Add the mayonnaise, lemon juice, soy sauce and pepper and puree until combined.

3. Fold the dressing into the chicken mixture to coat. Place 2 lettuce leaves on each of 4 chilled salad plates. Divide the salad among the plates. Dust each with 1½ teaspoons of the pecans and serve.

NUTRITIONAL INFORMATION PER SERVING: 285 CALORIES, 6.7 G FAT, 28.3 G PROTEIN, 27.5 G CARBOHYDRATE, 68 MG CHOLESTEROL, 768 MG SODIUM.

To toast chopped nuts: Preheat the broiler. Place the nuts in a thin, even layer on a broiler-safe pan under the broiler. Check after 1 to 2 minutes, and check every 30 seconds after that to see if the nuts are dark brown.

DELICATESSEN-STYLE MACARONI SALAD

MAKES 5 CUPS, SERVES 6

CHICAGO HAS SEVERAL old Jewish neighborhoods, which are home to some outstanding delicatessens. My mom never made a macaroni salad. My first taste probably came at one those delis. A half-cup serving, however, can contain more than 10 grams of fat. Then I discovered whipped nonfat salad dressing, and I looked through several old cookbooks for classic macaroni salad recipes. I created this deli salad by borrowing some of the best parts of each.

1¼	cups nonfat whipped salad dressing, such as Kraft Miracle Whip
2	tablespoons white-wine vinegar
1	tablespoon Dijon-style mustard
½	teaspoon salt
¼	teaspoon fresh-ground black pepper
½	pound elbow macaroni, cooked, rinsed under cold water and drained
1	cup sliced celery
½	cup chopped green bell pepper
½	cup chopped red bell pepper
¼	cup chopped red onion

1. In a medium glass or ceramic bowl, whisk together the salad dressing, vinegar, mustard, salt and pepper until combined.

2. Add the macaroni, celery, peppers and onion. Stir to combine. Cover and chill for 2 to 3 hours to enhance the flavor. Serve cold.

NUTRITIONAL INFORMATION PER ½-CUP SERVING: 133 CALORIES, 0.5 G FAT, 2.9 G PROTEIN, 19.4 G CARBOHYDRATE, 0 CHOLESTEROL, 597 MG SODIUM.

CHOPPED SALAD WITH BLACK PEPPER DRESSING

SERVES 8

IN EARLY SUMMER, when sun-warmed tomatoes are ripe, a chopped salad is the perfect use for them. Chop up a head of chilled iceberg lettuce, whirl up some homemade peppered mayonnaise and voilà! A delightful lunch. The original version of this salad had over 100 grams of fat and almost 1,000 calories from the dressing.

DRESSING

½   cup nonfat mayonnaise
½   cup nonfat buttermilk
1   teaspoon red-wine vinegar
½   teaspoon fresh-squeezed lemon juice
2   teaspoons coarse-ground black pepper

SALAD

1   head iceberg lettuce, washed and coarsely chopped
2   large ripe tomatoes, peeled, seeded and coarsely chopped
Salt (optional)

1. **Dressing:** In a small glass or ceramic bowl, whisk together the mayonnaise, buttermilk, vinegar, lemon juice and pepper. Set aside.

2. **Salad:** Place the lettuce and tomatoes in a large salad bowl. Pour about half of the dressing over all and toss until the salad ingredients are well coated. Salt to taste. Pass the remaining dressing at the table.

NUTRITIONAL INFORMATION PER SERVING (WITHOUT SALT): 36 CALORIES, 0.28 G FAT, 0.8 G PROTEIN, 7 G CARBO-HYDRATE, TRACE CHOLESTEROL, 221 MG SODIUM.

SMOTHERED SUMMER CUCUMBER SALAD

SERVES 10

WHEN I WAS GROWING UP, a high-fat version of this salad was always on the picnic table when we ate outdoors at my grandparents' house. The dawn of fat-free mayonnaise and sour cream brought this velvety salad roaring back to my own summer table. Using a sweet onion, like a Vidalia, balances the astringency of the vinegar, making it unnecessary to add sugar.

3   large cucumbers, peeled, seeded and thinly sliced
1   small sweet onion, finely chopped
2   tablespoons distilled white vinegar
2   teaspoons salt
¾   cup nonfat mayonnaise
1   cup nonfat sour cream
2   rounded tablespoons finely chopped fresh dill,
     plus more for garnish
¼   teaspoon fresh-ground black pepper
⅛   teaspoon hot red pepper sauce

1. Place the cucumbers, onion, vinegar and salt into a medium glass or ceramic bowl. With a rubber spatula, toss and stir until combined. Cover and let stand for 30 minutes. Drain well, pressing to extract as much liquid as possible.

2. In a medium glass or ceramic bowl, whisk together the mayonnaise, sour cream, dill, pepper and hot sauce. Add the cucumbers and onion to the bowl and, with a rubber spatula, stir and fold until the cucumbers are coated with the dressing. Cover and chill for 2 to 3 hours. Top with additional dill just before serving.

NUTRITIONAL INFORMATION PER ½-CUP SERVING: 51 CALORIES, TRACE FAT, 0.8 G PROTEIN, 6.7 G CARBOHYDRATE, 3.3 MG CHOLESTEROL, 325 MG SODIUM.

DILL AND RED PEPPER POTATO SALAD

SERVES 12

MY FRIENDS KRIS AND SCOTT invited us to their home for a Fourth of July celebration. For me, the Fourth of July isn't a celebration without potato salad. By using nonfat sour cream and very low-fat mayonnaise, Kris saved me over 22 grams of fat.

DRESSING

1	16-ounce container nonfat sour cream
½	cup low-fat mayonnaise
1	1-ounce package Hidden Valley Ranch Original Salad Dressing mix
¼	cup dried dill
2	tablespoons chopped fresh parsley
½	teaspoon crumbled dried oregano

SALAD

3	pounds red or white potatoes, boiled in their skins and chilled
½	medium red bell pepper, diced
1½	small yellow onions, diced
½	cup diced celery

1. **Dressing:** In a large bowl, whisk together all the dressing ingredients until combined. Set aside.

2. **Salad:** Cut the potatoes into ⅜-inch cubes. Place the cubed potatoes in the mixing bowl with the dressing and add the red pepper, onions and celery. Stir and fold until the salad ingredients are completely coated. Cover and chill. Serve cold.

NUTRITIONAL INFORMATION PER SERVING: 177 CALORIES, 0.9 G FAT, 2.8 G PROTEIN, 31 G CARBOHYDRATE, 5.5 MG CHOLESTEROL, 272 MG SODIUM.

Hot German Potato Salad

SERVES 8

AFTER SUSAN AND I were married, more than 20 years ago, we would visit her sister Darlene regularly. Darlene often made dinner for us and prepared her wonderful German potato salad. I convinced her to share the recipe with me.

I took it as a challenge to figure out how to make what turned out to be a very high-fat salad into a low-fat one. I replaced the high-fat bacon with Canadian bacon. Instead of cooking the vegetables in some of the bacon fat, I switched to vegetable-oil spray.

½ pound Canadian bacon, diced

1 medium onion, peeled and sliced ½ inch thick

1 large green bell pepper, seeded and diced

½ cup distilled white vinegar

¾ cup granulated sugar

½ teaspoon fresh-ground black pepper

2½ pounds red potatoes, scrubbed, cooked until tender and cut into ⅜-inch slices

2 tablespoons chopped fresh parsley

1. Preheat the oven to 325 degrees F.

2. Place a nonstick skillet over medium heat and spray lightly with vegetable oil. Add the Canadian bacon and cook until beginning to brown. Add the onion and green pepper and cook, stirring, until the onion has softened, about 4 minutes. Remove the skillet from the heat, drain off any liquid and set aside.

3. Add the vinegar, sugar and pepper to a small nonaluminum saucepan. Place over medium-high heat and bring the mixture to a boil, stirring. Remove from the heat and set aside.

4. Lightly spray the bottom and sides of a 9-by-12-by-2-inch casserole dish with vegetable oil and distribute the potato slices evenly around the bottom. Sprinkle the bacon mixture evenly over the potatoes. Pour the vinegar-sugar mixture over all.

5. Bake, uncovered, for 40 minutes, or until bubbling. Serve hot from the oven, dusted with the parsley.

NUTRITIONAL INFORMATION PER SERVING: 202 CALORIES, 1.6 G FAT, 8.2 G PROTEIN, 39.6 G CARBOHYDRATE, 12 MG CHOLESTEROL, 408 MG SODIUM.

Tangy Cabbage Salad

SERVES 8

I LOVE A GREAT CABBAGE SLAW and make up a big batch on Sunday so I can enjoy it with my dinners throughout the week. This one is virtually fat-free.

DRESSING

¾ cup nonfat mayonnaise

¼ cup nonfat plain yogurt

2 tablespoons fresh-squeezed lemon juice

2 teaspoons distilled white vinegar

1 tablespoon granulated sugar

1 teaspoon celery seeds

1 teaspoon salt

¼ teaspoon fresh-ground white pepper

SALAD

1 small head green cabbage (about 1½ pounds), shredded

1 medium red bell pepper, minced

3 green onions (white and green parts), minced

2 medium carrots, coarsely grated

1. **Dressing:** In a large glass or ceramic bowl, whisk together all of the dressing ingredients until combined.

2. **Salad:** Add the salad ingredients and, with a rubber spatula, stir and fold until they are completely coated with the dressing. Cover and chill for 1 hour. Serve cold.

NUTRITIONAL INFORMATION PER SERVING: 59 CALORIES, 0.3 G FAT, 2.8 G PROTEIN, 13.4 G CARBOHYDRATE, TRACE CHOLESTEROL, 586 MG SODIUM.

Sweet and Lean Slaw

SERVES 12

INSPIRED BY A RECIPE for cabbage salad that contained currants, I added chopped golden raisins to my slaw. I had a winner.

DRESSING

1½	teaspoons dry mustard
1	tablespoon poppy seeds
1	tablespoon sesame seeds
¾	teaspoon onion powder
¾	teaspoon garlic powder
½	teaspoon salt
½	teaspoon sweet paprika
½	teaspoon fresh-ground white pepper
½	teaspoon crumbled dried basil
½	teaspoon dried dill
¼	teaspoon fresh-ground black pepper
⅛	teaspoon cayenne pepper
1½	cups nonfat mayonnaise
1	tablespoon clover honey

SALAD

1	head green cabbage, shredded (about 6 cups)
2	medium carrots, peeled and grated
½	cup golden raisins, chopped
¼	cup green onions (white parts only), thinly sliced
¼	cup red bell pepper, finely diced

1. Dressing: In a medium mixing bowl, combine all the dry dressing ingredients. If the mustard is lumpy, press and break up with the back of a spoon, then stir together. Whisk in the mayonnaise and honey until smooth and combined.

2. Salad: Add the salad ingredients, stirring and folding with a rubber spatula until all the ingredients are completely coated with the dressing. Cover and chill for at least 30 minutes. Serve cold.

NUTRITIONAL INFORMATION PER ½-CUP SERVING: 74 CALORIES, 1 G FAT, 1 G PROTEIN, 16.4 G CARBOHYDRATE, 0 CHOLESTEROL, 491 MG SODIUM.

LeanTip: Use ⅓ cup of this slaw in a turkey breast sandwich in place of lettuce.

Asian Cabbage Salad

SERVES 8

Seasoned rice vinegar whisked together with aromatic sesame oil gives this salad its distinctive Asian spin. Rice vinegar has almost the exact aroma of cider vinegar but is seasoned with sugar and salt. Since sesame seeds are high in fat (4.5 grams per tablespoon), I use them sparingly. Lightly toasting the almonds increases their flavor.

⅓ cup seasoned rice vinegar*
2 teaspoons toasted sesame oil*
1 head green cabbage, shredded
4 green onions (white and green parts), chopped
1 tablespoon sesame seeds
1 tablespoon toasted almonds, finely chopped**

1. In a medium glass or ceramic bowl, whisk together the rice vinegar and sesame oil until combined, 20 to 25 seconds.

2. Add the cabbage, green onions, sesame seeds and almonds. With a rubber spatula, stir and fold together until evenly moistened. Cover and refrigerate for at least 30 minutes before serving.

NUTRITIONAL INFORMATION PER SERVING: 60 CALORIES, 2 G FAT, 1.9 G PROTEIN, 10.4 G CARBOHYDRATE, 0 CHOLESTEROL, 177 MG SODIUM.

Toasted sesame oil and rice vinegar can be found in most major supermarkets in the Asian section, or in health or natural food stores, as well as in all Asian markets.

**To toast nuts, see page 80.*

Tuna and Apple Salad

MAKES ABOUT 2 CUPS

MY MOTHER was the person who introduced me to apples in a tuna salad. It refreshes the flavor of this salad.

2   6.5-ounce cans tuna, packed in water
1   cup nonfat mayonnaise or whipped salad dressing,
      such as Kraft Miracle Whip
1   small Red Delicious apple, cored, quartered and chopped
2   celery stalks, stringed and chopped
4   tablespoons sweet pickle relish
2   tablespoons chopped green onion (white and green parts)
¼   teaspoon celery salt
¼   teaspoon fresh-ground black pepper

1. Drain the tuna of all water and add to a medium glass or ceramic mixing bowl, breaking it up with a fork.
2. Add the remaining ingredients and stir together to combine. Refrigerate. Serve cold.

NUTRITIONAL INFORMATION PER ½-CUP SERVING: 193 CALORIES, 1.2 G FAT, 22 G PROTEIN, 24 G CARBOHYDRATE, 41 MG CHOLESTEROL, 1,051 MG SODIUM.

CRANBERRY WALDORF SALAD

SERVES 8

WALDORF SALAD is classically made with apples, celery and walnuts and then coated with a thin mayonnaise-based dressing. It is attributed to the Waldorf-Astoria Hotel in New York. To some people, altering a Waldorf recipe in any significant way would be tantamount to sacrilege. That may be so, but the original is very high in fat from the walnuts (16 grams per ounce) and mayonnaise.

My brother, Tom Mauer, who is a chef, suggested that rather than make a pale, scaled-back version, it would be better to create a new classic with a tip of the hat to the original.

Tom suggested using dried fructose-sweetened cranberries with bright green and astringent Granny Smith apples as well as celery. Then, as I quickly scribbled down the quantities, he stirred together a simple dressing with nonfat mayonnaise. Finally, he suggested reducing the quantity of walnuts to just 2 ounces, chopping them fine and dusting the salad with them when serving.

The divine result is perfect for a winter holiday meal, since all the ingredients are readily available.

DRESSING
½   cup nonfat mayonnaise or whipped salad dressing,
     such as Kraft Miracle Whip
     Juice of ½ lemon
1   tablespoon water

SALAD
3   Granny Smith apples, washed, cored and coarsely chopped
2½   cups diced celery
6   ounces dried sweetened cranberries* (1¼ cups)
16   Bibb lettuce leaves, rinsed, spun dry and chilled

5 tablespoons finely chopped walnuts (about 2 ounces)

1. Dressing: In a large glass or ceramic mixing bowl, whisk together the dressing ingredients until smooth and combined.

2. Salad: Add the apples, celery and cranberries. Toss and stir with a rubber spatula until the ingredients are evenly coated with the dressing. Cover and refrigerate for at least 30 minutes, or until well chilled.

3. Place 2 of the Bibb lettuce leaves on each of 8 salad plates. Mound a generous portion of the salad in the center of each plate, dust with equal amounts of walnuts, and serve.

NUTRITIONAL INFORMATION PER SERVING: 159 CALORIES, 4.4 G FAT, 2.5 G PROTEIN, 31 G CARBOHYDRATE, 0 CHOLESTEROL, 235 MG SODIUM.

LeanTip: To enhance the flavor of the walnuts, you can toast them briefly under the broiler. If you wish to reduce the fat to almost zero, omit the walnuts and add ½ teaspoon of black-walnut flavoring to the dressing.

* Dried cranberries are available at some supermarkets as well as specialty food shops .

Holiday Cranberry Salad with Sour Cream Dressing

SERVES 12

THANKSGIVING AND CHRISTMAS would not be the same at my parents' dinner table without my mother's cranberry salad. It's poured into a ring mold and comes out a deep rosy pink hue. She used real sour cream to make this smooth and help round off the sharp edge of the raspberries and cranberries. Total fat grams per serving? Over 15.

My mother agreed to try her salad with nonfat sour cream and a reduced amount of pecans. She was skeptical, but it turned out to be a huge hit—and it now has fewer than 2 fat grams.

SALAD
2   packages raspberry-flavored gelatin
1   cup hot water
1   pint nonfat sour cream
1   15-ounce can jellied cranberry sauce

DRESSING
8   ounces nonfat sour cream
2   tablespoons powdered sugar

24   Bibb lettuce leaves, cleaned, dried and chilled
2½   tablespoons finely chopped pecans, toasted*

1. Salad: Place the gelatin and hot water in a large bowl. With an electric mixer, mix at medium speed until the gelatin is dissolved. Stop the mixer and add the sour cream and cranberry sauce. Mix until completely combined. Lightly spray the bottom and sides of a 6-cup gelatin mold with vegetable oil. Pour the prepared gelatin mixture into the mold and refrigerate overnight.

2. Dressing: In a small bowl, whisk together the sour cream and powdered sugar until completely combined. Cover and refrigerate.

3. Place the gelatin mold in warm water for 30 to 60 seconds, covered with a dish towel. Remove the mold from the water bath and wipe dry the bottom and sides of the mold. Place a serving plate slightly larger than the mold over the top and invert. Remove the mold.

4. Place 2 lettuce leaves on each of 12 salad plates. Serve a slice of the mold on top of the leaves. Spoon some of the sauce over the top of the gelatin. Dust with a pinch of the toasted pecans. Pass the remaining sauce at the table.

NUTRITIONAL INFORMATION PER SERVING: 190 CALORIES, 1.6 G FAT, 3.5 G PROTEIN, 18 G CARBOHYDRATE, 8.3 MG CHOLESTEROL, 126 MG SODIUM.

* To toast chopped nuts, see page 80.

SALAD DRESSINGS

"THIS REALLY TICKS ME OFF," I said. My outburst occurred while grocery shopping at my local supermarket. I was checking out a line of new salad dressings. The words "fat-free" were splashed all over the neck and front label of a bottle of Italian dressing. I had turned the bottle over to read the back label. First, I saw the food fact list at the top. I scanned the calories: they seemed higher than normal for a nonfat dressing. Next, I checked the fat line: "zero fat grams." I glanced down to the ingredient list in tiny type at the bottom: the fourth ingredient, soybean oil, jumped out at me.

"What's this?" I exclaimed loudly.

Several nearby shoppers swiveled their heads around, shooting me one of those looks. To myself, I said, "Has soybean oil suddenly become free of fat or what?"

Suddenly I remembered that the new labeling laws must be at play here. Those folks in the package-design department were toying with me again.

The labeling law allows manufacturers to claim zero fat grams if their product has one-half gram of fat or less per serving. Granted, half a gram is certainly better than the 8 to 13 grams that old-style salad dressings contained. But 0.5 grams is not zero.

The new labeling reminds me of the first *Back to the Future* movie, in which the character played by Michael J. Fox goes to a drugstore soda fountain and orders a Pepsi-Free. The soda jerk explains they don't give them away.

I guess "fat-free" can mean there is free fat, no extra charge.

My supermarket journey taught me two important lessons.

First, read food labels with a skeptical eye. Do not take for granted that "fat-free" actually means free of fat. It can mean that some products contain a little fat. Second, next time I will talk to myself more quietly unless I want every nearby shopper to think I'm kooky.

I *am* obsessive when it comes to salad dressings because these dressings have been the downfall in many of my well-meaning but ill-conceived diets. My good intentions were frequently crushed under the weight of their high calories (a single tablespoon can have 90 calories) and fat (up to 9 grams).

Because the fat-free, low-calorie dressings commercially available six years ago were flavorless and gummy, with an off taste, I began creating my own dressings from scratch. I used pureed nonfat cottage cheese and nonfat plain yogurt as the foundation for creamy-style dressings. Nonfat mayonnaise allowed me to lower the fat and calories in mayonnaise-based dressings. For oil-based dressings, I turned to thickened chicken broths with touches of olive oil.

The following recipes contain either no fat or only a touch of fat. And unlike the food manufacturers, I clearly state exactly how much fat is in each serving.

RECIPES

THOUSAND ISLAND DRESSING

MAKES 1½ CUPS

EVER SINCE I WAS A CHILD, I have loved Thousand Island salad dressing. As a teenager, I would cut a head of cleaned iceberg lettuce into quarters, place a wedge of lettuce point side up and drizzle a generous amount of homemade dressing over both sides, allowing it to pool onto the plate below. Great eating.

It continued to be great eating until I discovered that my Thousand Island dressings contained almost 6 fat grams per tablespoon. My salad probably harbored at least 30 fat grams. When bottled fat-free Thousand Island dressings appeared in my supermarket, I tried them all. None had the depth of flavor of the high-fat versions, so I created my own. It took a few attempts before I perfected it. Tomato ketchup, chili sauce, pickle relish and a touch of mustard helped lift the texture and sweetness of my dressing far past the mundane.

1   cup nonfat mayonnaise
2   tablespoons skim milk
2   tablespoons bottled chili sauce (I prefer Bennett's)
2   tablespoons tomato ketchup
2   tablespoons sweet pickle relish
1   teaspoon Dijon-style mustard

In a medium glass or ceramic bowl, whisk together all the ingredients until thoroughly combined. Cover and refrigerate. Serve cold. The dressing will keep for at least 1 week, covered and refrigerated.

NUTRITIONAL INFORMATION PER TABLESPOON: 13 CALORIES, 0.02 G FAT, 0.1 G PROTEIN, 3 G CARBOHYDRATE, TRACE CHOLESTEROL, 178 MG SODIUM.

LeanTip: If the dressing is too thick, thin it with additional skim milk.

Family Salad Dressing

MAKES ABOUT 2 CUPS

EVEN THOUGH there are just 2 teaspoons of clover honey in this recipe, the dressing wouldn't be the same without it. The honey sweetens and softens the sour notes imparted by the vinegar and sour cream. Fresh thyme, basil, dill and chives bring the taste to life.

This dressing originally contained 5 fat grams and 60 calories per tablespoon. It still has some oil, since the flavor wasn't right without it. Switching to thickened, defatted chicken broth and nonfat sour cream helped vanquish 145 total fat grams and almost 1,300 calories.

½	cup plus 2 tablespoons defatted low-sodium chicken or vegetable broth
2½	teaspoons arrowroot or cornstarch
1	cup nonfat sour cream
1	tablespoon extra-virgin olive oil
2	tablespoons white-wine vinegar
1	green onion (white and green parts), finely chopped
1	small garlic clove, minced
½	teaspoon Dijon-style mustard
1	teaspoon nonfat mayonnaise
1	teaspoon Worcestershire sauce
2	teaspoons clover honey
1½	teaspoons finely chopped fresh thyme (or ½ teaspoon crumbled dried)
1½	teaspoons finely chopped fresh basil (or ½ teaspoon crumbled dried)
1	teaspoon finely chopped fresh dill
1	teaspoon finely chopped fresh chives

Salt (optional) and fresh-ground black pepper to taste

1. Measure 2 tablespoons of the broth into a small bowl and whisk it together with the arrowroot or cornstarch. Put the remaining broth in a small saucepan and bring to a boil. Whisk the arrowroot mixture into the boiling broth. Return to the boil, remove from the heat, cool and chill.*

2. Place the thickened chicken broth and the remaining ingredients in a pint glass jar. Screw the top on tightly and shake the dressing until thoroughly combined. Refrigerate.

NUTRITIONAL INFORMATION PER TABLESPOON (WITHOUT SALT): 14 CALORIES, 0.4 G FAT, 0.3 G PROTEIN, 0.9 G CARBOHYDRATE, 1 MG CHOLESTEROL, 21 MGS SODIUM.

To cool the thickened broth rapidly: Fill a 4-quart bowl half full of ice; add water to half-fill the bowl. Place the saucepan in the ice water and whisk the broth for 2 to 3 minutes until cooled. Proceed with recipe.

LeanTip: This dressing is wonderful on a green salad, and it can also be used to marinate chicken breasts before broiling or grilling.

VINAIGRETTE DRESSING

MAKES 1 PINT

Classic vinaigrette salad dressings are also classically high in fat. Usually 2 level tablespoons contain 20 grams of fat and 175 calories. The following dressing has had 125 calories removed and 15 grams of fat eliminated.

Originally, I used a mixture of water, pectin and sugar as my trusty substitution for oil in a vinaigrette. I got weak-tasting results. A hospital dietitian sent me a recipe for a pasta salad with a dressing that used thickened chicken broth as its base. It definitely had much more flavor than my pectin concoction, but I still missed the distinctive aroma and flavor that good-quality olive oil imparts.

I did the math and realized that, on a per-tablespoon basis, a reduced amount of oil whisked into the chicken broth would leave only 2.5 fat grams in a tablespoon.

What is not missing in this new dressing is flavor.

1	cup defatted low-sodium chicken broth*
5	teaspoons arrowroot**
½	cup good-quality red-wine vinegar
½	teaspoon salt
1	teaspoon Dijon-style mustard
½	cup extra-virgin olive oil

1. Measure 2 tablespoons of the broth into a small bowl and whisk it together with the arrowroot. Put the remaining broth in a small saucepan and bring to a boil over high heat. Whisk the arrowroot mixture into the boiling broth. Return it to the boil, remove from the heat, cool and chill (for a quick-cooling technique, see previous page).

2. In a medium glass or ceramic bowl, whisk the vinegar, salt and mustard together until combined. In a stream, whisk in the olive oil and then the cooled broth. Taste and adjust the seasonings. Pour the dressing into a pint bottle, cover and chill. Serve cold.

NUTRITIONAL INFORMATION PER TABLESPOON: 25 CALORIES, 2.5 G FAT, TRACE PROTEIN, TRACE CARBOHYDRATE, TRACE CHOLESTEROL, 71 MG SODIUM.

Vegetable broth may be substituted for the chicken broth.

**Arrowroot (also called arrowroot flour) produces a silky result rather than a gummy one, as cornstarch can easily do, and has a neutral flavor. It can be found in the herb-and-spice section of any supermarket. It can also be purchased inexpensively in bulk from most health food stores. Cornstarch may be used as a substitute.*

LeanSuggestions

■ Consider adding a different mustard to vary the flavor.

■ Fresh-ground black or white pepper will add zip.

■ Vary the dressing with fresh herbs, such as basil, tarragon, thyme, oregano, chives or mint.

■ Try different vinegars: balsamic, apple-cider, sherry-wine, white-wine, champagne or malt. Add smaller amounts of these vinegars initially and gradually increase the amount until the most appealing flavor is achieved.

■ If the prepared dressing contains no added herbs, place it in a clean spray bottle and mist it on a finished salad. The misted dressing will leave the salad glistening with a minimal amount of fat calories.

CREAMY FRENCH DRESSING

MAKES 1½ CUPS

I CAN BUY bottled fat-free creamy French salad dressings from the grocery store. But every time I read the ingredient list, I shudder. What are some of those ingredients, exactly? My home-made creamy French dressing has a wonderful flavor and a beautiful color. Instead of ¼ cup of oil with its 54 fat grams, I use my own homemade chicken broth and then reduce it to concentrate its flavor. Honey and imported paprika ensure the sweet edge I find appealing. Garlic powder is not acceptable here—only fresh garlic brings this dressing to life.

1	tablespoon dry mustard
¼	cup red-wine vinegar
¼	cup reduced defatted low-sodium chicken broth*
¾	cup nonfat mayonnaise
1	tablespoon clover honey
1	tablespoon sweet paprika
1	small garlic clove, minced

1. Place the mustard in a medium glass or ceramic bowl. Whisk in a little of the vinegar.

2. Whisk in the remaining vinegar and the chicken broth, mayonnaise, honey, paprika and garlic. Taste and adjust the seasonings. Cover and refrigerate. Serve cold.

NUTRITIONAL INFORMATION PER TABLESPOON: 12 CALORIES, 0.2 G FAT, 0.2 G PROTEIN, 2.7 G CARBOHYDRATE, 0 CHOLESTEROL, 101 MG SODIUM.

To reduce chicken broth: Put ¾ cup of defatted chicken broth in a small saucepan and place over high heat. Bring to a boil and boil until enough water evaporates to leave ¼ cup of broth. Cool to room temperature and use, or cover and chill. Vegetable broth may be substituted for the chicken broth.

CREAMY GARLIC SALAD DRESSING

MAKES ABOUT 2 CUPS

THIS IS A CLOSE APPROXIMATION of dressings served in several major restaurants, without all the fat. It goes together easily and tastes great poured over any tossed salad. It also keeps well, covered and refrigerated.

1½	cups nonfat mayonnaise
½	cup nonfat sour cream
¼	teaspoon hot red pepper sauce
1	garlic clove, minced
1	teaspoon prepared mustard
1	teaspoon dried oregano, crumbled (or 1 tablespoon fresh, chopped)
¼	teaspoon fresh-ground black pepper
¼	teaspoon Dijon-style mustard

In a medium glass or ceramic bowl, whisk together all the ingredients until thoroughly combined. Pour into a medium glass jar, cover and refrigerate. Serve cold.

NUTRITIONAL INFORMATION PER TABLESPOON: 13 CALORIES, TRACE FAT, 0.1 G PROTEIN, 2.4 G CARBOHYDRATE, TRACE CHOLESTEROL, 153 MG SODIUM.

CREAMY ITALIAN DRESSING

MAKES 2 CUPS

REAL HOMEMADE MAYONNAISE is sublime, especially when fresh egg yolks and the highest-quality oils are used. The price of excellence in this case, however, is the extremely high fat content (11 grams per tablespoon). Nonfat mayonnaise made it possible to cut 324 fat grams from this recipe. I solved the taste dilemma by adding fresh herbs to make my dressing assertive.

Whisk up a batch and see what you think. To taste it, take a clean lettuce leaf and dip it in. This will give you a true reading of the flavor. If at all possible, go with fresh herbs instead of dried.

1½	cups nonfat mayonnaise
2	tablespoons white-wine vinegar
2	tablespoons fresh-squeezed lemon juice
2	tablespoons water
1	tablespoon chopped fresh oregano
	(or 1 teaspoon crumbled dried)
1	tablespoon chopped fresh basil
	(or 1 teaspoon crumbled dried)
2	teaspoons Worcestershire sauce
2	teaspoons clover honey
2	garlic cloves, minced
½	teaspoon fresh-ground black pepper

In a medium glass or ceramic mixing bowl, whisk together all ingredients until thoroughly combined. Cover and chill for at least 1 hour to allow the flavors to blend. Serve over chilled mixed greens.

NUTRITIONAL INFORMATION PER TABLESPOON: 11 CALORIES, 0.03 G FAT, 0.06 G PROTEIN, 2.6 G CARBOHYDRATE, 0 CHOLESTEROL, 151 MG SODIUM.

HONEY MUSTARD SALAD DRESSING

MAKES 2⅔ CUPS

A READER OF MY COLUMN sent me a copy of the original version of this recipe, with some personal notes in the margin explaining how she made it lower in fat. I put my own spin on it and developed this wonderful recipe.

After I published it, a caller to a radio talk show said she tried my dressing. She claimed it was very similar to the one she had been trying for several years to get a restaurant to share with her.

2	tablespoons distilled white vinegar
2	tablespoons grated onion
2	tablespoons granulated sugar
½	cup clover honey
6	tablespoons medium brown mustard, such as Gulden's
¾	cup nonfat mayonnaise
⅔	cup buttermilk

In a glass or ceramic bowl, whisk together all the ingredients until well combined. Cover and chill at least ½ hour. Serve cold.

NUTRITIONAL INFORMATION PER TABLESPOON: 21 CALORIES, 0.2 G FAT, 0.1 G PROTEIN, 4.8 G CARBOHYDRATE, TRACE CHOLESTEROL, 121 MG SODIUM.

CREAMY ROQUEFORT DRESSING

MAKES 2¾ CUPS

TRUE ROQUEFORT SALAD DRESSING used to be a real favorite of mine. However, it contained at least 8 grams of fat per tablespoon. Recently, I tasted a commercial bleu-cheese-flavored nonfat dressing, and its flavor was as small as the type on the label.

Nonfat mayonnaise helped remove a lot of the fat. However, I knew that using real cheese was the key to maintaining flavor. I grated a small quantity of imported Roquefort into the dressing. My technique worked. Now I drizzle a half-cup of dressing on a large romaine-lettuce salad and bring out some warm-from-the-oven, hold-the-butter-please French bread. Total fat for my meal is a miserly 3.7 grams.

1½	cups nonfat mayonnaise
¾	cup skim milk*
2	teaspoons Worcestershire sauce
2	small garlic cloves, minced**
¼	teaspoon fresh-ground white pepper
2	ounces top-quality Roquefort cheese, finely grated

1. In a medium mixing bowl, whisk together the mayonnaise, milk, Worcestershire sauce, garlic and white pepper until smooth and combined.

2. Sprinkle in the Roquefort and stir until combined. Cover and refrigerate. Serve cold.

NUTRITIONAL INFORMATION PER TABLESPOON: 14 CALORIES, 0.46 G FAT, 0.44 G PROTEIN, 0.47 G CARBOHYDRATE, 1.4 MG CHOLESTEROL, 131 MG SODIUM.

Depending on the brand of nonfat mayonnaise you're using, more skim milk may be needed to thin this dressing to the desired consistency.

**If you are not a garlic lover, reduce the quantity to a single clove.*

Parmesan Salad Dressing

MAKES 1¾ CUPS

MY FRIEND TARRY had us over for dinner one evening and began the meal with a wonderful tossed salad. Knowing my lean ways, she topped it with this beguilingly sweet-and-sharp dressing. The imported Parmesan cheese, even though Tarry used only ¼ cup, brought the flavor forward. Using ½ teaspoon of fresh-ground black pepper delivered just the right amount of heat to balance the sweetness of the sugar.

1	cup nonfat mayonnaise
½	cup skim milk*
4	teaspoons granulated sugar
¼	scant cup fresh-grated Parmesan cheese
½	teaspoon fresh-ground black pepper

In a medium mixing bowl, whisk together all the ingredients until combined. Cover and chill for 1 hour. Serve cold.

NUTRITIONAL INFORMATION PER TABLESPOON: 14 CALORIES, 0.2 G FAT, 0.4 G PROTEIN, 2.6 G CARBOHYDRATE, 0.7 MG CHOLESTEROL, 127 MG SODIUM.

LeanTips
■ Dress and toss the salad 15 minutes before serving, so it wilts slightly.
■ Two packets of Equal or NutraSweet sweetener may be substituted for the sugar without changing the flavor significantly.

If the dressing is too thick, thin it with additional skim milk.

BUTTERMILK SALAD DRESSING

MAKES 2½ CUPS

Most commercial salad dressings, especially buttermilk-flavored ones, are stratospherically high in fat, containing 90 percent of calories from fat. Those dressings use high-fat sour cream as their base. This recipe gets less than 11 percent of its calories from fat, but the flavor is sensational. It is worth the time to make your own. You can double this to make enough to last a week or more. The flavor gets even better after a day or two.

1	cup buttermilk
1	cup nonfat sour cream
¼	cup nonfat mayonnaise
1	tablespoon grated Parmesan cheese
2	small garlic cloves, minced
1	tablespoon minced fresh parsley
1	teaspoon grated onion
½	teaspoon fresh-ground white pepper
¼	teaspoon dry mustard
¼	teaspoon salt

In a glass or ceramic bowl, whisk together all the ingredients until completely combined. Cover and chill. Serve cold.

NUTRITIONAL INFORMATION PER TABLESPOON: 10.5 CALORIES, 0.08 G FAT, 0.4 G PROTEIN, 0.8 G CARBOHYDRATE, 1.1 MG CHOLESTEROL, 45 MG SODIUM.

LeanSuggestion: This dressing also makes a good dip for raw vegetables, baked potato chips or tortilla chips.

LINCOLN HIGHWAY DRESSING

MAKES 2⅔ CUPS

WHEN THE CHICAGO SUN-TIMES first featured me in its food section, my friend Marge challenged my lean recipe skills with her recipe for a dressing that she and her family had been enjoying for many years. It originated at a restaurant on the Old Lincoln Highway in Illinois.

The recipe contained ⅔ cup vegetable oil. I was stumped for months. Finally, I hit on a combination of thickened defatted chicken broth and arrowroot.

- ⅔ cup defatted low-sodium chicken broth*
- 3 teaspoons arrowroot*
- ½ cup granulated sugar
- ¾ cup tomato ketchup
- ¼ cup distilled white vinegar
- 1 teaspoon salt
- ½ cup grated onion

1. Set aside 1 tablespoon of the chicken broth. Bring the remaining chicken broth to a boil in a small saucepan. Whisk together the reserved tablespoon of broth with the arrowroot. Gradually whisk the diluted arrowroot solution into the boiling broth. Boil for about 1 minute, or until the broth is thick enough to coat the back of a spoon. Allow the broth to cool (for a quick-cooling technique, see page 101).

2. Add the chilled, thickened broth and the remaining ingredients to a 1-quart glass jar. Place a nonmetallic lid on the jar and shake until all the ingredients are well combined. Chill. Serve cold.

NUTRITIONAL INFORMATION PER TABLESPOON: 7.5 CALORIES, TRACE FAT, TRACE PROTEIN, 2 G CARBOHYDRATE, 0 CHOLESTEROL, 52 MG SODIUM.

Vegetable broth may be substituted for the chicken broth. Cornstarch may be used as a substitute for the arrowroot.

Soups

WHEN I WAS A NOVICE COOK, soup was one of the very first things I learned to make. Today, good homemade broths are the basis for more of my dishes than I can count. There is nothing as spiritually warming as a broth pot, loaded to the top with meats and vegetables, slowly simmering away. My whole house carries the aroma on the drifting breezes created by my home heating system. I always wish for friends to stop by, so they can exclaim, "What smells so good?"

After I lost weight, I yearned for substantive foods that were healthy and low in fat. Soup filled the bill quite nicely, thank goodness. And I have figured out how to make every one of my favorite soups either low in fat or nonfat, whether they are cream-based or not.

When you refrigerate soup broths, the fat rises to the top and solidifies. It does not matter whether the broth comes from your own pot or from a can. All broths can be made fat-free by refrigerating them and scraping the solid fat off the surface. This simple procedure ensures that every broth you start with has no fat. There's no need to purchase those high-priced fat-free ones.

I use several other tricks to create low- or nonfat soups. You can revamp your own cherished cream-soup recipe as follows: Instead of the cream or half-and-half that's called for, use an equivalent amount of skim milk and whisk in 3 tablespoons of cornstarch or arrowroot. After you have pureed the soup and returned it to the pot, whisk in the skim-milk mixture. If you are concerned it won't have enough flavor, whisk in one ½-ounce packet of Butter Buds.

I also increase the quantity of vegetables I use in my cream-style soups. For example, in my mushroom soup, I use 1 pound of mushrooms, which makes up for the loss of cream or butter. As a rule of thumb, increase the vegetable called for by half again.

A creamed soup can be thickened by pureeing 1 to 1½ cups of cooked rice and stirring it in at the end. This adds complex carbohydrates but no fat. Or you can add ⅔ cup uncooked rice to the pot at the beginning of cooking and puree everything at the end. Or add about 1 pound of peeled and chopped potatoes at the beginning and puree the finished soup.

As you will see, I add no salt to my broths, preferring to salt the soup at the end. If you are using canned broths, be aware that, unless the label indicates otherwise, most are heavy in sodium. Taste before adding any additional salt, since the broth probably already contains more than enough.

Clear broth can be used for a variety of things besides soup. In fact, I accomplish much of my kitchen magic with it. For example, instead of greasing a broiler pan and placing a fish on it, I spoon some broth on the pan instead. The fish doesn't stick, and the broth imparts additional flavor.

I use thickened or reduced broths as a substitute for some, if not all, of the oil in salad dressing. The broth adds richness, and since it has been thickened, it clings to the salad ingredients just like oil.

I also sauté with broth instead of oil. This is easy to do as long as you keep adding liquid to the pan, which is important because oils don't evaporate but broths do. By reducing whatever remains of the broth at the end of the sautéing process, I obtain a highly flavored yet virtually nonfat sauce.

I cook vegetables in broth and serve them in a bowl with some of the broth. At the table, when I've finished the vegetables, I use a spoon and slurp up the tasty broth, so that I get all the natural vitamins and minerals. No need for butter sauces at my table.

I cook beans to succulent softness using vegetable or chicken broth. Rice becomes flavorful and fluffy when cooked in my homemade chicken, beef or vegetable broth instead of water. No canned broth ever made a great sauce or gravy, but homemade broth certainly does.

RECIPES

HEARTY BEEF BROTH

MAKES 4 QUARTS

THE FIRST TIME I made a beef broth, it ended up clear, not brown. I couldn't imagine why. I finally spoke about it with my brother, who is a chef. "Did you brown the bones before making the broth?" he asked.

"No, I didn't know I had to," I said.

"You must brown them to within an inch of their life. That way they'll color your broth and give it an even richer flavor."

He was right. I got the beef bones together, placed them in a broiler pan and browned them till they were almost black. Then I made my broth. What a difference. It looked almost like root beer and the flavor was incredible.

7-8	pounds beef bones, with some meat
5	quarts water
1	tablespoon cider vinegar
1	large onion, peeled, quartered and studded with 4 cloves
4	medium carrots, sliced on the diagonal into 1-inch pieces
4	celery stalks, sliced on the diagonal into 1-inch pieces
1	white turnip, quartered
12	sprigs fresh parsley, rinsed, trimmed and coarsely chopped
4	garlic cloves, peeled
1	large leek
12	mixed peppercorns (white, green, black)
1	bay leaf
2	teaspoons dried thyme, crumbled

1. Preheat the broiler.

2. Cover a large broiler pan with heavy-duty aluminum foil. Spread out all the bones in the pan and place the pan 6 inches from the heat source. Broil the bones for 12 to 14 minutes, until they begin to blacken. Remove the pan from the broiler, turn all the bones over and return the pan to the broiler for an additional 12 to 14 minutes, until the other side begins to blacken. Remove the pan from the broiler. Set aside.

3. Add the water and vinegar to a large stock pot. Place all the bones, plus any accumulated liquid from the bottom of the broiler pan, into the pot. Add the remaining ingredients. Over high heat, bring the broth to a boil, skimming any froth. Lower the heat and simmer gently, uncovered, for at least 4 hours or up to 8 hours.

4. Remove the pot from the heat. Allow the broth to cool to room temperature. Pour the broth through a colander into a large bowl. Discard the colander contents. Pour the remaining broth through a fine sieve into four 1-quart bottles. Place a piece of plastic wrap over each opening and screw on the cap. Place the bottles in the coldest part of the refrigerator.

NUTRITIONAL INFORMATION PER SERVING: NOT AVAILABLE. AFTER THE BROTH HAS BEEN SKIMMED OF FAT, IT CONTAINS FEWER THAN 10 CALORIES PER ¼ CUP AND NEGLIGIBLE AMOUNTS OF FAT, PROTEIN, CARBOHYDRATE, CHOLESTEROL AND SODIUM.

LeanTips

■ To save energy, after the broiling step is completed remove the upper oven rack and place the remaining rack in the lowest position. Preheat the oven to 350 degrees F. When the broth begins to boil, cover and place the pot in the oven. The broth can simmer, unstirred, for up to 8 hours.

■ If the fat that has risen to the top of each bottle remains unbroken, the broth may be kept refrigerated for 2 weeks. If the broth is placed in a plastic freezer container and frozen, it may be kept for up to 6 months. Once the fat seal is broken, it will keep refrigerated for up to 3 days. Before using the broth, remove the small layer of fat.

■ Try freezing some of the broth in an ice cube tray. Once frozen, remove the broth cubes to a freezer bag and store the bag in the freezer.

HOMEMADE CHICKEN BROTH

MAKES 4 QUARTS

EVERY OTHER SUNDAY is broth day at the Mauer house. My glorious chicken broth begins slowly simmering in midmorning, and by early evening has turned into something closely akin to gold. I make several soups from this sublime liquid, as well as sauces and gravies.

5 pounds chicken backs, necks and wings,
    rinsed under cold water
5 quarts water
1 tablespoon cider vinegar
4 celery stalks, rinsed, cut on the diagonal into 1-inch sections
3 large carrots, peeled, cut on the diagonal into 1-inch sections
1 large onion, peeled, ends trimmed, quartered
1 apple, rinsed, stem removed, quartered
4 garlic cloves, peeled, crushed
8 sprigs fresh parsley, rinsed and trimmed, coarsely chopped
1 small sprig fresh marjoram, rinsed (or ¼ teaspoon dried)
8 whole black peppercorns
4 whole cloves
2 teaspoons dried thyme, crumbled
1 point star anise (or 3-4 whole anise seeds)
1 small bay leaf

1. Preheat the broiler.

2. Cover a large broiler pan with heavy-duty aluminum foil. Spread the backs, necks and wings out in the pan and place the pan 6 inches from the heat source. Broil for 12 to 14 minutes, until the chicken skin begins to brown. Remove the pan from the broiler, turn all the chicken parts over and return the pan to the broiler for an additional 12 to 14 minutes, or until they are evenly browned. Remove the pan from the broiler.

3. Put the water and vinegar in a large stock pot. Set over medium-high heat. Add the broiled chicken pieces and any accumulated liquid from the broiler pan along with the remaining ingredients. Bring to a boil, lower the heat and simmer gently for 3 to 4 hours, uncovered, until the broth is well-flavored. (The broth may be simmered longer for added flavor.)

4. Remove the pot from the heat. Allow the broth to cool to room temperature. Pour the broth through a colander into a large bowl. Discard the colander contents. Pour the remaining broth through a fine sieve into four 1-quart bottles. Place a piece of plastic wrap over each opening and screw on the cap. Place the bottles in the coldest part of the refrigerator.

NUTRITIONAL INFORMATION PER SERVING: NOT AVAILABLE. AFTER THE BROTH HAS BEEN SKIMMED OF FAT, IT CONTAINS FEWER THAN 10 CALORIES PER ¼ CUP AND NEGLIGIBLE AMOUNTS OF FAT, PROTEIN, CARBOHYDRATE, CHOLESTEROL AND SODIUM.

* See LeanTips for Hearty Beef Broth (page 117).

FISH BROTH

MAKES ABOUT 1½ QUARTS

WHENEVER A RECIPE called for fish broth, I used to substitute bottled clam juice. I never knew how wonderful homemade fish broth was until I made my first one. My local fish market gave me the bones and trimmings for free. I don't use homemade every time, but having two quarts sitting in the refrigerator waiting for a good recipe gets me headed in the fish or seafood direction sooner.

This is also the perfect liquid in which to poach a delicate fish. It will come out flavorful and moist every time.

2   pounds bones and trimmings of any white fish,
        such as sole, flounder or whiting, chopped
2   cups sliced onions
1   medium carrot, thinly sliced
1   celery stalk, thinly sliced
24 parsley sprigs
4   tablespoons fresh-squeezed lemon juice
      Salt to taste
7   cups water
1   cup dry white wine

1. Lightly spray the bottom and sides of a heavy nonstick saucepan with vegetable oil. Add the fish bones and trimmings, onions, carrot, celery, parsley, lemon juice and salt and place over medium heat. Cover and bring to a simmer and cook for 5 minutes, or until the onions begin to soften, but not brown.

2. Add the water and wine and bring to a boil, skimming any froth. Lower the heat and simmer the broth for 20 minutes, uncovered.

3. Pour the broth through a colander into a large bowl. Discard the colander contents. Let the broth cool. Pour the remaining broth through a fine sieve into two 1-quart bottles, filling each three-fourths full. Cover the opening of each with plastic wrap and screw on the cap. Chill the broth.*

NUTRITIONAL INFORMATION PER SERVING: NOT AVAILABLE. AFTER THE BROTH HAS BEEN SKIMMED OF FAT, IT CONTAINS FEWER THAN 10 CALORIES PER ¼ CUP AND NEGLIGIBLE AMOUNTS OF FAT, PROTEIN, CARBOHYDRATE, CHOLESTEROL AND SODIUM.

The broth may be kept frozen for up to 3 months.

VEGETABLE BROTH

MAKES ABOUT 2 QUARTS

I CREATED THIS BROTH after receiving many requests from vegetarian readers of my column. It has a richness even though no meat has ever touched it. Olive oil adds to the flavor, but when the broth is chilled, the fat is removed.

3	medium onions, chopped
3	tablespoons extra-virgin olive oil
2	leeks (white and pale green parts), washed well and chopped
2	medium carrots, chopped
2	celery stalks, chopped
¼	pound white button mushrooms, cleaned and chopped
1	cup potato peelings
⅓	cup plus 4 quarts water
¼	cup lentils, picked over
6	garlic cloves, unpeeled, smashed with the side of a chef's knife
10	whole black peppercorns
½	teaspoon dried thyme, crumbled
1	bay leaf
12	sprigs fresh parsley
1	teaspoon salt

1. In a stock pot or kettle, cook the onions in the olive oil over medium heat, stirring, until they are golden, 8 to 10 minutes. Add the leeks, carrots, celery, mushrooms, potato peelings and ⅓ cup water. Simmer, covered, stirring occasionally, for 5 minutes, or until foam appears on the surface.

2. Skim the foam and add the remaining 4 quarts water, lentils, garlic, peppercorns, thyme, bay leaf, parsley and salt. Bring the stock to a boil, reduce the heat to low and simmer, uncovered, for 2 hours. Remove from the heat and let cool to room temperature.

3. Pour the broth through a colander into a large bowl. Discard the colander contents. Pour the remaining broth through a fine sieve into three 1-quart bottles, filling each about three-fourths full. Cover the opening of each with plastic wrap and screw on the cap. Chill the broth.*

NUTRITIONAL INFORMATION PER SERVING: NOT AVAILABLE. AFTER THE BROTH HAS BEEN SKIMMED OF FAT, IT CONTAINS FEWER THAN **10** CALORIES PER ¼ CUP AND NEGLIGIBLE AMOUNTS OF FAT, PROTEIN, CARBOHYDRATE, CHOLESTEROL AND SODIUM.

Before using the broth, remove the small layer of fat solidified on the top of each bottle.

Beef and Cabbage Soup

MAKES 3 QUARTS

THIS IS ONE OF MY FAVORITE SOUPS. It goes together very fast, especially when a food processor is used. Rice was not originally an ingredient in this soup. However, I always make it as a full dinner and needed the complex carbohydrates that rice provides. It also improves the flavor.

½	pound 95% lean ground beef
1	cup diced onion
6	cups defatted low-sodium beef broth, preferably homemade
1	16-ounce can whole tomatoes, chopped, juice included
2	tablespoons tomato ketchup
4	cups coarsely chopped cabbage
1½	cups thinly sliced carrots
½	teaspoon salt
¼	teaspoon fresh-ground black pepper
½	teaspoon crumbled dried basil
½	teaspoon crumbled dried oregano
1	small bay leaf
¼	teaspoon crumbled dried thyme
¼	teaspoon celery seeds
½	cup long-grain white rice

1. Spray the bottom of a large saucepan with vegetable oil. Over medium-high heat, cook the beef and onion for about 5 minutes, or until the meat has lost its pink color, using the edge of a plastic spoon or spatula to break up the beef as it cooks. Pour off any accumulated fat.

2. Add the beef broth and the remaining ingredients except for the rice, and bring to a boil. Reduce the heat to low, cover and simmer gently for 40 minutes. Add the rice and simmer for 20 minutes more, until the rice is cooked. Remove the bay leaf and serve.

NUTRITIONAL INFORMATION PER CUP: 90 CALORIES, 1.1 G FAT, 7 G PROTEIN, 13.2 G CARBOHYDRATE, 10 MG CHOLESTEROL, 282 MG SODIUM.

LeanSuggestion: Ground all-white-meat turkey can be substituted for the beef. You can also substitute chicken or turkey broth for the beef broth.

Chicken, Rice and Cabbage Soup

SERVES 8

ILOVE CABBAGE in all its forms. If handled properly, it is great in soup, too. Blanching it before adding it makes for milder flavor. This soup has a rough, farmhouse look and a spicy bite. Using an aromatic rice, whether basmati or jasmine, brings the flavor to perfection.

6   cups defatted low-sodium chicken broth,
     preferably homemade
2   medium-size sweet onions, sliced
½   cup white basmati rice* (for example, Texmati)
½   large head green cabbage, coarsely chopped
2   lemon slices
½   pound cooked skinless, boneless chicken breast,
     shredded (about 4 half breasts)
3   tablespoons chopped fresh parsley
1   teaspoon salt
½   teaspoon fresh-ground white pepper
⅛   teaspoon cayenne pepper
1   tablespoon cornstarch (or arrowroot),
     mixed into ¼ cup chicken broth

1. Place the chicken broth in a medium saucepan. Bring to a boil over high heat. Add the onions and rice. Reduce the heat to low and gently simmer, covered, for 12 minutes.

2. Meanwhile, in a large pan of boiling water, boil the cabbage for 2 minutes and drain.

3. Add the cabbage and lemon slices to the saucepan with the chicken broth and simmer for 5 minutes. Add the chicken, parsley, salt, white pepper and cayenne, and simmer until the chicken is heated through. Stir in the cornstarch mixture and return to a simmer. Serve hot.

NUTRITIONAL INFORMATION PER SERVING: 159 CALORIES, 1 G FAT, 18 G PROTEIN, 18 G CARBOHYDRATE, 34 MG CHOLESTEROL, 375 MG SODIUM.

LeanSuggestion: This soup makes a meal when served with North Carolina Skillet Cornbread (page 388) drizzled with some flavorful honey.

If you cannot find basmati or jasmine rice, substitute any long-grain white rice.

WILD RICE AND MUSHROOM SOUP

MAKES 7 CUPS, SERVES 6

I HAVE NEVER BEEN FOND OF WILD RICE as a side dish with a meal, but I love it in soup. The earthy flavor is an ideal complement to the woodsy flavor of mushrooms. Curry powder makes this soup glow, and sherry rounds and smooths all the flavors.

1   cup wild rice, rinsed in a sieve under cold water
      until water runs clear
1   tablespoon extra-virgin olive oil
1   medium onion, chopped
1   cup sliced shiitake mushrooms
      (stems removed before slicing)*
1   cup sliced white button mushrooms
½   cup thinly sliced celery
¼   cup all-purpose flour
6   cups defatted low-sodium chicken broth,
      preferably homemade
2   teaspoons mild curry powder
1   teaspoon salt
½   teaspoon dry mustard
½   teaspoon crumbled dried thyme
¼   teaspoon fresh-ground white pepper
⅓   cup dry sherry
¼   cup minced fresh parsley

1. In a medium saucepan of boiling salted water, gently simmer the rice, covered, for 45 minutes, or until tender. Drain.

2. Heat the olive oil in a large saucepan over medium heat. Add the onion and cook, stirring, until softened, 4 to 5 minutes. Add the shiitakes, button mushrooms and celery and cook the mixture until the vegetables are tender, 3 to 4 minutes. Gradually stir in the flour and cook the mixture, stirring, for 3 minutes. Stir in the wild rice, chicken broth, curry powder, salt, mustard, thyme and white pepper. Return the mixture to a simmer and cook for 5 minutes. Stir in the sherry. Serve sprinkled with the parsley.

NUTRITIONAL INFORMATION PER CUP (WITHOUT SALT): 165 CALORIES, 2.6 G FAT, 6.6 G PROTEIN, 25.4 G CARBOHYDRATE, 0 CHOLESTEROL, 381 MG SODIUM.

LeanTip: If, like me, you enjoy food with a little more heat, add hot curry powder instead of the mild.

* If shiitake mushrooms are not available, use 2 cups white button mushrooms in all.

Chicken Vegetable Noodle Soup

SERVES 4

THERE IS ABSOLUTELY NO COMMERCIAL SOUP that beats a homemade one, especially for fat content and flavor. I like my soups packed with good ingredients.

4	cups defatted low-sodium chicken broth, preferably homemade
4	ounces fine egg noodles or vermicelli, broken into short pieces
⅓	cup finely chopped onion
1	medium carrot, cut into julienne
1	small zucchini, cut into 1½-inch sections and julienned
½	cup finely diced celery
½	cup frozen or fresh corn kernels
½	cup frozen or fresh baby peas
½	pound cooked chicken breast, diced
½	teaspoon salt
¼	teaspoon fresh-ground pepper

In a large saucepan, over medium heat, bring the broth to a simmer. Add the remaining ingredients and simmer for 10 minutes. Taste, adjust the seasonings and serve.

NUTRITIONAL INFORMATION PER SERVING: 237 CALORIES, 2.4 G FAT, 22.5 G PROTEIN, 30.5 G CARBOHYDRATE, 61 MG CHOLESTEROL, 432 MG SODIUM.

LeanTips

■ For an even quicker soup, omit the carrot, zucchini, celery, corn and peas. Substitute one 12-ounce package frozen mixed vegetables. Prepare as above.

■ A wide variety of pasta shapes in your supermarket can be substituted for the fine noodles.

Leek and Potato Soup with Garlic

SERVES 4

GARLIC AND POTATOES are meant for each other. Prepare this soup when you need to be warmed from the inside out. It is an excellent chill-chaser.

1	teaspoon extra-virgin olive oil
1	leek (with some green parts), cleaned and chopped
½	large sweet onion, chopped
6	garlic cloves, peeled and put through a garlic press
2	large potatoes (1 pound), peeled and coarsely chopped
2	cups defatted low-sodium chicken broth, preferably homemade
½	teaspoon salt
	Couple grinds black pepper, or to taste

1. Place a large saucepan over medium heat and add the oil. When it is hot, add the leek and onion and cook until just softened, about 5 minutes.

2. Add the garlic, potatoes and chicken broth and simmer for 30 minutes. Remove the pan from the heat.

3. Place the soup in a food processor fitted with the steel blade and puree. Return to the saucepan, add the salt and pepper and simmer. Taste and adjust the seasonings.

NUTRITIONAL INFORMATION PER SERVING: 142 CALORIES, 1.3 G FAT, 4.5 G PROTEIN, 29 G CARBOHYDRATE, 0 CHOLESTEROL, 317 MG SODIUM.

LeanSuggestion: If you really love garlic, double the amount.

Cold and Creamy Carrot Soup

SERVES 8

THE ADDITION OF CARROTS to this vichyssoise (cold potato soup) is perfect. Since potatoes and carrots are both root vegetables, they carry an earthy yet sweet flavor, and the carrots color the soup and provide a healthy dose of betacarotene. Nonfat sour cream makes the soup smooth as silk, creamy to the palate and as close to fat-free as possible.

1	pound carrots, peeled and chopped*
1	pound boiling potatoes, peeled and chopped
2	large leeks (white part only), split lengthwise, washed well and chopped
7	cups defatted low-sodium chicken broth, preferably homemade
1	teaspoon minced peeled fresh gingerroot
¾	teaspoon ground cinnamon
¼	teaspoon ground allspice
½	teaspoon salt
½	teaspoon fresh-ground white pepper
1	cup nonfat sour cream
2	tablespoons finely chopped fresh parsley

1. In a large saucepan, simmer the carrots, potatoes and leeks in the chicken broth with the ginger, cinnamon, allspice, salt and pepper, covered, for 30 minutes.

2. In a blender, puree the soup in small batches, transferring each batch to a large bowl. Once it is pureed, whisk in the sour cream and chill the soup, covered, for at least 4 hours or overnight. Taste and adjust the seasonings before serving. Dust the top of each bowl with chopped parsley and place a carrot curl (see LeanSuggestion opposite page) in the center.

NUTRITIONAL INFORMATION PER SERVING: 134 CALORIES, 0.5 G FAT, 7 G PROTEIN, 27 G CARBOHYDRATE, 4 MG CHOLESTEROL, 465 MG SODIUM.

LeanSuggestion: After peeling the carrot, press hard against it with the peeler and remove 1 to 2 flat lengthwise strips. With a sharp knife, cut the strips lengthwise into ⅛-inch strips. Place the strips in a bowl of ice water and chill along with soup. They will curl. Garnish each soup bowl with a carrot curl.

I prefer using carrots purchased with the fresh greens still attached, not those that are trimmed and packed in plastic bags. They have a fresher flavor.

Quick Corn Chowder

SERVES 8

FALL IS THE TIME for this soup of corn, potatoes and tomatoes. I used to thicken it with a cup of heavy whipping cream. As always, the cream brought along 88 grams of highly saturated fat. I now thicken it with skim milk and cornstarch. It looks almost exactly the same and is just as smooth, but I banished all that nasty fat, as well as more than 700 calories. By precooking the potatoes, I can have this soup appear on my dinner table in a flash.

2	teaspoons extra-virgin olive oil
1	cup finely chopped sweet onion, such as Vidalia
2	garlic cloves, minced
2	cups defatted low-sodium chicken broth, preferably homemade
1½	cups fresh corn kernels (about 2 ears)
½	pound potatoes, cooked, peeled and diced
2	ripe tomatoes, peeled, seeded and chopped
1	tablespoon cornstarch or arrowroot
1	cup skim milk
1	teaspoon salt
¼	teaspoon fresh-ground black pepper
⅛	teaspoon cayenne pepper
1	teaspoon minced fresh basil
1	jalapeño pepper, seeded and minced

1. Put the oil in a large heavy-bottomed saucepan and place over medium heat. Add the onion and cook until soft, about 5 minutes. Add the garlic and cook for 1 minute more.

2. Add the broth, corn, potatoes and tomatoes and bring to a boil. Reduce the heat to low and simmer, un-covered, for 5 minutes.

3. Whisk the cornstarch or arrowroot into the skim milk in a small bowl and stir the mixture into the soup. Return the soup to a simmer, stirring. Add the salt, black pepper, cayenne and basil. Top each serving with ¼ teaspoon of the jalapeño pepper.

NUTRITIONAL INFORMATION PER SERVING: 96 CALORIES, 1.7 G FAT, 3.4 G PROTEIN, 17.7 G CARBOHYDRATE, 0.5 MG CHOLESTEROL, 310 MG SODIUM.

TURKEY GUMBO

SERVES 4

I LOVE THE THICK, RICH TEXTURE and wonderful earthy flavor of gumbos. Even though turkey breast is not traditional, I thought it might work well. I used a traditional shrimp-gumbo recipe as the basis for this soup. After a tweak here (substituting Canadian bacon for fatback) and a boost there (bumping up the seasonings), this gumbo had all the taste of a traditional gumbo.

⅓ cup trimmed and chopped Canadian bacon (about 2½ ounces)
1 small onion, chopped
1 tablespoon all-purpose flour
1 8-ounce can whole tomatoes, undrained
1 garlic clove, minced
¾ teaspoon salt
½ teaspoon fresh-ground black pepper
1 bay leaf
1 cup chopped skinless raw turkey breast
1 quart defatted low-sodium turkey broth, preferably homemade
    (or canned defatted chicken broth; if using, omit the salt)
10 ounces fresh okra, sliced crosswise into ½-inch pieces
    (or a 10-ounce package frozen cut okra)
1½ teaspoons gumbo filé powder*
2 cups hot cooked rice (prepared without added fat)

1. Lightly spray a small nonstick sauté pan with vegetable oil. Place over medium heat and when it is hot, add the Canadian bacon. Stir and cook until the bacon is lightly browned, 6 to 7 minutes. Drain the cooked bacon on a double layer of paper towels.

2. Lightly spray a large saucepan with vegetable oil and place over medium heat. Add the onion and spray again lightly with vegetable oil. Cook until tender, stirring, for 3 to 4 minutes. Stir in the flour; cook for 4 to 5 minutes, stirring constantly. Add the bacon, tomatoes with their juice, garlic, salt, pepper, bay leaf, turkey and turkey broth, stirring well. Bring the soup to a boil and reduce the heat to low. Gently simmer, uncovered, for 1 hour.

3. Stir in the okra and gumbo filé and simmer for 15 minutes more. Remove the bay leaf. Ladle the gumbo over the hot rice.

NUTRITIONAL INFORMATION PER SERVING (INCLUDING RICE): 232 CALORIES, 1.9 G FAT, 18 G PROTEIN, 34.6 G CARBOHYDRATE, 26 MG CHOLESTEROL, 757 MG SODIUM.

* Gumbo filé, which is powdered sassafras leaves, seasons and thickens gumbos. Since I live in North Carolina, I find this seasoning on every supermarket shelf. If you cannot locate some, omit it.

LeanTip: 1 pound of cleaned deveined shrimp can be substituted for the turkey. Add to the soup at the same time as the gumbo filé and okra. Proceed as directed.

CREAMY MUSHROOM SOUP

SERVES 4

LUNCHTIME WHEN I WAS A KID often meant cream of mushroom soup. I loved to break a bunch of saltines into my bowl and let them get soft . . . then slurp away. Today, I know just how much fat (7 grams per serving, not including the crackers) was in that fondly remembered soup. I have also learned that 4 ounces of saltines contain almost a tablespoon of fat (13.5 more fat grams).

I had to come up with a way to improve it. I began by substituting skim milk for the cream. Since cream, when heated, naturally thickens a soup, I used cornstarch to create the rich consistency. Because my soup would not have the same complexity of flavor, I used a whole pound of mushrooms. Since it still didn't have the buttery flavor to which I was accustomed, I added a packet of Butter Buds. A superb mushroom soup was the result, with less than a single fat gram per serving.

3	cups defatted low-sodium chicken broth, preferably homemade (or canned defatted chicken broth; if using, omit salt)
⅓	cup finely chopped onion
1	pound white button mushrooms, cleaned, stems trimmed and sliced
1	½-ounce packet Butter Buds
1	teaspoon salt
½	teaspoon fresh-ground black pepper
	Pinch nutmeg (fresh-grated, if possible)
3	tablespoons cornstarch
1	cup skim milk
1	tablespoon finely chopped fresh parsley

1. In a medium saucepan, over medium heat, bring the broth to a simmer.

2. Meanwhile, spray a nonstick skillet with vegetable oil and place over medium-high heat. Add the onion and cook for 1 minute, stirring. Add the mushrooms and continue to cook, stirring, until the mushrooms begin to give up their liquid and the onion is softened. Remove the skillet from the heat.

3. Add the cooked mushroom mixture, Butter Buds, salt, pepper and nutmeg to the chicken broth and simmer for 3 minutes. Whisk the cornstarch into the milk in a small bowl and stir the mixture into the soup. Return the soup to a simmer and cook for 1 minute. Ladle the soup into serving bowls and sprinkle with the parsley.

NUTRITIONAL INFORMATION PER SERVING: 94 CALORIES, 0.8 G FAT, 4.3 PROTEIN, 15 G CARBOHYDRATE, 1 MG CHOLESTEROL, 629 MG SODIUM.

LeanSuggestion: For a nice flavor, stir in 2 tablespoons dry sherry (not cooking sherry), just before serving.

Sweet and Sour Cabbage Soup

SERVES ABOUT 8 AS A MAIN COURSE

THIS SOUP BEGAN LIFE in the kitchen of a close friend of mine. The wonderful aromas, tinged with the brown sugar welling up from the soup pot, always made my mouth water. Unfortunately, the soup was based on beef broth and prepared with chunks of beef chuck: flavorful, but very fatty. Skimming the broth only partly helped, since the meat still retained much of its natural fat content.

Why not make this a chicken-broth-based soup with the leanest meat possible, say, turkey breast? I admit that it is slightly less rich, but the sweet flavor of the brown sugar and the sour of the lemon still shine through. And it has less than 1 fat gram per serving.

2	quarts defatted low-sodium chicken broth, preferably homemade
1	pound skinless, boneless turkey breast, cut into ½-inch cubes (about 3 cups)
1½	pounds green cabbage, coarsely chopped (6-7 cups)
2	medium tomatoes, peeled and chopped
1	medium onion, chopped (about ⅔ cup)
1	small green bell pepper, finely diced (about ¾ cup)
1	large celery stalk, strings removed, thinly sliced (about ¾ cup)
1	large carrot, peeled and thinly sliced (about ¾ cup)
⅓	cup tomato paste
¼	cup ketchup
¼	cup light brown sugar
⅓	cup fresh-squeezed lemon juice (about 1½ lemons)
1	teaspoon salt
½	teaspoon fresh-ground black pepper

1. Heat the broth in a large soup pot over medium-high heat. Add the turkey and bring to a boil. Lower the heat and gently simmer for about 30 minutes, skimming any froth from time to time.

2. Add the cabbage, tomatoes, onion, green pepper, celery and carrot. Stir in the tomato paste, ketchup, brown sugar, lemon juice, salt and black pepper. Cover and simmer gently for 1½ hours, stirring occasionally. Serve hot.

NUTRITIONAL INFORMATION PER SERVING: 154 CALORIES, 0.9 G FAT, 20.3 G PROTEIN, 18 G CARBOHYDRATE, 35 MG CHOLESTEROL, 572 MG SODIUM.

Beef

FOR AT LEAST TWO YEARS AFTER I LOST WEIGHT, I had beef only once a month. I missed it big time and began exploring leaner methods to cook beef so I could enjoy it with greater frequency. Early on, I found out that ground beef comes in many different guises. Regular ground beef is 73 percent lean. Sounds pretty good—but it's not. According to the National Livestock and Meat Board, 73 percent raw lean ground beef contains 27 percent fat, by weight. Therefore, one pound of regular ground beef contains 4.32 ounces of fat. I did the math and discovered that an astounding 78.6 percent of the calories in 73 percent lean ground beef come from fat.

Ground beef that is 95 percent lean is the leanest there is. An entire pound contains only 0.8 ounces fat, with only 34.4 percent of the calories from fat. By percent, then, there is 82 percent less fat in 95 percent lean than in 73 percent lean—a big savings.

Here's even better news. If you pan-fry that pound of 95 percent lean ground beef in a nonstick skillet and drain off the fat, the fat content will be 0.66 ounces. If you put the browned beef in a mesh strainer and rinse it with hot water, you will reduce the fat content even further. My conservative estimate of what's left is about one-half ounce of fat or less.

The only bad news here is that since there is so little fat in 95 percent lean ground beef, you should cook it to no more than medium-rare because it dries out fast.

Bring your burger to the table with a baked potato served with nonfat sour cream and a nonfat liquid butter substitute, and your calories from fat for the meal will come in at close to 13.7 percent. Add another vegetable to your dinner plate and serve a salad with nonfat dressing, and your percent of calories from fat for this feast goes down even further.

There are other cuts of beef that are pretty lean, too. Consider a well-trimmed flank steak. A 4-ounce serving of broiled flank steak alone has 11.5 fat grams, with 44 percent of its calories from fat. However, add a baked potato with nonfat sour cream and nonfat liquid butter substitute and 4 ounces of steamed green beans, and you'll dine on a 500-calorie meal, with 12 grams of fat and 21 percent of the calories from fat.

Or look at beef top round. A lean 4-ounce piece, trimmed of visible fat and roasted, contains 6.7 grams of fat and gets only 28.2 percent of its calories from fat (less than 95 percent lean ground beef). Add potatoes and green beans to the meal, and you get a terrific dinner with a total 7.2 grams of fat and 13.3 percent of the calories from fat.

One more example: If you love a tender steak, the answer is beef tenderloin. A 4-ounce piece of tenderloin contains 11.5 grams of fat, with 43 percent of its calories from fat. With a baked potato and baby peas, this indulgent meal will contain only 12 fat grams, with just 19 percent of the calories from fat. The least expensive way to enjoy this dandy cut of meat is to purchase the whole tenderloin. Trim it of all visible fat. Cut the thin end into ½-inch cubes and make beef stroganoff—using nonfat sour cream, of course. Slice the remaining thicker parts into 1-inch-thick steaks. Broil or grill what you want and freeze the rest.

If you select the proper cuts of beef and prepare them in a variety of lean ways, you won't have to make beef a once-a-month treat.

RECIPES

Beef, Tomato and Peppers Skillet Dinner

SERVES 4

CHINESE RESTAURANTS, especially those on main-street America, have used flank steak in beef dishes for decades. Flank steak is lean, flavorful and, if improperly handled, tough as leather. Fortunately, slicing it across the grain makes it melt-in-your-mouth tender. I used to love ordering a dish just like this one in Chinese restaurants. It mixes the wonderful salty flavor of soy sauce with the smoky contribution of Scotch whisky.

You won't need a fancy wok or other special tools to create a restaurant-quality version of this dish at home. A whisk, skillet, sharp knife and spatula will have this meal on the table in a flash. Begin by cooking the rice and everything will come out at the same time.

MARINADE

3	tablespoons sodium-reduced soy sauce
1	tablespoon dry sherry (not cooking sherry) or Scotch whisky
2	teaspoons arrowroot or cornstarch
1	garlic clove, minced
½	teaspoon granulated sugar
¾	pound lean flank steak, trimmed of all visible fat
1	medium green bell pepper, seeded and cut into ½-inch-wide strips
1	medium red bell pepper, seeded and cut into ½-inch wide strips
1	16-ounce can plum tomatoes, drained and chopped, reserving ½ cup of the juice

3 cups hot cooked rice (1 cup uncooked)

1. Marinade: In a medium bowl, whisk together the marinade ingredients until the sugar dissolves. Set aside.

2. With a knife held in a slanted position almost parallel to the cutting surface, slice the steak crosswise into the thinnest possible slices. Stir and mix the sliced beef into marinade and set aside for 10 minutes.

3. Spray a large nonstick skillet with vegetable oil. Over medium-high heat, cook the peppers and tomatoes, stirring constantly, until the peppers are crisp-tender, 2 to 3 minutes. Transfer the mixture to a bowl.

4. Spray the skillet again with vegetable oil, increase the heat to high and quickly sauté the drained marinated beef, stirring, for 3 to 4 minutes until beef has just lost its pink color. Add the marinade, reserved tomato juice and cooked vegetables to the skillet, stirring until it comes to a boil. Serve over hot cooked rice.

NUTRITIONAL INFORMATION PER SERVING (INCLUDING RICE): 376 CALORIES, 9 G FAT, 29 G PROTEIN, 43.2 G CARBOHYDRATE, 57 MG CHOLESTEROL, 873 MG SODIUM.

LeanSuggestions
■ Add a little fresh grated gingerroot to your rice-cooking liquid for flavor.
■ Use this as a stuffing for halved pita pocket bread that has been briefly warmed in the microwave.

Beef with Snow Peas

SERVES 4

BEEF, MARINATED IN A SLIGHTLY SWEET MIXTURE of soy sauce and sherry, is cooked in a flash with bright green snow peas seasoned with black pepper and spring onions. This seemingly uncomplicated marriage of flavors is hauntingly delicious.

MARINADE
1 teaspoon cornstarch
2 teaspoons sodium-reduced soy sauce
2 teaspoons dry sherry
½ teaspoon granulated sugar

½ pound beef flank steak, trimmed of all visible fat
2 teaspoons cornstarch, mixed with 2 teaspoons water
   Fresh-ground black pepper
½ teaspoon granulated sugar
1 teaspoon grated fresh gingerroot
½ pound snow peas, rinsed, strings removed
½ cup defatted low-sodium beef broth
1 bunch green onions (white parts only),
   cut at angles into ½-inch pieces

1. **Marinade:** In a small bowl, whisk together the marinade ingredients until the sugar dissolves. Set aside.

2. Holding the knife at 45-degree angle, slice the beef crosswise into very thin slices. Place it in the marinade and turn to coat. Marinate for 10 minutes.

3. In a small bowl, whisk together the cornstarch mixture, pepper and sugar. Set aside.

4. Heat a nonstick skillet over medium-high heat. Spray the skillet lightly with vegetable oil. Add the ginger; cook for 5 seconds. Add the snow peas, stir and toss. Add the beef broth, stir until steam appears and transfer everything to a bowl.

5. Reheat the skillet and spray lightly with vegetable oil. Add the green onions; stir for 1 minute. Add the beef with its marinade and stir quickly for about 2 minutes, or until the beef just loses its pink color. Return the ginger, snow peas and beef broth to the skillet, and stir in the cornstarch mixture. Continue stirring until the sauce thickens. Serve immediately.

NUTRITIONAL INFORMATION PER SERVING: 164 CALORIES, 5.8 G FAT, 17 G PROTEIN, 8.5 G CARBOHYDRATE, 38 MG CHOLESTEROL, 212 MG SODIUM.

LeanSuggestion: Serve this with Garlic Sesame Rice (page 313).

Asian Beef and Bell Peppers

SERVES 4

I LIKE SERVING THIS COLORFUL DISH to dinner guests on a Saturday evening. It is always received with the oooohs and ahhhhs associated with a colorful fireworks display. There is some definite heat generated by the red pepper flakes, but they are a wonderful counterpoint to the sweet peppers and onions. Serve over hot rice garnished with the chopped green onion.

MARINADE
1	tablespoon dry sherry (not cooking sherry) or Scotch whisky
1	tablespoon sodium-reduced soy sauce
1	teaspoon toasted sesame oil*
1	large garlic clove, minced
1	teaspoon hot red pepper flakes

½	pound flank steak, thinly sliced crosswise
3	teaspoons canola oil
1	small red bell pepper, cored and thinly sliced
1	small yellow bell pepper, cored and thinly sliced
1	small green bell pepper, cored and thinly sliced
4	green onions, white parts cut at angles into ½-inch pieces, green parts chopped
3	cups hot cooked rice (1 cup uncooked)

1. Marinade: In a medium bowl, whisk together all the marinade ingredients. Add the sliced beef. Let stand, uncovered, for at least 15 minutes and up to 1 hour.

2. Heat 2 teaspoons of the canola oil in a large nonstick skillet over medium-high heat. Drain the beef, reserving the marinade, and stir-fry the beef for 1 minute, or until it has just lost its pink color. Transfer to a clean bowl.

3. Add the remaining 1 teaspoon oil to the skillet and when it is hot, add the bell peppers. Cook, stirring, for 2 minutes. Add the white parts of the green onions and stir for 1 minute more. Stir in the beef and marinade, and cook until heated through, about 1 minute.

NUTRITIONAL INFORMATION PER SERVING: 285 CALORIES, 10.5 G FAT, 18.5 G PROTEIN, 27 G CARBOHYDRATE, 38 MG CHOLESTEROL, 182 MG SODIUM.

Toasted sesame oil can be found in most major supermarkets in the Asian section.

SPICY CHINESE BEEF SAUTÉ

MAKES 4 SERVINGS

THIS IS NOT A DISH FOR A KITCHEN NOVICE. Prepare the ingredients ahead and lay them all out on a large serving plate, cover with plastic wrap and chill. Then, when ready, heat your skillet and cook everything quickly. A grand Saturday evening dinner will be on the table in no time, and the reviews for it will all be raves. And not one diner will ever suspect how low-in-fat this dish really is.

2 cups defatted low-sodium beef broth, preferably homemade
1 cup long-grain white rice

THICKENING SAUCE

3 tablespoons reduced-sodium soy sauce
2 tablespoons distilled white vinegar
1 teaspoon granulated sugar
½ teaspoon hot red pepper flakes

1 tablespoon canola oil
½ pound lean beef flank steak, cut across the grain into thin strips
2 medium carrots, peeled and sliced thinly or julienned (1½ cups)
1 medium red bell pepper, cut into thin strips
1 medium green bell pepper, cut into thin strips
1 bunch green onions (white and green parts), chopped
2 garlic cloves, pressed through a garlic press
2 cups shredded Chinese cabbage
½ pound white button mushrooms, sliced
16 water chestnuts, sliced

1. Bring the beef broth to a boil in a medium nonstick saucepan and stir in the rice. Cover the pan, reduce the heat to low and simmer for 17 minutes, or until all the broth has been absorbed. Turn the heat off and let the pan remain on the burner.

2. Thickening sauce: In a small bowl, whisk together all the ingredients until the sugar dissolves. Set aside.

3. Heat 1 teaspoon of the canola oil in a large nonstick skillet over medium-high heat. Add the beef and sauté for 3 to 4 minutes, until it has lost its pink color. Transfer the cooked beef to a small clean bowl and set aside.

4. Add the remaining 2 teaspoons oil to the skillet and add the carrots, bell peppers, green onions and garlic. Cook, stirring occasionally, for 4 minutes. Add the cabbage, mushrooms and water chestnuts. Increase the heat to high and cook, stirring frequently, for 4 to 5 minutes. Add the beef and the thickening sauce and cook, stirring constantly, for 2 minutes, until heated through. Serve over the cooked rice.

NUTRITIONAL INFORMATION PER SERVING (INCLUDING RICE): 359 CALORIES, 7.5 G FAT, 14.5 G PROTEIN, 60 G CARBOHYDRATE, 19 MG CHOLESTEROL, 439 MG SODIUM.

APPLESAUCE MEAT LOAF

SERVES 8

I LEARNED TO USE APPLESAUCE as a substitute for shortening in cakes, muffins and brownies. Applesauce can also be used instead of tomatoes to create an absolutely fabulous meat loaf. Just as applesauce helps to maintain the moisture of a baked good, it does the same for this meat loaf.

1	large whole egg
2	large egg whites
1½	pounds 95% lean ground beef
2	tablespoons minced onion
1	teaspoon salt
½	teaspoon fresh-ground black pepper
½	teaspoon ground allspice
¾	cup old-fashioned or quick-cooking (not instant) oats
1	cup unsweetened applesauce

GLAZE

½	cup light brown sugar
½	teaspoon ground cloves
2	tablespoons hot water

1. Preheat the oven to 350 degrees F.
2. In a small bowl, whisk together the egg and egg whites until combined. Set aside.

3. Place the egg mixture, ground beef, onion, salt, pepper, allspice, oats and applesauce in a large mixing bowl. Working with clean hands, combine all the ingredients well, but do not overwork. Pat the mixture into a 9-by-5-by-3-inch loaf pan.

4. Glaze: In a small bowl, stir together the brown sugar, cloves and water. Brush the glaze over the top of the meat loaf. Bake for 1½ hours, or until a thermometer inserted into the center of the loaf registers 160 degrees. Remove the meat loaf from the oven and allow it to rest for 10 minutes before serving.

NUTRITIONAL INFORMATION PER SERVING: 203 CALORIES, 5.5 G FAT, 21 G PROTEIN, 17.8 G CARBOHYDRATE, 73 MG CHOLESTEROL, 357 MG SODIUM.

Mom's Corn Pone Pie

SERVES 6

SINCE MY MOM was a full-time teacher and simultaneously brought up three sons, she didn't have much time for kitchen experimentation. However, there was at least one meal I always looked forward to: Corn Pone Pie.

A richly flavored, cumin-scented chili is the heart of this "pie." It's a chili that suited my mom's tight schedule, simmering for only 15 minutes. Instead of topping this with a regular high-fat pie crust, my mother used a cornbread batter. I recreated her cornbread batter minus the ½ cup butter and used 95 percent lean ground beef. A wedge of this pie has fewer than 8 fat grams.

1½	pounds 95% lean ground beef
⅔	cup chopped onion
1	tablespoon chili powder
½	teaspoon salt
2	teaspoons Worcestershire sauce
1	16-ounce can whole tomatoes
1	15-ounce can red kidney beans, drained

CORNBREAD BATTER

1½	cups yellow cornmeal
½	cup all-purpose flour
1	tablespoon baking powder
1	tablespoon granulated sugar
1	large whole egg
½	cup drained unsweetened applesauce
1	cup skim milk

1. Lightly spray a large nonstick skillet with vegetable oil and place over medium-high heat. Add the ground beef and onion and cook, flipping and breaking up the beef. Once the beef has lost all its pink color and the onion is soft, drain any excess liquid from the skillet.

2. Return the skillet to the heat and add the chili powder, salt, Worcestershire sauce and tomatoes with their juice. Break up the tomatoes with the edge of a spatula or spoon. Reduce the heat to low, cover and simmer for 15 minutes. Stir in the kidney beans and remove the skillet from the heat.

3. Cornbread batter: Meanwhile, in a small bowl, whisk or stir together the cornmeal, flour and baking powder until thoroughly combined. Set aside.

4. Preheat the oven to 425 degrees F.

5. In a medium mixing bowl, whisk together the sugar, egg, drained applesauce and milk until the mixture is completely combined and the sugar has dissolved. Add the cornmeal mixture to the bowl and continue whisking until the dry ingredients are just moistened, 15 to 20 seconds.

6. Lightly spray the bottom and sides of a large casserole dish with vegetable oil. Add all the beef mixture to the casserole and smooth the top as flat as possible. Top with the cornbread batter, spreading carefully with a wet knife. Bake for 20 to 25 minutes, or until the cornbread is golden. Cut into wedges and serve immediately.

NUTRITIONAL INFORMATION PER SERVING: 447 CALORIES, 7.8 G FAT, 36 G PROTEIN, 58 G CARBOHYDRATE, 98 MG CHOLESTEROL, 888 MG SODIUM.

SLOPPY SAMMIES

MAKES 8 SANDWICHES

I'VE TRIED MAKING SLOPPY JOES using the canned products found in supermarkets. I hate the result: most brands are too sweet and they have way too much salt. My wife, Susan, created this great Sloppy Joe adaptation. The ingredient list of these sloppy sandwiches may appear intimidating, but the dish truly is quick and easy to make.

1	tablespoon molasses
¾	tablespoon chili powder
⅛	teaspoon cayenne pepper
1	8-ounce can tomatoes, including the juice
⅓	cup white-wine vinegar
½	cup tomato ketchup
½	cup dark corn syrup
½	cup water
½	cup fresh-squeezed orange juice
½	teaspoon salt
½	teaspoon fresh-ground black pepper
1	pound 95% lean ground beef or 97% lean ground all-white-meat turkey
½	medium onion, chopped
½	medium green bell pepper, chopped
8	hamburger buns, toasted

1. In a medium heavy-bottomed saucepan, stir together the molasses, chili powder and cayenne pepper. Whisk in the tomatoes, vinegar, ketchup, corn syrup and water. Bring the mixture to a boil, reduce the heat so the sauce barely simmers and cook, uncovered, for 30 minutes, stirring occasionally. Whisk in the orange juice, salt and pepper and continue simmering for 5 minutes more.

2. Meanwhile, sauté the ground beef or turkey in a medium nonstick skillet over medium heat for 5 to 6 minutes, or until it is no longer pink. Add the onion and green pepper and continue cooking until they have softened slightly, about 5 minutes. Add the sauce to the meat mixture, reduce the heat to low and simmer for 5 minutes, or until it slightly thickens. Serve over the toasted hamburger buns.

NUTRITIONAL INFORMATION PER SANDWICH (WITH BEEF): 261 CALORIES, 5.2 G FAT, 16.4 G PROTEIN, 37 G CARBOHYDRATE, 31 MG CHOLESTEROL, 631 MG SODIUM.
WITH TURKEY: 247 CALORIES, 3.1 G FAT, 17.8 G PROTEIN, 37 G CARBOHYDRATE, 23 MG CHOLESTEROL, 627 MG SODIUM.

MIDDLE EASTERN BEEF KEBABS

SERVES 4

Until I tasted Middle Eastern cuisine, cinnamon as a flavoring for meat was a strange concept to my very American taste buds. I wanted to create a kebab that didn't use high-fat ground lamb. I switched to 95 percent lean ground beef, but used the traditional seasonings. I bound the mixture with an egg white, formed it into ovals and grilled them. Then I laid the finished kebabs on torn romaine leaves and sprinkled colorful red onion over all.

1½	pounds 95% lean ground beef
½	cup minced fresh parsley
2	tablespoons minced fresh cilantro
⅓	cup grated onion
1	large egg white
1	teaspoon ground cumin
½	teaspoon ground cinnamon
½	teaspoon salt
½	teaspoon fresh-ground black pepper
4	cups torn romaine leaves, rinsed and spun dry
½	cup minced red onion

1. In a large bowl, combine the ground beef, parsley, cilantro, onion, egg white, cumin, cinnamon, salt and pepper. Chill the mixture, covered, for at least 1 hour and up to 6 hours.

2. Preheat the broiler.

3. Form the beef mixture into sixteen (1¾-ounce) 2-by-1-inch ovals and thread 4 ovals onto each of 4 metal skewers, pressing the ovals onto the skewer.

4. Place the kebabs in a foil-lined pan and broil about 4 inches from the heat for 2 to 3 minutes on each side, or until they are browned and just cooked through.

5. Divide the romaine among 4 plates, arrange a kebab on each plate, sprinkle with the red onion and serve immediately.

NUTRITIONAL INFORMATION PER SERVING: 250 CALORIES, 8.8 G FAT, 37 G PROTEIN, 4 G CARBOHYDRATE, 93 MG CHOLESTEROL, 423 MG SODIUM.

LeanSuggestions

■ For added flavor, these can also be grilled on a barbecue.

■ Pita bread makes a great accompaniment. Warm the separated breads in a microwave oven on high for 15 seconds. Serve immediately.

■ The meat kebabs can be interspersed with large pieces of green or red bell pepper, chunks of sweet onion, large mushrooms or chunks of eggplant about the same size as each meat kebab. Brush the kebabs while they are cooking with a mixture of one ½-ounce packet of Butter Buds and ½ cup warm defatted beef broth.

Southwestern Beef and Black Bean No-Tomato Chili

SERVES 12

How can a chili have no tomatoes? It can omit them when it has the flavor, texture and color of this one. Tablespoonfuls of oregano, chili powder, coriander and cumin give this a deep, rich taste. Flour and pureed corn provide body.

1	teaspoon extra-virgin olive oil
1½	pounds 95% lean ground beef
1	cup chopped mild fresh chilies
⅔	cup chopped red onion
⅔	cup chopped celery
⅔	cup chopped red bell pepper
⅔	cup chopped leek (white part only)
2	garlic cloves, minced
2	tablespoons crumbled dried oregano
½	cup all-purpose flour
4	cups defatted low-sodium beef broth, preferably homemade
3	cups frozen corn kernels, thawed
2½	tablespoons chili powder
2	tablespoons ground coriander
1	tablespoon ground cumin
1½	teaspoons salt, plus more to taste
1	teaspoon clover honey
2	15-ounce cans black beans, drained
	Fresh-ground black pepper to taste

1. Place the olive oil in a large saucepan and set it over medium-high heat. Add the ground beef and cook, breaking it up with the edge of a spoon. When it has begun to lose its pink color, reduce the heat to medium-low and add the chilies, onion, celery, bell pepper, leek, garlic and oregano. Cook, stirring occasionally, for 15 minutes, or until the vegetables are softened.

2. Add the flour and cook the mixture over low heat, stirring, for 15 to 20 minutes. (The flour will stick to the bottom and brown, but don't worry.) Stir in 3 cups of the beef broth. Return to a simmer, scraping up the brown bits from the bottom of the pan.

3. To a blender, add the remaining 1 cup beef broth and 1¼ cups of the corn. Blend until pureed and add to the chili with the remaining 1¾ cups corn, chili powder, coriander, cumin, salt, honey and beans. Simmer, stirring occasionally, for 15 minutes. Taste, season with additional salt and pepper and serve.

NUTRITIONAL INFORMATION PER SERVING: 237 CALORIES, 5.4 G FAT, 18 G PROTEIN, 28 G CARBOHYDRATE, 31 MG CHOLESTEROL, 448 MG SODIUM.

LeanTip: As with most chilis, this one is even better after it has been chilled and reheated.

LeanSuggestion: This is tremendous served with slices of North Carolina Skillet Cornbread (page 388) drizzled with some honey and a salad of chilled, crisp lettuce topped with slices of ripe tomato, cucumber and nonfat dressing.

PORK

JUSTIN WILSON, Cajun cookbook author and PBS cooking-show host, says something that rings in my ears every time I think of pork. He calls it, "P-I-G-hog." I have always enjoyed pig-hog in all its forms. There is nothing that sings Christmas louder to me than a beautifully roasted and glazed ham, with the bone in. I savor Szechuan-style pork dishes from that heat-loving area of China. When I weighed over 300 pounds, I used to purchase my bacon from a small German butcher shop on the far north side of Chicago. They slab-cured their own with whole peppercorns pounded in the rind of fat. I can still smell it sizzling in my skillet on Sunday morning. I used to save the grease from that slab bacon and store it in a jar in my refrigerator. Whenever I wanted to fry up some pork chops, I'd dip into my jar of bacon grease.

Today, on the rare occasions that I use bacon, I roast it on a rack over a jelly-roll pan in a very hot oven for about 20 minutes. I carefully trim off all the remaining fat and use only the lean portions. For a special dish, I use one—or at the most two—teaspoons of the rendered bacon fat to sauté some of the vegetables for the dish. The smoky flavor it imparts is worth the 1 or 2 fat grams per serving it costs. That way I don't ever feel deprived.

I use pork tenderloin as often as possible. Why? It's the leanest portion on the P-I-G. I trim off any visible fat and turn the tenderloin into luxuriously rich dishes. I especially like it for sausage.

Almost every sausage commercially produced, unless it's low-fat, gets 80 percent or more of its calories from fat. For a long time, all sausage was on my "Nope, can't-have-it" list. I began missing it so much that I started experimenting with my own ground pork tenderloin and seasonings. Ultimately I created some exquisite sausages that generally derive 25 percent of their calories from fat. They are lower in fat than any pork sausage commercially available. What they aren't short on is flavor. For example, my Lean Italian Sausage (page 170) is better than any I have ever bought or had in a restaurant. My recipes will show you how to make it by using the freshest ingredients and easy-to-learn techniques.

RECIPES

MUSTARD-COATED ROAST PORK TENDERLOIN

SERVES 4

PORK PRODUCED in the United Sates has become leaner over the years, but I don't for one second buy into the widely publicized concept that pork is "the other white meat." Not until pigs fly past my kitchen window will I be convinced that the two are the same.

Hey, who would want chickens and pigs to be alike anyhow? I think the flavor of pork is terrific, and the fact that it is now leaner makes my life easier. Pork tenderloin is the leanest pork; 3 ounces of raw tenderloin, trimmed of all visible fat, has only 2.1 fat grams.

One night, when I was in a big hurry to put dinner on the table, I turned to a pork tenderloin that I had bought earlier in the week. I smeared it heavily with some good-quality Dijon-style mustard and roasted it. The mustard sealed in the juices.

1   1-pound pork tenderloin, trimmed of all visible fat
     Dijon-style mustard

1. Preheat the oven to 425 degrees F, with a rack in the center.
2. Thickly coat the pork tenderloin with the mustard.
3. Line the interior of a small broiler pan with aluminum foil. Place a wire rack in the center of the pan. Spray the rack lightly with vegetable oil. Place the tenderloin on the rack and roast for 25 minutes, or until a meat thermometer registers 160 degrees. Remove from the oven and let the tenderloin rest for 5 minutes. Slice crosswise into thin slices and serve.

NUTRITIONAL INFORMATION PER SERVING: 145 CALORIES, 4.4 G FAT, 24 G PROTEIN, 0 CARBOHYDRATE, 74 MG CHOLESTEROL, 282 MG SODIUM.

LeanSuggestion: A good baked potato (baked without a foil wrapping), with nonfat sour cream and nonfat butter substitute, and Celery with Dill and Sour Cream (page 360) round out this quick and easy meal.

Bratwurst Lean Sausage

SERVES 8

Bill, a reader of my Illinois column, dropped me a note with a request. Seventy-eight years young and a widower, he said, "I love sausage, but being on a low-cholesterol, low-fat diet, I need some recipes for it." So I gave Bill a call and we talked. Ten years ago, Bill's doctor told him he had to stop eating high-fat and salty luncheon meats and sausages. He put up quite a fuss. He asked his doctor, "What, do you want me to become a vegetarian?"

I offered Bill a few hints about how the fat in homemade sausage could easily be reduced. I suggested he use cuts of meat that are very low in fat to substitute for the higher fat ones called for. If pork is needed, use well-trimmed pork tenderloin. I also suggested that he consider substituting skinless, boneless chicken or turkey breast, such as the 97 percent lean ground all-white-meat turkey available. My final suggestion was not to add any fat. I told him to increase the ground meat by the same weight as the fat called for. He'd save about 25 grams of fat for every ounce of fat he omitted.

Bill told me he also loved bratwurst, so I shared my recipe. Break out the poppy seed buns and get ready to pass the mustard and onions.

1½	pounds pork tenderloin, trimmed of all visible fat
½	pound 95% lean ground beef
3	tablespoons ice water
2	teaspoons salt*
1	teaspoon fresh-ground black pepper
1	teaspoon ground coriander
1	teaspoon sweet paprika
½	teaspoon dry mustard
¼	teaspoon ground mace
½	cup amber beer

1. Cut the pork tenderloin into 1-inch pieces and place about one-third of the meat in a food processor fitted with the metal blade. Pulse until the meat looks like it has been ground through the large-hole plate of a meat grinder. Place the processed pork in a large bowl. Process the remaining pork in 2 batches and place in the bowl when completed.

2. Add the ground beef, mix and toss until combined. Add the water, salt, black pepper, coriander, paprika, mustard and mace; mix until the flavorings are evenly distributed. Do not overhandle.

3. Divide the mixture into eight 4-ounce pieces. Roll and form into sausage shapes. Place on a plate, cover with plastic wrap and refrigerate for 4 hours or overnight.

4. Pour the beer into a nonstick skillet and place over medium heat. Add the bratwurst and cover. When the beer begins to simmer, remove the cover; turn and cook the sausages until the beer evaporates, 5 to 6 minutes. Continue to sauté the sausages until they are nicely browned and cooked through. Serve immediately.

NUTRITIONAL INFORMATION PER SERVING: 158 CALORIES, 4.8 G FAT, 25.6 G PROTEIN, 1 G CARBOHYDRATE, 78 MG CHOLESTEROL, 708 MG SODIUM.

LeanSuggestion: Serve on warm poppy seed buns, hot dog style, with plenty of dark, coarse mustard.

If you are on a sodium-restricted diet, omit the salt.

Lean Italian Sausage

MAKES ABOUT 2 POUNDS

I HAVE LOVED PIZZA for most of my life. My all-time favorite pizza used to be cheese and sausage. (Commercial Italian sausage contains approximately 80 percent of calories from fat.) After I lost weight, I came up with this recipe, made with lean pork tenderloin instead of high-fat pork shoulder, so that I could have Italian sausage on and in some dearly loved dishes.

2	pounds pork tenderloin, trimmed of all visible fat
½	medium onion, minced
1	medium garlic clove, minced
1½	teaspoons salt*
½	teaspoon hot red pepper flakes (optional)
½	teaspoon fresh-ground black pepper
1	teaspoon fennel seeds
1	teaspoon sweet paprika
½	small bay leaf, crushed
	Pinch dried thyme
¼	cup dry red wine or defatted low-sodium chicken broth

1. Cut the tenderloin into 1-inch cubes and feed through a meat grinder in batches with the onion and garlic. Alternatively, the tenderloin can be chopped in a food processor by carefully pulsing with the steel blade.

2. Place the ground pork in a large glass or ceramic mixing bowl. Add the remaining ingredients except the wine or chicken broth; mix thoroughly. Add the wine or broth. Mix well, but take care not to overmix and compress the sausage. Use fresh sausage immediately. Any remaining sausage may be divided into 8-ounce portions. Place each portion in freezer bags and freeze until needed. It keeps for up to 6 months.

NUTRITIONAL INFORMATION PER 3 OUNCES: 98 CALORIES, 2.6 G FAT, 15.4 G PROTEIN, 1.5 G CARBOHYDRATE, 48 MG CHOLESTEROL, 297 MG SODIUM.

LeanTip: To defrost sausage, remove from the freezer and place in the refrigerator for 12 hours. Spray the surface of a nonstick skillet with vegetable oil. Over medium-high heat, sauté the sausage, breaking it up, until lightly browned. Add to spaghetti sauce or use as a pizza topping

LeanSuggestion: Coarsely ground 95 percent lean ground beef can be substituted for the pork tenderloin. (Ground pork, commonly found in the meat section of supermarkets, is very high in fat and not comparable to ground pork tenderloin.)

If you are on a sodium-restricted diet, omit salt.

Southern-Style Ham Pilaf

SERVES 6

AFTER I MOVED TO NORTH CAROLINA, I began to understand two things about Southern food. First, it is some of the tastiest on Earth. Second, it is generally very high in fat. I made it a personal goal to begin enjoying Southern cuisine. All I had to do was figure out how to make it leaner.

One of my first success stories was this pilaf. It has a terrific flavor—like no other pilaf. Mine has okra in it, which adds both a great Southern taste and an interesting texture. Normally, because of its unique and wonderful flavor, I make this with real country-cured ham, trimmed of all visible fat. However, because some people don't live where that is available, this recipe calls for baked ham.

3	slices bacon (2.5 ounces), preferably slab bacon
1	cup chopped sweet onion, such as Vidalia
½	cup chopped green bell pepper
1	cup thin-sliced okra
½	pound leanest possible baked ham, cut into julienne pieces
1	cup peeled and cubed eggplant
6	fresh plum tomatoes, peeled and chopped
1	medium garlic clove, minced
1	tablespoon chopped fresh thyme
1½	teaspoons chopped fresh basil
⅛	teaspoon cayenne pepper
1	cup long-grain white rice
2	cups defatted low-sodium chicken broth, preferably homemade

1. Preheat the oven to 425 degrees F, with a rack in the highest position.

2. Line a jelly-roll pan with foil and place a wire rack on the pan. Lay the bacon slices on the rack and place in the oven. Bake for 20 minutes, turning once after 10 minutes. Remove from the oven and place the cooked bacon on paper towels to drain. Set aside 2 teaspoons of bacon fat; discard the remainder.

3. Reposition the rack to the center of the oven.

4. Trim the bacon of all fat and chop the remaining lean parts. Place a large, nonstick, oven-safe skillet over medium-high heat and add the bacon fat. When hot but not smoking, add the onion, green pepper and okra and sauté until just softened. Add the ham, eggplant, tomatoes and garlic and continue cooking for about 5 minutes. Add the bacon, thyme, basil, cayenne, rice and chicken broth and bring to a boil. Shake the pan to distribute the ingredients evenly and place, uncovered, in the oven.

5. Reduce the oven temperature to 325 degrees and bake for 30 to 35 minutes, or until the rice is tender. Serve hot.

NUTRITIONAL INFORMATION PER SERVING: 235 CALORIES, 4.3 G FAT, 15.3 G PROTEIN, 33.4 G CARBOHYDRATE, 27 MG CHOLESTEROL, 585 MG SODIUM.

Pork Chops with Sauerkraut

SERVES 4

M Y WIFE created this recipe using the organic reduced-sodium sauerkraut that I found in my local health food store. We usually serve these pork chops with fat-free mashed potatoes and LeanStyle Chicken Gravy (page 260).

4   4-ounce lean center-cut pork chops, trimmed of all visible fat
2   teaspoons rubbed dried sage
    Salt (optional)
    Fresh-ground black pepper
2   cups defatted low-sodium chicken broth
4   large shallots, thinly sliced
2   garlic cloves, minced
2   tablespoons Cognac, brandy or dry sherry
2   pounds reduced-sodium sauerkraut, undrained*
1   teaspoon caraway seeds

1. Preheat the oven to 350 degrees F.

2. Sprinkle each pork chop with some sage, salt (if using), and pepper to taste. Rub the seasonings into the pork chops so they will adhere. Set aside.

3. Place a large nonstick skillet over medium-high heat and pour ½ cup of the chicken broth into it. When the broth begins to boil, add the shallots and garlic and sauté for 30 seconds. Add the pork chops and some broth. Allow the broth to almost evaporate and brown the chops on one side, 4 to 5 minutes. Add ½ cup more broth to the skillet and turn the chops. Allow the broth to almost evaporate as the chops brown on the other side, 4 to 5 minutes. Remove the chops from the skillet and add the remaining broth and Cognac or other spirits. Stir and scrape the brown bits from the bottom of the skillet. Allow the liquid to reduce until slightly thickened. Remove the skillet from the heat.

4. Place half of the sauerkraut in the bottom of a casserole dish large enough to hold the chops. Sprinkle the sauerkraut with ½ teaspoon of the caraway seeds. Place the browned chops on top of the sauerkraut and pour the reduced skillet liquid over each of the chops. Distribute the remaining sauerkraut evenly over the chops and sprinkle the remaining ½ teaspoon caraway seeds over all. Cover the casserole and place it in the oven. Bake for 1½ hours, or until the pork is very tender. Remove the casserole from the oven. Remove the cover carefully, since steam will billow out. Serve each chop with some sauerkraut. Drizzle some of the liquid from the casserole over each.

NUTRITIONAL INFORMATION PER SERVING (WITHOUT SALT): 240 CALORIES, 6.2 G FAT, 28.5 G PROTEIN, 13 G CAR-BOHYDRATE, 72 MG CHOLESTEROL, 870 MG SODIUM.

LeanSuggestion: Since the cooking time is long for this flavorful dish, I like to prepare it on a lazy Sunday afternoon for our Sunday dinner. That leaves two chops for a weeknight meal.

* If the sauerkraut is not reduced-sodium, reserve ½ cup of the liquid, discard the remaining liquid and rinse and drain the kraut. When adding the sauerkraut to the casserole dish, sprinkle each layer with some of the reserved liquid.

Garlicky Pork with Snow Peas

SERVES 4

JUST THE MENTION of Asian cuisine gets my mouth watering. Classically, it uses the freshest possible ingredients, and that's an important principle for Mr. Lean and Lovin' It. However, it is very difficult to ask the kitchen of an Asian restaurant to prepare dishes with the least amount of fat. The response usually is, "No problem. We use vegetable oil, no cholesterol, no cholesterol." There is more than just a language difficulty here.

My solution is to make it at home. This is a dish I usually reserve for special guests. You may wish to also.

MARINADE

1	tablespoon sodium-reduced soy sauce
1½	tablespoons Scotch whiskey
1½	tablespoons minced garlic
1	tablespoon arrowroot or cornstarch

½   pound pork tenderloin, trimmed of all visible fat

SAUCE

½	cup defatted low-sodium chicken broth
6	tablespoons oyster sauce*
1½	tablespoons Scotch whisky
1	teaspoon sodium-reduced soy sauce
1½	teaspoons arrowroot or cornstarch

2   teaspoons toasted sesame oil
1   tablespoon minced garlic

3   tablespoons minced green onions (white parts only),
     plus 1 cup 1-inch pieces green tops
1½ tablespoons minced fresh gingerroot
1   5-ounce can sliced water chestnuts, rinsed under cold water
12 ounces fresh snow peas, ends trimmed and strings removed

1. **Marinade:** In a medium bowl, whisk together the marinade ingredients until combined. Set aside.

2. Cut the tenderloin with the grain in half lengthwise. Slice it across the grain into the thinnest possible slices. Add the tenderloin to the marinade, cover with plastic wrap and let marinate at room temperature for 30 minutes.

3. **Sauce:** Meanwhile, in a small bowl, whisk together the sauce ingredients until combined. Set aside.

4. Heat a large nonstick skillet over high heat. Add 1 teaspoon of the sesame oil (it will smoke) and add the drained pork tenderloin (reserve the marinade). Cook, stirring, until the pork has lost all of its pink color. Transfer the pork to a clean bowl.

5. Add the remaining 1 teaspoon sesame oil to the skillet. Add the garlic, minced green onions and ginger and sauté for 10 seconds. Add the water chestnuts and sauté for 30 seconds, or until heated through. Add the snow peas, remaining pork marinade and sauce mixture and heat until thickened, stirring continuously. Add the green onion tops and cooked pork, toss lightly to coat and serve immediately.

NUTRITIONAL INFORMATION PER SERVING: 202 CALORIES, 5.3 G FAT, 17.8 G PROTEIN, 18 G CARBOHYDRATE, 50 MG CHOLESTEROL, 237 MG SODIUM.

Oyster sauce can be found in the Asian food section of most large supermarkets, as well as in Asian markets.

LeanSuggestion: Jasmine rice, prepared with defatted chicken broth instead of water, makes this a complete meal.

Old-Fashioned Braised Tenderlean Pork

SERVES 6

IN MY FAT DAYS, I used to make this dish with regular pork chops, sautéing them in bacon grease for added flavor. Canned cream of mushroom soup added its portion of fat, too. Now I substitute pork tenderloin for the chops. I use a nonstick skillet and the barest minimum of olive oil to sear the pork. Finally, I make my own nonfat mushroom gravy that tastes better than anything from a can. The sherry adds just the right note.

2	¾-pound pork tenderloins
1½	teaspoons salt
½	teaspoon fresh-ground black pepper
1	tablespoon fresh sage, chopped (or 1 teaspoon crumbled dried)
1	teaspoon extra-virgin olive oil
1	medium onion, chopped
2	large garlic cloves, minced
1	pound white button mushrooms, cleaned, tough bottoms of stems removed; chopped
2⅔	cups defatted low-sodium chicken broth, preferably homemade
1	cup skim milk
1	tablespoon dry sherry
4	tablespoons cornstarch, mixed with ¼ cup water

1. Preheat the oven to 325 degrees F.

2. Cut each pork tenderloin crosswise into thirds. One by one, place a tenderloin piece, rounded side up, on a piece of plastic wrap. With a rubber mallet or the back of a small iron skillet, pound slightly to start to flatten, then place plastic wrap on top of the pork and pound to flatten until it is approximately ½ inch thick. Mix ½ teaspoon salt, pepper and sage and sprinkle each piece with some of the mixture, pressing the seasonings into the surface.

3. Heat the oil in a large, nonstick, oven-safe skillet over medium heat. When hot, add the pork and cook until it is light golden brown on both sides, 8 to 10 minutes. Remove to a plate, loosely cover and set aside.

4. Add the onion and garlic to the pan and sauté until softened, 5 to 6 minutes. Add the mushrooms and sauté until lightly browned, 6 to 7 minutes. Add the chicken broth, milk and sherry and bring to a low boil. Add the remaining 1 teaspoon salt and the cornstarch mixture. Return to a boil while stirring and allow to thicken, about 1 minute.

5. Return the pork to the skillet, cover and place in the oven. Bake for 1 hour, turning the tenderloins and spooning the sauce over them once during that time, until tender. Serve immediately with some of the sauce spooned over each tenderloin.

NUTRITIONAL INFORMATION PER SERVING: 217 CALORIES, 5 G FAT, 26 G PROTEIN, 12.5 G CARBOHYDRATE, 74 MG CHOLESTEROL, 471 MG SODIUM.

LeanSuggestion: I love serving this with Decadent Fat-Free Whipped Potatoes (page 368) so I can use the sauce in which the pork is cooked for a lean and tasty gravy. Steamed carrots dusted with a little snipped fresh dill provide color and flavor.

Pork Tenderloin in Bourbon-Brown Sugar Marinade

SERVES 6

IT's NOT ALWAYS EASY to find good ways to prepare pork tenderloin. This excellent marinade imparts an intriguing flavor. Any cold leftovers, sliced paper-thin across the grain, make tasty sandwiches with a dab of spicy mustard.

½	cup bourbon
½	cup dark brown sugar
⅓	cup sodium-reduced soy sauce
½	bunch fresh cilantro, coarsely chopped
¼	cup fresh-squeezed lemon juice
1½	teaspoons Worcestershire sauce
1	cup water
2	sprigs fresh thyme, chopped (or ½ teaspoon crumbled dried)
2	1-pound pork tenderloins, trimmed of all visible fat

1. In a shallow glass casserole dish, combine the bourbon, brown sugar, soy sauce, cilantro, lemon juice, Worcestershire sauce, water and thyme, stirring until the sugar is dissolved. Add the pork tenderloins, cover and marinate in the refrigerator, turning occasionally, for 8 to 12 hours.

2. Preheat the oven to 450 degrees F.

3. Place the tenderloins, side by side without touching, on a wire rack in a shallow roasting pan. Roast for 30 minutes, or until a meat thermometer inserted into the center registers 160 degrees, basting occasionally with the marinade. Discard any unused marinade. Allow the tenderloins to rest for 5 minutes so the meat sets up. Slice them at a 45-degree angle, across the grain, into ¼-inch rounds. Serve immediately.

Nutritional information per serving: 291 calories, 5 g fat, 50 g protein, 15 g carbohydrate, 98 mg cholesterol, 566 mg sodium.

LeanSuggestion: For a special treat, serve these with Oven-Browned Potatoes (page 372).

Pork Tenderloin with Cumin-Mustard Sauce

SERVES 4

T HERE IS NOTHING UNIQUE about the ingredients of this recipe. But when they are put together, they are wonderful. After trying the dish, many people come back to me with the same response, "The flavor of that pork tenderloin was on my mind throughout the next day."

I once used 4 tablespoons of rendered bacon fat when I prepared this. Not anymore. A meager teaspoon of olive oil is all that's needed.

2	½-pound pork tenderloins
½	teaspoon salt
	Fresh-ground black pepper
1	teaspoon extra-virgin olive oil
⅓	cup finely chopped onion
1	garlic clove, minced
2	tablespoons white-wine vinegar
½	cup defatted low-sodium chicken broth
1	scant tablespoon tomato paste
1	small bay leaf
½	teaspoon dried thyme
1-2	teaspoons ground cumin, to taste
2	tablespoons Dijon-style mustard
3	tablespoons chopped fresh parsley

1. Preheat the oven to 200 degrees F.

2. Cut each of the tenderloins crosswise into 4 equal pieces. Put the slices between sheets of plastic wrap and, on a counter or other flat surface, pound with a mallet to flatten them to about 3⁄16 inch thick. Sprinkle each piece with salt and pepper to taste.

3. Add the oil to a large nonstick skillet and brown the pork over medium heat, turning to brown evenly, 8 to 10 minutes. Transfer the cooked meat to a plate, cover and place in the oven.

4. Add the onion and garlic to the skillet, stirring until they start to brown. Add the vinegar and bring to a boil. Add the chicken broth, stir, then add the tomato paste, bay leaf, thyme, cumin and any juice accumulated around the pork. Bring the mixture to a boil and add the mustard, whisking it into the liquid. Simmer for 1 minute. Remove the bay leaf. Divide the pork among 4 dinner plates and spoon the sauce over. Serve topped with the parsley.

NUTRITIONAL INFORMATION PER SERVING: 174 CALORIES, 5.9 G FAT, 24.5 G PROTEIN, 3.4 G CARBOHYDRATE, 74 MG CHOLESTEROL, 554 MG SODIUM.

LeanTip: If the sauce is too thick, whisk in 1 to 2 tablespoons chicken broth.

Poultry

DURING THE SIX YEARS that I lost and kept off more than 100 pounds, I turned to chicken breast constantly, creating more recipes for it than anything else. Chicken breast, after all, is very lean. A 4-ounce skinless chicken breast has 1.5 grams of fat, with only 10 percent of its calories from fat. Only 0.4 gram of that is saturated. Unfortunately, the lack of fat can make for a very dry result, because the breasts will lose water as they cook.

My problem at the end of the first year was how to continue eating chicken and make it taste good so I didn't get bored and switch to fattier cuts of meat. So I searched for the best recipes I could find. Then, using every lean trick I knew, I recreated them to fit my high standards.

I used to love fried chicken, whether it came from a restaurant or my own kitchen, fried in half an inch of fat. I started baking chicken instead of frying it and came up with several different ways to impart great taste and crunch without adding unnecessary fat. I learned how to poach a chicken breast in a full-flavored liquid to keep it succulent in anything from casserole to salad. I also learned that marinating chicken and basting it with the marinade help maintain its moist tenderness.

In all these dishes, the quality of the chicken is pivotal. I purchase free-range chicken from a butcher who can be counted on for quality.

As for turkey, until about six years ago, everything I ever wanted to know about it happened on or around Thanksgiving. Then my life changed. I started closely watching how much fat was a part of my daily food plan, and up popped turkey breast—just like those little thermometers—as the leanest meat. It's even leaner than chicken breast. However, this race was won by a gobble, since by the ounce, white-meat turkey has one-tenth of a gram less fat than white-meat chicken.

One of the first things I made with ground all-white-meat turkey was meat loaf. At the time, there was no commercially available lean ground turkey; all of it had fat and skin ground in. So I made my own. I bought a large, bone-in, skin-on turkey breast. I pulled all the meat off the bones and removed the skin and all visible fat. Then I cut the breast meat into chunks and ground it. My first "turkey" meat loaf was great, giving off almost no fat whatsoever. It was fabulous warm and even better cold in sandwiches.

I found out that poaching a turkey breast in homemade turkey broth produced a moist and flavorful piece of meat. Once chilled and sliced, it makes the best turkey sandwiches and turkey salads I have ever eaten.

I also make some wonderful soups with the bones from the turkey breast. I take the liquid in which I poach the breast and add the skin and bones. Then I add six wings that I have broiled for about 12 minutes per side until brown. In go carrots, celery, onions, peppercorns and thyme. I add a heaping teaspoon of spaghetti sauce seasoning—my grandmother's secret to a fabulous-tasting turkey soup.

But when I made turkey burgers, I found that by the time I had broiled or grilled them until they were done, they had dried out. So I added moisture by using nonfat sour cream. I also discovered the moisture is retained when I add ice. To do this, I slice the uncooked burgers horizontally and open them like a sandwich. Then I take a heaping tablespoon of crushed ice and sprinkle it around the inside of each and put the burgers back together. I gently seal the edges all the way around and take them out to the grill. While the burger is cooking, the ice slowly melts, and moister burgers are the result. (This trick works with 95 percent lean ground beef, too.)

I also took my chili and substituted 97 percent lean ground all-white-meat turkey for the beef. A woman told me she made it for a huge gathering for a Super Bowl Sunday. A double batch was eaten right down to the last bean.

RECIPES

Chicken Léanique

SERVES 4

My version of Chicken Véronique resided in limbo for a while, until I made some changes. Unfortunately, it had depended on butter to produce the smooth and silken sauce that coats the gently cooked chicken breast. Following the classic recipe, I always made it with green grapes. But a small amount of extra-virgin olive oil made an admirable stand-in for the butter. Cornstarch-thickened homemade chicken broth produced a glossy and rich finish. Finally, I switched to red grapes, which have slightly more sweetness than green and a beautiful color. This retains all the terrific flavors of the original but now is much lower in fat.

2	whole chicken breasts, split, skinned and boned
1	teaspoon extra-virgin olive oil
½	teaspoon salt
¼	teaspoon fresh-ground white pepper
2	tablespoons finely chopped green onions (white parts only)
¼	cup dry white vermouth
1	teaspoon fresh-squeezed lemon juice
2	teaspoons cornstarch
½	cup defatted low-sodium chicken broth
1	cup seedless red grapes, rinsed, dried and quartered

1. Trim any visible fat from the breasts. Slice the breasts across the grain into ½-inch-wide strips.

2. In a large nonstick skillet, heat the oil over medium-high heat. Add the chicken strips and sprinkle with the salt and white pepper. Sauté the chicken, stirring constantly, until just cooked through, 3 to 4 minutes. With a slotted spoon, remove the chicken from the skillet to a warm plate and set aside.

3. Return the skillet to the heat and add the green onions; cook, stirring, until softened. Add the vermouth, lemon juice and any juice that has accumulated on the chicken plate. Stir until the liquid reaches a boil. Whisk the cornstarch into the chicken broth; add it and the grapes to the skillet. Lower the heat slightly and cook for 3 to 4 minutes, stirring occasionally. Return the cooked chicken to the pan and heat through. Serve, spooning the grapes and sauce over the chicken.

NUTRITIONAL INFORMATION PER SERVING: 174 CALORIES, 2.7 G FAT, 28 G PROTEIN, 5.8 G CARBOHYDRATE, 68 MG CHOLESTEROL, 354 MG SODIUM.

LeanSuggestion: Steamed young carrots make a terrific side dish.

Herb-Seasoned Broiled Chicken

SERVES 4

To enhance the mild flavor of chicken breast, I mix garlic and onion powder with dry mustard, paprika, cumin, basil, oregano and thyme. Then I add fresh-ground white and black pepper in equal proportions and press the blend through a fine sieve. I coat the chicken with the spice mixture as if with flour—in effect, sealing them. Under a hot broiler, the breasts turn out moist and wonderful.

2	whole chicken breasts, split, skinned and boned
1	teaspoon salt
1	teaspoon dry mustard
1	teaspoon onion powder
1	teaspoon sweet paprika, preferably Hungarian
¾	teaspoon garlic powder
¾	teaspoon ground cumin
¾	teaspoon crumbled dried basil
¾	teaspoon crumbled dried oregano
½	teaspoon crumbled dried thyme
¼	teaspoon fresh-ground white pepper
¼	teaspoon fresh-ground black pepper

1. Preheat the broiler, with a rack about 4 inches from the heat source.

2. Rinse the chicken breasts under cold water and dry with a clean paper towel. Trim all remaining visible fat. Set aside.

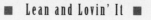

3. Cover a broiler pan with foil and lightly spray with vegetable oil. Set aside.

4. Put the salt and all the herbs and spices in a fine sieve placed over a small bowl. Shake and rub the spices through the sieve into the bowl. Discard any hard pieces that will not go through. Shake the spice mixture so it flattens and spreads to the edge of the bowl. Press a chicken breast into the spice mixture to coat it with the seasonings on both sides. Place, boned side up, on the broiler pan. Continue with the remaining breasts.

5. Broil the breasts for 4 minutes. Turn the breasts over. Adjust the broiler rack to the uppermost position and return the chicken to the broiler. Broil for 3½ minutes more, or until breasts are cooked through but not blackened. Serve immediately.

NUTRITIONAL INFORMATION PER SERVING: 144 CALORIES, 2 G FAT, 27 G PROTEIN, 2.3 G CARBOHYDRATE, 68 MG CHOLESTEROL, 612 MG SODIUM.

Southern-Style Oven-Fried Chicken

SERVES 6

SINCE I NOW LIVE IN NORTH CAROLINA, I've seen how some of the best fried chicken is prepared. It's seasoned and then skillet-fried in at least half an inch of fat. I use the seasonings that make Southern-style fried chicken taste so good. I choose white-meat chicken breasts (less than half the fat of dark-meat chicken). I remove the skin (that's where the majority of the fat resides) and use bread crumbs to protect the meat from drying out. I bake it in a very hot oven to duplicate the heat of a frying pan.

3½	cups fresh white bread crumbs
2	teaspoons crumbled dried thyme
1	teaspoon fresh-ground black pepper
1	teaspoon crumbled dried basil
1	teaspoon crumbled dried oregano
1	teaspoon curry powder
1	teaspoon ground cumin
1	teaspoon garlic powder
½	teaspoon salt
½	teaspoon hot red pepper flakes
2	large egg whites
¼	cup buttermilk
2	teaspoons Dijon-style mustard
3	whole skinless, boneless chicken breasts, split

1. Preheat the oven to 450 degrees F.

2. In a medium mixing bowl, stir together the bread crumbs, thyme, black pepper, basil, oregano, curry powder, cumin, garlic powder, salt and red pepper flakes. Set aside.

3. In a small bowl, whisk together the egg whites, buttermilk and mustard. Set aside.

4. Dip each chicken breast in the buttermilk mixture and then drop into the bread-crumb mixture, coating well. Firmly press the crumbs into each breast. Place each breast, without letting the sides touch, on a nonstick jelly-roll pan. Bake for 16 minutes, turning once after 8 minutes, or until golden and cooked through. Serve immediately.

NUTRITIONAL INFORMATION PER SERVING: 275 CALORIES, 3.7 G FAT, 33 G PROTEIN, 25 G CARBOHYDRATE, 69 MG CHOLESTEROL, 562 MG SODIUM.

LeanSuggestion: For extra-crunchy Southern-style oven-fried chicken, add 1 cup all-purpose flour to the spice mixture, omit the bread crumbs and place the mixture in a small brown paper bag. In a separate bowl, place 3½ cups corn flakes that have been lightly crushed (place them in a resealable bag and roll them with a rolling pin). Add the breasts to the seasoning mix and shake. Dip each breast in the egg-mustard mixture. Coat the breast with the crushed corn flakes. Bake as directed above.

GRILLED MARINATED CHICKEN BREASTS

SERVES 4

WHEN OUTDOOR TEMPERATURES begin to rise, it's time for me to fire up the old barbecue. For lean eaters, a barbecue is a blessing, since meats and vegetables have much more flavor when cooked over charcoal.

The first time I prepared chicken on my grill, I let it cook on the first side without checking. Upon lifting the cover, I discovered both chicken halves were on fire. Due to that unfortunate incident, I was immediately stripped of my Grillmeister status. My spatula, tongs and basting brush were returned only after successfully retaking the Grill Proficiency Test (GPT), administered by my skeptical wife.

1	tablespoon grated fresh gingerroot
1	large garlic clove, minced
¼	cup fresh lime juice
1	teaspoon olive oil
1	bay leaf, chopped or broken into small pieces
1½	teaspoons fresh thyme, chopped (or ½ teaspoon crumbled dried)
½	teaspoon salt
¼	teaspoon fresh-ground white pepper
2	whole chicken breasts, split

1. In a small glass or ceramic bowl, whisk together the ginger, garlic, lime juice, olive oil, bay leaf, thyme, salt and pepper. Set aside.

2. Place the breasts, skin side down, in a glass dish just large enough to hold them. Pour the marinade over the chicken, cover and refrigerate for 1 hour, turning once.

3. Prepare a charcoal or gas grill. When the coals are hot, drain the chicken and place it, skin side down, on the grill. Cook until nicely browned, about 8 minutes, basting with the marinade every 4 minutes. Turn the breasts skin side up. Baste them with the marinade. Grill for 8 minutes more, basting every 4 minutes, until the chicken is cooked through. Remove the skin before serving.

NUTRITIONAL INFORMATION PER SERVING: 153 CALORIES, 2.7 G FAT, 27 G PROTEIN, 3.3 G CARBOHYDRATE, 68 MG CHOLESTEROL, 345 MG SODIUM.

BAKED CHICKEN BREASTS
MARINATED IN ORANGE AND BROWN SUGAR

SERVES 4

MY WIFE DISCOVERED a recipe that used orange juice to marinate fish. It inspired her to create her own marinade using fresh-squeezed orange juice. Although there is added oil, the flavor would be greatly diminished without it.

I took the recipe to the next step by marinating skinned and boned chicken breasts in this mixture, then breading and baking them. The flavors march to an Asian drummer.

½	cup fresh-squeezed orange juice
1	tablespoon light brown sugar
2	tablespoons sodium-reduced soy sauce
1	teaspoon grated fresh gingerroot
1	garlic clove, minced
½	teaspoon toasted sesame oil*
2	whole chicken breasts, split, skinned and boned
2	cups fresh white bread crumbs (about 4 slices)

1. In a medium glass or ceramic bowl, whisk together the orange juice, brown sugar, soy sauce, ginger, garlic and sesame oil. Add the chicken breasts, spoon the marinade over them, cover and refrigerate for 1 hour.

2. Preheat the oven to 450 degrees F. Lightly spray a nonstick jelly-roll pan with vegetable oil. Set aside.

3. Spread the bread crumbs on a dinner plate. Take each chicken breast from the marinade and coat it with the bread crumbs, pressing them on. Shake off the excess crumbs and place the breast on the prepared pan. Coat the remaining breasts.

4. Bake for 16 to 18 minutes, turning once after 8 minutes, until cooked through. Serve warm.

NUTRITIONAL INFORMATION PER SERVING: 256 CALORIES, 3.3 G FAT, 31 G PROTEIN, 24 G CARBOHYDRATE, 68 MG CHOLESTEROL, 500 MG SODIUM.

Toasted sesame oil can be found in the Asian food section of most large supermarkets, as well as in Asian markets.

Sweet-Smelling Baked Chicken Breasts

SERVES 4

THE FIRST TIME I prepared these chicken breasts for guests, everyone seemed to find a reason to come through the kitchen doorway to see what smelled so good. If you're looking for a mouth-watering delight, this is it (as long as you don't mind a little company in the kitchen). The toasted bread crumbs give the outside crunch, and the spices permeate the chicken.

COATING

1	cup toasted bread crumbs
1¼	teaspoons garlic powder
1	teaspoon onion powder
1	teaspoon crumbled dried basil
1	teaspoon sweet paprika
½	teaspoon crumbled dried oregano
½	teaspoon ground cumin
½	teaspoon salt
½	teaspoon fresh-ground black pepper
½	teaspoon fresh-ground white pepper
½	cup fresh-squeezed lemon juice
½	teaspoon hot red pepper sauce
2	whole chicken breasts, split and skinned

1. Preheat the oven to 425 degrees F, with a rack in the upper third.

2. Coating: Place all the coating ingredients in a small mixing bowl and stir together until well combined. Set aside.

3. Place the lemon juice and hot sauce in a small glass or ceramic bowl. Dip each chicken breast first in the lemon juice mixture and then into the coating mixture. Press the crumb mixture and seasoning firmly into each breast, shaking off the excess. As each breast is coated, place it skinned side down on a small nonstick baking sheet, making sure the sides do not touch.

4. Bake for 9 minutes, or until the breasts begin to feel firm when pressed. Turn and bake for 7 minutes more, or until cooked through and golden. Serve immediately.

NUTRITIONAL INFORMATION PER SERVING: 175 CALORIES, 2 G FAT, 28 G PROTEIN, 8.9 G CARBOHYDRATE, 68 MG CHOLESTEROL, 410 MG SODIUM.

Zippy Marinated Chicken Breasts

SERVES 6

This is how I avoid weeknight hassles: I shop for free-range chicken breasts on Saturday afternoon. On Sunday, I do steps 1, 2 and 3 of this recipe. By Tuesday, my marinating chicken breasts are infused with flavor and ready to be cooked.

While I am preheating the oven, I take the chicken out of the refrigerator so it loses some of the chill. Then onto the pan it goes and into the oven. Unless the breasts are unusually large, they are done in 10 minutes. The yogurt and lemon make them meltingly moist. The tingle on the tongue comes from the jalapeño, which asserts its heat without being overwhelming, and cumin adds an East Indian spin. Leftovers make a good quick lunch or a great sandwich.

3	pounds (approximately 3 large whole) chicken breasts, split and skinned
1½	teaspoons salt
6	tablespoons fresh-squeezed lemon juice
1	cup nonfat plain yogurt
1-2	fresh jalapeño peppers, seeds removed, coarsely chopped
1	large garlic clove, peeled
1	small onion, chopped
2	teaspoons ground cumin
2	teaspoons crumbled dried thyme
2	teaspoons crumbled dried oregano
1	teaspoon finely grated fresh gingerroot
¼	cup minced fresh parsley

1. Cut 2 parallel diagonal slits on the meaty sides of each breast, cutting all the way through to the bone but being careful not to cut through.

2. In a small bowl, whisk together the salt and lemon juice until the salt dissolves. Put the chicken breasts and the lemon-juice mixture into a resealable plastic bag. Press the air from the bag and seal. Squeeze the bag to coat the breasts with the liquid and marinate at room temperature for 20 minutes.

3. In a blender, puree the yogurt with the peppers, garlic, onion, cumin, thyme, oregano and ginger. Transfer the yogurt puree to the resealable bag with the chicken. Press all the air from the bag and seal. Turn and press the breasts to make certain they are completely coated. Refrigerate, turning the bag once or twice, for at least 8 hours and up to 2 days.

4. Preheat the oven to 550 degrees F, with a rack in the upper third. Cover the inside of the broiler pan with aluminum foil. Remove the breasts from the bag, letting the excess marinade drip off, and place each breast on the pan; arrange them in one layer, without touching. Discard the remaining marinade.

5. Roast, turning once, for 10 minutes, or just until the breasts are cooked through. Transfer the breasts to a heated platter, sprinkle them with the parsley and serve.

NUTRITIONAL INFORMATION PER SERVING: 136 CALORIES, 1.5 G FAT, 28 G PROTEIN, 0.9 G CARBOHYDRATE, 68 MG CHOLESTEROL, 84 MG SODIUM.

LeanSuggestion: Serve with basmati rice prepared with defatted chicken broth, to which 2 teaspoons of mild or hot curry powder have been added.

Hearty Chicken Stew

SERVES 4

ONE COLD DECEMBER EVENING, I wanted to make a real stick-to-your-ribs stew. Beef was out for two reasons: too much fat and too long a cooking time. I had all the remaining ingredients for a beef stew in my refrigerator, plus chicken. When I make beef stew, I use rosemary or thyme for flavoring. Since Susan and I both love tarragon with chicken, I tossed it in.

After I added the flour, some brown pieces of vegetable and chicken stuck to the bottom of the pot. When I poured in the broth and began to stir, everything became unstuck, and the cooking liquid took on a beautiful dark golden glow. The flavors were unbelievably rich. We did not miss the beef—not for one single second.

2	whole chicken breasts split, skinned, boned and cut into ¾-inch pieces
	Salt and fresh-ground black pepper
2	teaspoons extra-virgin olive oil
4	parsnips, peeled, cut crosswise into ¼-inch slices
3	large carrots, peeled, cut crosswise into ¼-inch slices
3	medium leeks (white and pale green parts only), halved lengthwise, rinsed of all sand, cut crosswise into ¼-inch slices
1	pound small new potatoes, scrubbed, cut into ¼-inch slices
3	tablespoons all-purpose flour
3	cups defatted low-sodium chicken broth
1	medium bay leaf
2	teaspoons crumbled dried tarragon (or 1 tablespoon minced fresh)
¼	cup nonfat sour cream

1. Sprinkle the chicken pieces with salt and pepper. Heat the oil in a large nonstick saucepan over medium heat and add the chicken. Cook, tossing and stirring until it is light brown, about 5 minutes. Transfer to a warm plate.

2. Add the parsnips, carrots, leeks and potatoes to the saucepan and cook, stirring and tossing every 2 minutes, for a total of 8 minutes. Add the flour and cook, stirring, for 2 minutes. Gradually stir in the chicken broth. Increase the heat and bring to a boil, scraping up all the brown bits at the bottom of the pan. Return the chicken to the saucepan along with the bay leaf and tarragon. Lower the heat, cover and gently simmer, stirring occasionally, for 30 minutes. Remove and discard the bay leaf, stir in the sour cream and serve.

NUTRITIONAL INFORMATION PER SERVING: 328 CALORIES, 2 G FAT, 34 G PROTEIN, 39 G CARBOHYDRATE, 79 MG CHOLESTEROL, 447 MG SODIUM.

LeanTip: Some warm French bread, with no added butter, is an excellent aid to mopping up the delicious gravy created by this stew.

Arroz con Pollo

(RICE WITH CHICKEN)

SERVES 8

LEAN ARROZ CON POLLO IS COLORFUL, tastes fabulous and is incredibly low in fat (less than 10 percent of the calories). Saffron, although used in small quantities, brings much wonderful flavor to this dish. Baby peas and pimiento contribute splendid sweetness and dynamic color. I start my meal with a big tossed salad and a nonfat dressing. Two words describe the meal: filling and fantastic.

3	whole chicken breasts, skinned, boned and cut into ½-inch cubes
1	teaspoon salt
½	teaspoon fresh-ground black pepper
½	teaspoon sweet paprika
2	teaspoons extra-virgin olive oil
1	medium onion, chopped
1	large garlic clove, minced
2	cups defatted low-sodium chicken broth, preferably homemade
1	28-ounce can whole tomatoes, coarsely chopped
1	bay leaf
½	teaspoon crumbled dried oregano (or 1½ teaspoons chopped fresh)
½	teaspoon saffron (5-6 threads), crushed
½	teaspoon salt
2	cups long-grain white rice
1	10-ounce package frozen baby peas, defrosted
3	bottled pimientos, finely diced

1. Preheat the oven to 350 degrees F. Lightly spray a large casserole dish with vegetable oil.

2. Season the chicken breast with the salt, pepper and paprika. In a large nonstick skillet over medium-high heat, heat the oil. When hot but not smoking, sauté the chicken until lightly golden, 3 to 4 minutes. Remove the chicken to the casserole.

3. Add the onion and garlic to the skillet; sauté until tender. Add the chicken broth and scrape up the browned bits from the skillet bottom while heating. Add the tomatoes and their liquid, the bay leaf, oregano, saffron and salt. Bring to a boil, stirring.

4. Pour the tomato mixture over the chicken. Add the rice, stir, cover the casserole and bake for 25 minutes. Carefully uncover the casserole (steam will billow out), and stir in the peas. Distribute the pimiento pieces over the top, cover and return to the oven for 10 minutes more. Serve immediately.

NUTRITIONAL INFORMATION PER SERVING: 335 CALORIES, 2.8 G FAT, 27 G PROTEIN, 49 G CARBOHYDRATE, 51 MG CHOLESTEROL, 613 MG SODIUM.

LeanTip: Buying saffron in small quantities keeps the price reasonable and means it will be fresh whenever you reach for it.

LEAN AND EASY CHICKEN PAPRIKA

SERVES 6

MY CHICKEN PAPRIKA, which uses nonfat sour cream, is so rich that you won't believe less than 13 percent of its calories come from fat. The last person for whom I made this knew a Hungarian restaurant in Chicago where the high-fat version was the signature dish. He proclaimed this to be its equal.

1½	teaspoons extra-virgin olive oil
2	whole chicken breasts, split, skinned and boned
½	cup sliced white onion
½	cup defatted low-sodium chicken broth
½	teaspoon salt
2	tablespoons sweet paprika
¼	cup chopped peeled fresh or canned tomato
1	medium green bell pepper, seeded, cut into julienne strips
12	ounces broad, flat noodles made without egg yolks
1	tablespoon all-purpose flour
½	cup nonfat sour cream

1. Place a large nonstick skillet over medium-high heat and add the oil. When it is hot, add the chicken breasts. Cook for 3 minutes, turn and cook for 3 minutes more to sear. Remove the breasts to a warm plate.

2. Reduce the heat to medium, add the onion to the skillet and sauté for 2 minutes, or until shiny and just beginning to give off steam. Add the chicken broth, salt, paprika, tomato and green pepper, and stir to combine. Return the breasts to the skillet. Spoon the sauce over the breasts, cover, reduce the heat to low and gently simmer for 18 to 20 minutes.

3. Meanwhile, bring a pot of salted water to a boil and stir in the egg noodles. When the water returns to the boil, cook for about 8 minutes, stirring occasionally. Drain and rinse under hot water.

4. Transfer the chicken to the serving plates. Blend the flour with the sour cream and add to the ingredients in the skillet, stirring constantly. Cook for 3 minutes, until the sauce begins to thicken, taking care not to bring to a boil.

5. Divide the cooked noodles among the serving plates, spoon some sauce and vegetables over the noodles, place the chicken breast on top and distribute the remaining sauce and vegetables over each. Serve immediately.

NUTRITIONAL INFORMATION PER SERVING: 357 CALORIES, 4.9 G FAT, 27.5 G PROTEIN, 46 G CARBOHYDRATE, 48 MG CHOLESTEROL, 277 MG SODIUM.

Jamaican Chicken

SERVES 3

Jamaican jerk-flavored foods are terrific—sizzling hot and spicy with great taste. When I used to make this, I used an ocean of butter. I replaced it with a small amount of canola oil. Now it tastes absolutely splendid.

MARINADE

1   teaspoon Worcestershire sauce
2   teaspoons reduced-sodium soy sauce
3   tablespoons Jamaican rum
1   garlic clove, minced
¼   cup snipped fresh chives

3   split chicken breasts, skinned and boned
2   teaspoons canola oil
2   tablespoons light brown sugar
1   medium onion, chopped

1. Marinade: In a medium glass bowl, whisk together the marinade ingredients until well combined. Set aside.

2. Rinse the chicken breasts under cold water. Pat them dry with a paper towel. Place them in the bowl with the marinade, turning to coat. Marinate at room temperature for 10 minutes.

3. Place a large nonstick skillet over medium heat and add the oil and brown sugar. Cook until the sugar is almost completely melted. Remove the chicken from the marinade and place it in the skillet. Sauté on both sides until light brown, 6 to 7 minutes total. Add the marinade and the onion and cook 10 minutes more, or until the chicken is cooked through and the onion is soft.

4. Remove the skillet from the heat. Place a breast on each plate, spoon the sauce over and serve.

NUTRITIONAL INFORMATION PER SERVING: 241 CALORIES, 4.5 G FAT, 27.3 G PROTEIN, 11.8 G CARBOHYDRATE, 68 MG CHOLESTEROL, 211 MG SODIUM.

LeanSuggestion: Rice goes well with this chicken, especially when prepared with garlic and ginger. Fresh spinach, cooked lightly and doused with a touch of balsamic vinegar and fresh-ground black pepper, is the perfect accompaniment.

Spicy Chicken

SERVES 2

TWO OF MY FAVORITE FLAVORS are onions and garlic. Few things smell better in a kitchen when they are being prepared together. This chicken is ideal served with rice to bring complex carbohydrates into play and to soak up all the delicious sauce.

1½	cups defatted low-sodium chicken broth, preferably homemade
2	tablespoons white-wine vinegar
2	teaspoons brown sugar
1	teaspoon sodium-reduced soy sauce
1	large (1 pound) whole chicken breast, split, skinned and boned
2	large garlic cloves, minced
1	medium onion, finely chopped
1	bay leaf
¼	teaspoon cayenne pepper
2	teaspoons cornstarch, mixed with 1 tablespoon water
¼	teaspoon salt

1. In a saucepan over medium-high heat, combine the chicken broth, vinegar, brown sugar and soy sauce and boil the mixture until reduced by half. Set aside.

2. Meanwhile, place a large nonstick skillet over medium-high heat and lightly spray with vegetable oil. Add the chicken and sauté, turning, until golden, 6 to 8 minutes. Transfer the chicken to a plate.

3. Return the skillet to the heat and cook the garlic, onion, bay leaf and cayenne over medium heat, stirring, until the onion is softened. Add the reduced-broth mixture and the chicken along with any juices that have collected on the plate. Lower the heat and slowly simmer the chicken, turning, until it is cooked through, 10 to 12 minutes.

4. Divide the chicken between 2 dinner plates. Stir the cornstarch mixture into the sauce and cook until clear and thickened. Discard the bay leaf, stir in the salt, pour the sauce over the chicken and serve.

NUTRITIONAL INFORMATION PER SERVING: 206 CALORIES, 1.6 G FAT, 30 G PROTEIN, 15.2 G CARBOHYDRATE, 68 MG CHOLESTEROL, 488 MG SODIUM.

LeanSuggestion: Oven-Browned Potatoes (page 372) are sensational with this. I also enjoy quickly cooked baby peas with a little Butter Buds (mixed with hot water according to the package directions) drizzled over them.

LEAN AND MEAN TURKEY CHILI

SERVES 12

THIS RECIPE HAS CONTINUED EVOLVING for almost 30 years. At first, the seasonings came from a store-bought spice packet. As I grew older and wiser, I began experimenting with spices from my own rack.

Over the years I also replaced the beef and pork with lean ground turkey. Now I substitute cocoa for unsweetened baking chocolate. Baking chocolate has too much fat (76 percent of calories), whereas cocoa has much less (24 percent of calories), and it adds an extra dimension, as it does in some Mexican sauces.

2	teaspoons extra-virgin olive oil
1½	pounds 97% lean all-white-meat ground turkey
2	large yellow onions, coarsely chopped
4	large garlic cloves, minced
1	rounded tablespoon chili powder
1	tablespoon ground cumin
1	tablespoon sweet paprika
1	teaspoon fresh-ground black pepper
2	16-ounce cans whole tomatoes, chopped (reserve juice)
1	28-ounce can tomato sauce
1	cup dry red wine (optional)
1	cup defatted low-sodium beef broth
2	tablespoons unsweetened cocoa powder
2	teaspoons clover honey
½	teaspoon hot red pepper sauce
1	large bay leaf
2	16-ounce cans pinto beans (or kidney beans)

1. Heat a large saucepan over medium-high heat and add the oil. Add the turkey and begin to break it up with the edge of a spoon. Add the onions, garlic, chili powder, cumin, paprika and pepper. Sauté for 6 to 7 minutes, or until the turkey has lost its pink color and the onions have softened.

2. Add the tomatoes with their reserved juice, tomato sauce, optional wine and beef broth, stirring to combine. Stir in the cocoa, honey, hot sauce and bay leaf. Reduce the heat to low and gently simmer for 1 hour.

3. Add the pinto or kidney beans, stirring to combine. Heat for 5 minutes, until the beans are heated through. Remove and discard the bay leaf before serving.

NUTRITIONAL INFORMATION PER SERVING: 224 CALORIES, 1.9 G FAT, 20.5 G PROTEIN, 29 G CARBOHYDRATE, 35 MG CHOLESTEROL, 758 MG SODIUM.

LeanSuggestions

■ Top each bowl with a large dollop of nonfat sour cream. The addition of shredded fat-reduced or nonfat cheese is wonderful. Pass a bowl of chopped sweet onions.

■ This is great when turned into a "chili Mac." Prepare macaroni elbows according to the package directions. Drain and place ½ cup of the prepared macaroni in the bottom of each serving bowl. Top with the chili.

BEST-EVER TURKEY MEAT LOAF

SERVES 8 AS A MAIN COURSE

T HIS WAS ONE OF MY FEATURED RECIPES in a 1992 article about my weight-loss success in the *Chicago Sun-Times*. The readers found the dish to be delicious. Ketchup or freshly prepared tomato sauce served over a slice of this loaf makes it just as good as a beef meat loaf. Cold and thinly sliced, it makes one terrific sandwich.

1	16-ounce can whole tomatoes with juice, chopped
2	large egg whites, slightly beaten
3	green onions (white and green parts), chopped
1	scant cup old-fashioned or quick-cooking (not instant) oats
1	teaspoon salt
½	teaspoon fresh-ground black pepper
1½	pounds 97% lean ground all-white-meat turkey
	Sweet paprika

1. Preheat the oven to 350 degrees F.

2. In a large mixing bowl, combine the tomatoes and juice, egg whites, green onions, oats, salt and pepper. Add the turkey. With clean hands, mix the turkey well with the other ingredients, but do not overwork.

3. Pat the mixture into a 9-by-5-by-3-inch loaf pan. Smooth the surface and dust generously with the paprika.

4. Bake for 60 to 65 minutes, or until a meat thermometer inserted into the center registers 160 degrees. Let the turkey loaf stand at room temperature for 10 minutes before slicing.

NUTRITIONAL INFORMATION PER SERVING: 151 CALORIES, 1.3 G FAT, 25 G PROTEIN, 9.3 G CARBOHYDRATE, 55 MG CHOLESTEROL, 334 MG SODIUM.

TURKEY DIVAN

SERVES 6

I PUT A WHOLE NEW SPIN on this favorite potluck-supper dish. Since I said "so long" to so much fat in this casserole, I needed to replace the lost flavor. I add blanched fresh broccoli spears instead of the frozen because they have far more flavor and texture. If you use roasted turkey breast and reduced-fat cheese, this is fabulous. The big plus? It's easy.

2   large (1½-pound) heads of broccoli, rinsed, trimmed
      and cut into spears
1   10-ounce can condensed fat-reduced cream of celery soup
⅓   cup dry white wine
1   pound sliced cooked turkey breast
1   cup shredded fat-reduced Cheddar cheese (4 ounces)

1. Preheat the oven to 350 degrees F.

2. Cook the broccoli spears in a pot of unsalted, boiling water for 1 to 1½ minutes, or until they are bright green; drain well.

3. In a medium mixing bowl, whisk together the celery soup and white wine. Set aside.

4. Lightly spray a medium casserole dish with vegetable oil. Evenly arrange the broccoli spears in the bottom of the casserole. Pour half the soup mixture over the broccoli. Arrange the turkey slices over the broccoli and pour the remaining soup mixture over the top.

5. Bake for 25 minutes. Sprinkle the top of the casserole with the cheese and bake for 5 minutes more, or until the cheese melts. Serve immediately.

NUTRITIONAL INFORMATION PER SERVING: 182 CALORIES, 5.7 G FAT, 27 G PROTEIN, 7.2 G CARBOHYDRATE, 43 MG CHOLESTEROL, 1,259 MG SODIUM.

Turkey Fajitas

SERVES 4

THIS RECIPE TRANSFORMS leftover turkey meat into a delicious dish. It's very easy to make, and it's lower in fat than any restaurant version.

1	teaspoon extra-virgin olive oil
1	small onion, halved lengthwise, sliced into thin strips
2	cups sliced white button mushrooms
½	medium red bell pepper, sliced into thin strips
3	garlic cloves, minced
¾	pound cooked all-white-meat turkey, thinly sliced across the grain
1	teaspoon ground cumin
⅛	teaspoon hot red pepper flakes
1	cup frozen corn, thawed
2	tablespoons fresh-squeezed lime juice
1	tablespoon sodium-reduced soy sauce
4	8-inch nonfat flour tortillas
4	tablespoons nonfat sour cream

1. Heat the oil in a large nonstick skillet over medium-high heat. Add the onion, mushrooms, red bell pepper and garlic. Cook, stirring, for 4 minutes, or until softened. Add the turkey strips, cumin, red pepper flakes and corn. Cook, stirring, for 2 minutes, or until thoroughly heated. Remove from the heat. Stir in the lime juice and soy sauce.

2. Place the tortillas, wrapped in a paper towel, in a microwave oven, or wrapped in aluminum foil in a conventional oven preheated to 350 degrees F. Set the microwave on high and microwave for 25 seconds, or

warm for 2 minutes in a conventional oven. Divide the filling evenly among the warmed tortillas; top each with 1 tablespoon of the sour cream and roll up each tortilla. Serve immediately.

NUTRITIONAL INFORMATION PER SERVING: 262 CALORIES, 3.5 G FAT, 24.5 PROTEIN, 27.6 G CARBOHYDRATE, 56 MG CHOLESTEROL, 368 MG SODIUM.

LeanNote: One flour tortilla can have up to 3 grams of fat. Look for nonfat tortillas in the refrigerated section of most supermarkets.

Turkey Stew with Mushrooms

SERVES 5

AT FIRST, the concept of a turkey stew did not sound all that appealing to me. My opinion came in part from having grown up on beef stews. I started with my own beef stew recipe, altering it a little each time. This stew has a good rich flavor and makes a hearty dinner with Sweet and Lean Slaw (page 88) and warm French or Italian bread (without butter).

1	tablespoon extra-virgin olive oil
1¼	pounds skinless, boneless turkey breast, cut into ½-inch pieces
10	small red potatoes (new potatoes are best)
4	medium carrots, peeled, sliced crosswise into coins 1½ inches thick
4	celery stalks, stringed, sliced crosswise 1½ inches thick
1	large onion, chopped
4	garlic cloves, minced
2	tablespoons all-purpose flour
¾	cup defatted low-sodium chicken broth
1	cup dry white wine
1½	teaspoons chopped fresh rosemary (or 1 teaspoon crumbled dried)
½	teaspoon salt
½	teaspoon fresh-ground white pepper
½	pound white button mushrooms, cleaned and quartered
½	cup chopped fresh parsley

1. Preheat the oven to 350 degrees F.

2. Heat the oil in a large ovenproof skillet and sauté the turkey over medium-high heat until lightly browned, about 5 minutes. Add the potatoes, carrots, celery, onion and garlic. Sauté, stirring, for 5 to 6 minutes, or until the onion begins to soften.

3. Sprinkle the flour over the turkey mixture and cook for 1 minute more. Add the chicken broth, wine, rosemary, salt and pepper. Bring to a boil, stirring. Stir in the mushrooms.

4. Bake, uncovered, for 45 minutes, or until the vegetables are tender. Stir in the parsley and serve.

NUTRITIONAL INFORMATION PER SERVING: 306 CALORIES, 4.1 G FAT, 39 G PROTEIN, 26.6 G CARBOHYDRATE, 71 MG CHOLESTEROL, 339 MG SODIUM.

Roast Turkey Breast

When I make turkey for Thanksgiving, I no longer roast a whole turkey, I cook only the breast. That way I end up with flavorful, very lean meat.

2 cups defatted low-sodium chicken broth, preferably homemade
2 cups dry white wine
3 large carrots, coarsely chopped
4 celery stalks, coarsely chopped
1 medium onion, peeled and quartered
1 whole turkey breast, with bone and skin, rinsed well under cold water

1. Preheat the oven to 350 degrees F.

2. Place the chicken broth and wine in a quart jar. Cover and shake until combined. Set aside.

3. Line a roasting pan with heavy-duty aluminum foil. Add the carrots, celery and onion. Nestle the roasting rack among the vegetables and set it securely at the bottom of the pan. Lightly spray the rack with vegetable oil. Place the turkey breast on the rack. Roast for 25 minutes per pound, or until the juices run clear when pierced with a knife. Baste every 15 minutes with the broth-wine mixture.

4. Remove the turkey from the oven and place it on a carving board; discard the vegetables. Let the turkey rest for 10 minutes, then remove the skin and blot the surface with a paper towel. Slice and serve.

NUTRITIONAL INFORMATION PER 3-OUNCE SERVING: 94 CALORIES, 0.5 G FAT, 21 G PROTEIN, 0 CARBOHYDRATE, 53 MG CHOLESTEROL, 42 MG SODIUM.

LeanTip: The liquid in the bottom of the pan will make a great gravy. After the turkey has been removed, take out the rack, discard the vegetables, and pour any accumulated liquid into a fat separator. Or pour into a clear measuring cup and spoon off the fat on top. Use 2 cups of the defatted liquid to prepare gravy (see LeanStyle Chicken Gravy, page 260).

TURKEY STUFFING

SERVES 8

THANKSGIVING JUST ISN'T THANKSGIVING without stuffing. Because of his dietary restrictions, my stepfather could no longer eat high-fat stuffing on any occasion. So for him, I began trying to create the best lowest-fat stuffing I could. It meant two easy substitutions and the willingness to bake the stuffing in a casserole dish.

I used defatted chicken broth instead of water. Then, since most stuffing recipes start with a stick of butter (800 calories and 92 fat grams), I switched to Butter Buds.

1   cup diced celery
1   cup diced onion
2   cups sliced white button mushrooms
3   cups defatted low-sodium chicken broth, preferably homemade
1   ½-ounce packet Butter Buds
1   16-ounce package bread-cube stuffing

1. Preheat the oven to 350 degrees F.

2. Lightly spray a large sauté pan with vegetable oil. Add the celery, onion and mushrooms and sauté over medium-high heat until the onion is soft and the mushrooms give up their liquid, about 6 minutes. Add the broth. When it is hot, whisk in the Butter Buds. Add the stuffing and toss.

3. Let the stuffing cool. Lightly spray a large casserole dish with vegetable oil. Add the stuffing. Cover and bake for 45 minutes, or until hot.

NUTRITIONAL INFORMATION PER SERVING: 182 CALORIES, 2 G FAT, 5.4 G PROTEIN, 34 G CARBOHYDRATE, 0 CHOLESTEROL, 448 MG SODIUM.

LeanTip: If you wish to have a moister stuffing, use 3½ cups defatted chicken broth in all.

New-Fashioned Virginia Turkey Stuffing

MAKES 12 CUPS, ENOUGH TO STUFF A 12-TO-14 POUND TURKEY

THIS STUFFING IS WONDERFULLY FLAVORED. Yes, it is elaborate, but for a once-a-year effort, it's worth it. Only 17 percent of all the delicious calories come from fat.

BROTH

4	cups warm water
	Giblets from 1 turkey, capon or chicken
¾	cup diced celery
1	medium carrot, peeled and sliced
1	small onion, sliced
1	teaspoon salt

RICE

1	cup long-grain white rice
1	teaspoon extra-virgin olive oil

VEGETABLES

2	teaspoons extra-virgin olive oil
2	cups thinly sliced celery
2	cups chopped onions
½	pound white button mushrooms, thinly sliced
½	cup water
1	½-ounce packet Butter Buds

BREAD AND SEASONINGS

2	teaspoons olive oil
4	cups cubed corn bread
2	cups cubed day-old white bread
¼	cup finely chopped pecans
1	tablespoon poultry seasoning
½	teaspoon fresh-ground black pepper

1. Broth: Place the water, giblets, celery, carrot, onion and salt in a medium saucepan. Cover and simmer gently until the giblets are tender, 1½ to 2 hours. Discard vegetables and giblets, and reserve the broth.

2. Rice: In a medium nonstick saucepan over medium-high heat, lightly brown the rice in the olive oil. Add enough water to the reserved broth to measure 4 cups. Add the broth mixture to the rice and simmer for 12 minutes, or until the rice is almost tender.

3. Vegetables: Meanwhile, heat the oil in a large nonstick skillet over medium heat. Add the celery, onions and mushrooms and sauté for about 6 minutes, until the mushrooms begin to give up their liquid. Add the water. When the mixture is hot, add the Butter Buds, stirring until dissolved.

4. Bread and Seasonings: In a large bowl, combine the vegetable mixture, rice with its liquid, the corn bread, white bread, pecans, poultry seasoning and pepper and stir thoroughly, without compressing. To bake this stuffing in a casserole, see step 3 on page 221.

NUTRITIONAL INFORMATION PER ½ CUP: 119 CALORIES, 2.3 G FAT, 3.4 G PROTEIN, 21.2 G CARBOHYDRATE, TRACE CHOLESTEROL, 228 MG SODIUM.

MARINADES AND BARBECUE SAUCES

I F YOU HAVE EVER MARINATED MEATS or fish in the past, you know that most recipes call for some oil. I believe, as do many professional chefs, that oil in a marinade is not only unnecessary but actually prevents the marinade from being absorbed. Once the flesh is coated with oil, it acts as a barrier to the flavorings.

I created several marinades with no fat whatsoever. The flavors they impart are complex, rich and wonderful. Here's what to do: If you have a favorite recipe for a marinade that calls for oil, omit it. If that makes the marinade too dry, add an equal amount of wine (white or red, depending on the marinade's base flavor). Or add defatted homemade broth in equal measure. Or add about half the amount called for in the form of Scotch whisky, bourbon, cognac, brandy, sherry, port or marsala wine. Each of these substitutions will change the flavor of your marinade for the better.

Barbecue sauces, too, can make a big difference. I used to buy a terrific bottled Asian barbecue sauce that used molasses and soy sauce as the foundation for its exotic flavors. I cut up baby back ribs, put a cup of the barbecue sauce in a bowl and tossed the ribs in the sauce. Then I covered the bowl and refrigerated it overnight. The next evening, I placed them on a nonstick pan and roasted them for one hour, dipping them in additional sauce halfway through the roasting process. When I served this as an appetizer, dinner guests inevitably filled up on them so much that they would have a hard time finishing their meal.

Today I do the same thing, but I substitute pork tenderloin, which has 85 percent less fat, and use my own barbecue sauce made with plum sauce and molasses. Rather than roasting the pork in the oven—which is fine—I enhance the flavor by grilling. I keep turning and basting the tenderloin with the sauce until cooked through, then bring the meat to the table with more sauce to pass around and some of my homemade beans, to which I have also added some barbecue sauce.

If you have a favorite homemade barbecue sauce that calls for oil or butter, think about omitting it. If you need to cook onions or other ingredients for sauce, sauté them in homemade broth, or use wine, bourbon, Scotch or brandy. If butter is a major component, consider instead swirling in a packet of Butter Buds when the sauce is hot.

Any meat, poultry or fish can benefit from marinating or barbecuing. Marinate lean cuts, which are tougher, for 24 to 48 hours and cook them slowly. Don't poke the meat while it's cooking, because that will cause the natural juices to escape, drying it out. Quickly sear the outside to seal in the juices. Then reduce the heat and cook it very slowly until done.

A short kitchen-safety note: During the marinating, raw meat, poultry or fish sit in liquid. Since they have not yet been cooked, they can contaminate the marinade with bacteria. To be absolutely safe, bring the marinade to a boil before basting with it.

RECIPES

BOURBON MUSTARD MARINADE

MAKES ABOUT 1½ CUPS

USE THIS INCREDIBLE MARINADE for beef, chicken or pork. Marinate meat in the refrigerator overnight and baste with it during grilling or broiling.

    ¼   cup bourbon
    ¼   cup sodium-reduced soy sauce
    ¼   cup Dijon-style mustard
    ¼   cup firmly packed dark brown sugar
    1   small onion, minced
    1   teaspoon salt
    ¼   teaspoon Worcestershire sauce
    ½   teaspoon fresh-ground black pepper, or to taste

In a small glass or ceramic bowl, whisk together all the ingredients until the sugar has dissolved.

NUTRITIONAL INFORMATION PER ¼ CUP: 72 CALORIES, 0.7 G FAT, 1.3 G PROTEIN, 8.6 G CARBOHYDRATE, 0 CHOLESTEROL, 1,023 MG SODIUM.

BEER MARINADE

MAKES 4 CUPS

BEER AND BEEF seem to be one of those combinations that were meant for each other. For this beer marinade, I buy a bottle of the best beer I can find. The marinade makes flank steak tender and delicious.

1½	cups defatted low-sodium beef broth
1	12-ounce bottle amber beer
1	cup chopped, peeled and seeded fresh tomatoes
¼	cup chopped fresh parsley
1	teaspoon Worcestershire sauce
½	teaspoon fresh thyme (or pinch crumbled dried)
½	teaspoon fresh-ground black pepper
6	drops hot red pepper sauce
1	bay leaf

In a medium glass or ceramic bowl, whisk together all the ingredients until combined. Use immediately.

NUTRITIONAL INFORMATION PER ¼ CUP: 13 CALORIES, 0.1 G FAT, 0.2 G PROTEIN, 1.6 G CARBOHYDRATE, TRACE CHOLESTEROL, 150 MG SODIUM.

LeanNote: Once the marinade is made, pour it into a 1-gallon plastic resealable bag. Place the flank steak, trimmed of all visible fat and lightly scored on both sides, into the bag with the marinade. Remove as much air as possible from the bag and seal. Place the bag in the refrigerator for at least 4 hours or preferably overnight.

Prepare a barbecue grill. When the grill is hot, remove the steak from the bag and pour the marinade into a medium saucepan. Remove the bay leaf. Bring the marinade to a boil and reduce by half, 15 to 20 minutes. While the marinade is reducing, barbecue the steak on the grill for 5 minutes per side for rare, about 6 minutes per side for medium.

Remove the steak from the grill and let rest for 5 minutes. Holding the knife at a 45-degree angle, cut the steak crosswise into thin slices. Distribute the steak slices on serving plates, and pour a thin ribbon of the reduced marinade down the center of the steak slices. Pass the remaining marinade.

LeanTip: Flank steak can also be broiled. Place the prepared flank steak on a broiler pan and broil 6 inches from the heat source for the same time as for barbecuing. Proceed as above.

LeanSuggestions

■ A great side dish for barbecued flank steak is grilled leeks. Spray the leeks with a small amount of olive oil before grilling.

■ A sprig of fresh thyme is an elegant garnish for this dish.

FLANK STEAK MARINADE

MAKES ABOUT ⅓ CUP

I CAN THINK OF NOTHING that tastes as good as a flank steak marinated for two days in this flavorful liquid and then grilled. I have also used this marinade as a basis for a warm beef salad. I gather a variety of greens, including Chinese cabbage, slice them into thin strips, add some sliced water chestnuts and bean sprouts, layer the sliced grilled steak on top and drizzle on some Family Salad Dressing (page 100).

½	cup defatted low-sodium beef broth
1½	tablespoons reduced-sodium soy sauce
3	tablespoons minced green onions (white and green parts)
1½	teaspoons chopped fresh thyme
	(or ½ teaspoon crumbled dried thyme)
5	drops hot red pepper sauce
1	tablespoon fresh-squeezed lemon juice

1. In a small saucepan over high heat, reduce the broth to 2 tablespoons, about 5 minutes. Cool.
2. In a small mixing bowl, whisk together the broth with the remaining ingredients until combined.

NUTRITIONAL INFORMATION PER ¼ CUP: 26 CALORIES, 0.15 G FAT, 2.3 G PROTEIN, 5.4 G CARBOHYDRATE, 0 CHOLESTEROL, 648 MG SODIUM.

LeanSuggestion: Trim all visible fat from a small flank steak and lightly score in diamond shapes on both sides. Add the marinade and steak to a 1-gallon resealable plastic bag, press out the excess air and seal. Marinate in the refrigerator from 2 hours to 2 days.

Remove the steak from the bag and pour any marinade into a small glass or ceramic bowl. Broil or barbecue the steak for 5 minutes per side, brushing with any remaining marinade during cooking.

ASIAN MARINADE

MAKES ABOUT 1 CUP

Each INGREDIENT in this marinade can be easily purchased at any supermarket. Hoisin sauce, which imparts an important smoky, sweet and salty flavor, can be found in the Asian section or in health food stores. I use this marinade for closely trimmed pieces of lean pork tenderloin. I marinate them, refrigerated, overnight and then brush some marinade on as they slowly cook on my barbecue grill.

½	cup hoisin sauce
6	tablespoons medium-dry sherry or Scotch whisky
¼	cup minced green onions (white parts only)
¼	cup sodium-reduced soy sauce
4	garlic cloves, minced
2	teaspoons granulated sugar
2	teaspoons grated fresh gingerroot
1	teaspoon salt

In a medium glass or ceramic bowl, whisk together all the ingredients until combined.

NUTRITIONAL INFORMATION PER ¼ CUP: 92 CALORIES, 0 G FAT, 4 G PROTEIN, 12 G CARBOHYDRATE, 0 CHOLESTEROL, 4,160 MG SODIUM.

South-of-the-Border Marinade

MAKES ABOUT 1¾ CUPS

I MARINATE SHRIMP in this mixture before grilling, and I brush more on the shrimp while they are cooking. Then I chill the shrimp and eat them cold. For a more complex flavor, dip the shrimp in a good homemade horseradish-laced cocktail sauce (page 243).

This is also great for chicken. After it has marinated, I grill it until it is just done. I pop some nonfat whole wheat tortillas in the microwave to warm them slightly, shred the chicken and roll it up in the tortillas along with some nonfat sour cream and nonfat sharp cheese, plus some spicy taco sauce.

¾ cup fresh-squeezed lemon juice
¾ cup minced onion
¼ cup seeded minced jalapeño pepper
3 tablespoons minced fresh cilantro
1 teaspoon salt
2 garlic cloves, minced
Fresh-ground black pepper to taste

In a medium glass or ceramic bowl, whisk together all the ingredients until combined.

NUTRITIONAL INFORMATION PER ¼ CUP: 22 CALORIES, TRACE FAT, TRACE PROTEIN, 5.7 G CARBOHYDRATE, 0 CHOLESTEROL, 308 MG SODIUM.

LeanSuggestion: Marinate shellfish, chicken or fish, covered, in the refrigerator overnight. Remove from the marinade before grilling or broiling and brush with the marinade while cooking.

ZESTY BEEF MARINADE

MAKES ABOUT 1¾ CUPS

FOR THE FIRST TWO YEARS after I lost more than 100 pounds, I ate beef only on rare occasions. In order to make those times as wonderful as possible, I came up with this marinade. The pineapple juice tenderizes the beef. It also adds a sweet note that I find appealing.

1	cup pineapple juice
1	tablespoon defatted low-sodium beef broth
2	teaspoons sodium-reduced soy sauce
1	teaspoon red-wine vinegar
2	large garlic cloves, minced
1	teaspoon minced jalapeño pepper, including seeds
1	teaspoon chili powder
¼	teaspoon hot red pepper sauce
⅓	cup chopped fresh pineapple
2	thin slices red onion
1	small lime, sliced

1. In a medium glass or ceramic bowl, whisk together the pineapple juice, beef broth, soy sauce, vinegar, garlic, jalapeño, chili powder and hot sauce until thoroughly combined.

2. Stir in the pineapple, onion and lime.

NUTRITIONAL INFORMATION PER ¼ CUP: 40 CALORIES, 0.1 G FAT, TRACE PROTEIN, 10.3 G CARBOHYDRATE, 0 CHOLESTEROL, 134 MG SODIUM.

LeanSuggestion: Marinate flank steak or top round steak for at least 4 hours and up to 24 hours. Once the marinating is complete, the marinade can be brushed on the meat during broiling.

ORANGE HONEY MARINADE

MAKES ABOUT 2 CUPS

FRESH-SQUEEZED ORANGE JUICE is extra-good here, but if you don't have it, don't let that stop you from making this great marinade; orange juice from concentrate will work fine. I have used this for both chicken and turkey breast. It imparts a sweet citrus note. I grow lemon thyme in my garden and use it to great effect here.

½	cup fresh-squeezed orange juice
3	tablespoons honey (orange blossom or clover)
3	tablespoons red-wine vinegar
1	medium onion, chopped
1	tablespoon grated orange rind
1½	teaspoons chopped fresh thyme (or ½ teaspoon crumbled dried)
6	whole cloves
¼	teaspoon ground allspice
¼	teaspoon ground ginger
1	bay leaf, crumbled
½	teaspoon salt
½	teaspoon fresh-ground black pepper

In a medium glass or ceramic bowl, whisk together all the ingredients until combined.

NUTRITIONAL INFORMATION PER ¼ CUP: 40 CALORIES, 0.1 G FAT, TRACE PROTEIN, 10.3 G CARBOHYDRATE, 0 CHOLESTEROL, 134 MG SODIUM.

LeanSuggestion: Marinate chicken breasts, turkey breasts or pork tenderloin, covered, in the refrigerator overnight. Brush with the marinade while cooking.

LeanTip: Since I always like marinades to impart some fire to my dishes, I add half a jalapeño or serrano pepper, minced, including the seeds.

Barbecue Sauce

MAKES ABOUT 3½ CUPS

CAYENNE PEPPER is the major heat provider in this barbecue sauce. I suggest making it the first time with the amount called for. If it doesn't send your taste buds into orbit, double the amount the next time you prepare it. I guarantee that will bring perspiration to your forehead. This sauce is great for barbecuing just about anything. However, it seems particularly well suited to pork.

¼	scant cup dark brown sugar
1	tablespoon molasses
1	tablespoon chili powder
¼	teaspoon ground cayenne pepper
1	8-ounce can tomato sauce
½	cup white-wine vinegar
½	cup tomato ketchup
¼	cup Chinese plum sauce
¼	cup dark corn syrup
½	cup water
¼	cup fresh-squeezed orange juice

1. In a medium heavy-bottomed saucepan, stir together the brown sugar, molasses, chili powder and cayenne. Whisk in the tomato sauce, vinegar, ketchup, plum sauce, corn syrup and water.

2. Bring the mixture to a boil, reduce the heat so that the sauce barely simmers, and cook, uncovered, for 30 minutes. Stir occasionally.

3. Whisk the orange juice into the mixture and continue simmering, uncovered, for 5 minutes more.

NUTRITIONAL INFORMATION PER ¼ CUP: 55 CALORIES, 0.1 G FAT, 0.3 G PROTEIN, 14 G CARBOHYDRATE, 0 CHOLESTEROL, 232 MG SODIUM.

LeanTip: This sauce is good on baked beans, whether the beans are homemade or out of a can.

LeanSuggestion: When barbecuing whole pork tenderloins, start brushing on this sauce near the end of the cooking. Pass the remaining sauce at the table.

Tomato-Molasses Barbecue Sauce

MAKES ABOUT 4 CUPS

THIS RECIPE WAS HANDED DOWN through several generations. I know: it has a daunting list of ingredients. But the sauce has spent years being fine-tuned to perfection. Originally, a large amount of cholesterol-laden bacon fat was used, but not anymore. If the small bit of un-saturated oil used in the sautéing process still seems like too much fat, sauté the onion and celery in some defatted chicken broth.

This is wonderful with chicken breasts or pork tenderloin. If you have saved up some fat grams, try it with very lean baby back ribs.

2	cups finely chopped onions
1	cup finely chopped celery
2	teaspoons canola oil
3	cups canned tomato sauce
¾	cup dark molasses
¾	cup tomato ketchup
½	cup cider vinegar
2	tablespoons Worcestershire sauce
1	tablespoon Dijon-style mustard
1	cup firmly packed dark brown sugar
¾	cup finely chopped green bell pepper
1	garlic clove, minced
½	teaspoon salt
½	teaspoon fresh-ground white pepper
½	teaspoon baking soda
	Pinch freshly grated nutmeg
	Pinch ground cinnamon

1. In a large heavy-bottomed saucepan, sauté the onions and celery in the oil over medium heat, stirring occasionally, until they are softened but not browned, about 7 minutes.

2. Stir in the remaining ingredients, reduce the heat to low and gently simmer, stirring occasionally, for 1 hour, or until the mixture is thickened.

NUTRITIONAL INFORMATION PER ¼ CUP: 88 CALORIES, 0.7 G FAT, 0.9 G PROTEIN, 20.7 G CARBOHYDRATE, 0 CHOLESTEROL, 572 MG SODIUM.

LeanNote: The sauce may be made 1 week in advance and kept covered and chilled.

LeanTip: This is a fairly sweet barbecue sauce. If you wish additional heat, add ¼ to ½ teaspoon cayenne pepper.

Condiments

OVER THE YEARS, I've learned that reducing fat in a dish is not enough: Low-fat food can be bland, flat-tasting and lacking in zing and zip. Because fat carries flavor to the palate, reduced fat can mean reduced flavor. Increasing the seasonings won't necessarily do the trick, because fat also smooths and rounds tastes, so adding more herbs and spices can make the dish harsh or off-flavored.

Condiments are the answer. Seasoned just right, they add dimension and depth to a dish without overwhelming it. Tarheel Tartar Sauce (page 250) makes a simple broiled flounder explode with taste. Country Corn Relish (page 244) turns a mundane low-fat tuna salad into something exciting. My seasoned salt uses zero fat and no MSG, and yet makes all sorts of magical things happen to chicken, potatoes or whatever else I shake it on.

All of these condiments are simple to make and deliver a flavor wallop.

RECIPES

CRANBERRY RELISH

MAKES ABOUT 4 CUPS

CAROLE, A VIEWER OF MY CABLE-TELEVISION COOKING SHOW, sent me this wonderful recipe as a Thanksgiving gift. I immediately made it and found it to be as terrific as she said. Except for needing to sit overnight so the flavors blend, this relish goes together in a flash. It is great with roasted turkey breast, and when mixed with a little nonfat cream cheese and used instead of mayonnaise, it makes a turkey sandwich special.

1	navel orange
1	lime
1	12-ounce bag fresh cranberries, rinsed and picked over
¾	cup orange-blossom or clover honey

1. In a medium saucepan of boiling water, simmer the orange and lime for 5 minutes. Drain them and let cool.

2. Halve the orange and lime and reserve one-half of each for another use. Cut the remaining halves into pieces. In a food processor fitted with the steel blade, finely chop the orange and lime pieces. Transfer to a glass or ceramic bowl.

3. Place the cranberries in the food processor bowl and process until they are coarsely chopped. Add the cranberries to the orange-lime mixture. Stir in the honey. Let the relish chill, covered, for 12 hours or overnight. Covered and refrigerated, the relish will keep for 1 week.

NUTRITIONAL INFORMATION PER TABLESPOON: 14 CALORIES, TRACE FAT, TRACE PROTEIN, 5 G CARBOHYDRATE, 0 CHOLESTEROL, 0 MG SODIUM.

Carolina Coastal Cocktail Sauce

MAKES 2⅛ CUPS

THE SECOND SPRING I lived in North Carolina, I traveled to the Atlantic Ocean and stayed in a resort town called Emerald Isle. I bought lots of shrimp, brought them back to the ocean-front house and cooked them in Crab-Boil Spices (page 246). Then I brought out this cocktail sauce that I had made earlier. The half-cup of horseradish is just right.

1	cup chili sauce (Heinz or Bennett's)
½	cup well-drained grated horseradish
¼	cup granulated sugar
2	tablespoons distilled white vinegar
2	teaspoons minced onion
2	teaspoons Worcestershire sauce
2	teaspoons celery seed
1	teaspoon celery salt
½	teaspoon garlic powder
¼	teaspoon fresh-ground black pepper
¼	teaspoon hot red pepper sauce

1. In a medium glass or ceramic bowl, whisk together all the ingredients until completely combined and the sugar has dissolved.

2. Cover and refrigerate for at least 1 or preferably 2 days to give the flavors time to blend.

NUTRITIONAL INFORMATION PER TABLESPOON: 17 CALORIES, TRACE FAT, TRACE PROTEIN, 3.4 G CARBOHYDRATE, 0 CHOLESTEROL, 177 MG SODIUM.

LeanTip: Try this with raw oysters or cooked and chilled sea scallops.

Country Corn Relish

MAKES 3 PINTS

I've always loved condiments. Ketchup on a burger, relish on a hot dog, good mustard on just about anything. When growing up, I loved midsummer, when my Aunt Betty Condon would make a wonderful corn relish.

Today, corn relishes are available in some supermarkets and specialty shops, but none of them has the wonderful flavor of my Aunt Betty's. I finally figured out why. She made hers with honey from the farm, not sugar.

4	cups fresh corn, cut from the cob (about 6 ears fresh, or use frozen kernels)
¼	cup clover honey
1	teaspoon salt
1	tablespoon olive oil
2	jalapeño peppers, seeds removed, finely chopped
1	medium green bell pepper, chopped
1	medium red bell pepper, chopped
1	medium red onion, chopped
1	tablespoon celery seeds
2	teaspoons mustard seeds
1	teaspoon coarse-ground black pepper
¾	cup cider vinegar

1. In a large bowl, stir together the corn, honey and salt until the corn is coated. Set aside.

2. In a large nonstick skillet, heat the oil over medium heat. Add all the peppers and onion and sauté until softened, about 4 minutes. Add the corn mixture and cook for 2 to 3 minutes, or until the corn is almost

tender. Stir in the celery seeds, mustard seeds, pepper and vinegar and bring to a boil, stirring. Remove from the heat immediately.

3. Divide the hot relish among 3 sterilized pint jars, cover and refrigerate. It will keep for at least 1 month.

NUTRITIONAL INFORMATION PER TABLESPOON: 13 CALORIES, 0.2 G FAT, 0.2 G PROTEIN, 2.8 G CARBOHYDRATE, 0 CHOLESTEROL, 23 MG SODIUM.

LeanTip: This relish adds a wonderful twist to tuna salad, especially one made from grilled and chilled fresh tuna. It also makes a tasty dip for low-fat baked tortilla chips.

Crab-Boil Spices

MAKES ABOUT 1 CUP

YES, I KNOW YOU CAN BUY packaged crab boil. But freshness makes a big difference. This mixture, added to liquid, enhances any seafood that comes in contact with it.

¼   cup pickling spices
¼   cup sea salt
2   tablespoons mustard seeds
2   tablespoons whole black peppercorns
2   tablespoons hot red pepper flakes
1   tablespoon celery seeds
1   tablespoon minced dried chives
2   teaspoons ground ginger
2   teaspoons dried oregano
5   bay leaves

1. Add all of the ingredients to the bowl of a food processor fitted with the metal blade. Pulsing, process until the mixture forms a coarse powder.

2. For cooking shrimp, add ¼ cup of the spices, along with 2 teaspoons salt, to a large saucepan of boiling water or half water and half beer. For lobster or crab, use 1 part distilled white wine to 3 parts water. Add the seafood and cook for 2 minutes, or until just cooked through. Remove the seafood and serve or chill.

NUTRITIONAL INFORMATION PER TABLESPOON: 18 CALORIES, 0.9 G FAT, 0.3 G PROTEIN, 2.5 G CARBOHYDRATE, 0 CHOLESTEROL, 1,423 MG SODIUM.

LeanTip: This spice mixture can be kept in a tightly sealed container in a cool, dark place for several months. Or freeze them. That way, they'll keep for 6 months.

CUMIN TOMATO KETCHUP

MAKES 1 CUP

ORDINARY KETCHUP CAN GET BORING. This variation is great on grilled turkey burgers mixed with a little chili powder before grilling.

1   cup tomato ketchup
2   teaspoons ground cumin
2   teaspoons balsamic vinegar

In a small glass or ceramic bowl, whisk together the ketchup, cumin and vinegar until combined. Refrigerate any unused portion.

NUTRITIONAL INFORMATION PER TABLESPOON: 17 CALORIES, 0.2 G FAT, TRACE PROTEIN, 4.4 G CARBOHYDRATE, 0 CHOLESTEROL, 183 MG SODIUM.

MAUERY'S SEASONED SALT

MAKES A SCANT ½ CUP

THE MOST WELL-KNOWN SEASONED SALT available in the supermarket contains monosodium glutamate (MSG). Since my wife is sensitive to it, I created my own. This is the sensational result. I use this in a wide variety of ways. It's great on Oven-Browned Potatoes (page 372) and for dusting mild-flavored fish before broiling. Or sprinkle on meats or vegetables.

- 1 tablespoon sweet paprika, preferably Hungarian
- 1 tablespoon onion powder
- 1 tablespoon dry mustard
- 2 teaspoons salt
- 2 teaspoons garlic powder
- 2 teaspoons ground cumin
- 2 teaspoons crumbled dried basil
- 2 teaspoons crumbled dried oregano
- 1 teaspoon fresh-ground white pepper
- ½ teaspoon fresh-ground black pepper

1. Add all the ingredients to a small bowl and stir together until combined. Over a piece of waxed paper, put the mixture in a fine-screen sieve and rub the mixture through until only a couple of stem pieces remain. Discard what remains in the sieve.

2. Pour the mixture into a clean shaker bottle with a tight-fitting cover.

NUTRITIONAL INFORMATION PER ¼ TEASPOON: 2 CALORIES, 0.07 G FAT, 0.04 G PROTEIN, 0.32 G CARBOHYDRATE, 0 CHOLESTEROL, 58 MG SODIUM.

LeanTip: Use only impeccably fresh herbs and spices. I get mine from local stores that sell them in bulk.

REAL AND EASY HONEY MUSTARD

MAKES 1¼ CUPS

I NORMALLY RESTRICT MY CALORIES to 20 percent or less from fat. However, this is such a tasty mustard I want to share it with you. Be forewarned that 39 percent of the calories come from fat, 0.5 gram of fat per teaspoon.

If used in small amounts to enhance flavor, this will have little effect on your total fat intake. It makes a lean ham (18 percent fat calories) sandwich something special.

½ cup dry mustard
½ cup distilled white vinegar
3 tablespoons clover honey
1 large egg yolk

1. In a small glass or ceramic bowl, whisk together the mustard and vinegar until combined. Cover and let stand at room temperature for at least 4 hours.

2. In a small nonstick saucepan, mix the honey and egg yolk, then whisk in the mustard mixture. Cook until thickened over medium-low heat, stirring constantly, 8 to 10 minutes.

3. Remove from the heat, cool slightly, pour into a glass jar with a tight-fitting nonaluminum lid, cover and chill. Covered and chilled, this mustard keeps well for at least 1 month.

NUTRITIONAL INFORMATION PER TEASPOON: 9 CALORIES, 0.4 G FAT, 0.4 G PROTEIN, 1.2 G CARBOHYDRATE, 3 MG CHOLESTEROL, 0 SODIUM.

LeanSuggestion: Consider using flavored vinegars—for example, white-wine tarragon vinegar—to make this mustard unique.

TARHEEL TARTAR SAUCE

MAKES ⅔ CUP

NORTH CAROLINA is known as the "Tarheel State." I created this sauce there and named it for my new home. I serve the sauce on the side with broiled fresh flounder, but it goes well with any mild, lean fish.

½	cup nonfat mayonnaise
2	scant tablespoons drained sweet pickle relish
1	tablespoon grated onion
1	tablespoon minced celery
1	tablespoon minced green olives
1½	teaspoons Dijon-style mustard
1	teaspoon fresh-squeezed lemon juice
1	teaspoon chopped fresh tarragon
⅛	teaspoon cayenne pepper

1. In a small glass or ceramic bowl, whisk together all the ingredients until completely combined.
2. Cover and refrigerate for at least 1 hour to allow the flavors to blend.

NUTRITIONAL INFORMATION PER TABLESPOON: 17 CALORIES, 0.2 G FAT, TRACE PROTEIN, 3.6 G CARBOHYDRATE, 0 CHOLESTEROL, 212 MG SODIUM.

SPECIAL BURGER SAUCE

MAKES 1½ CUPS

WHEN I WAS GOING TO HIGH SCHOOL in Evanston, Illinois, a coffee shop called Walker Brothers was a favorite hangout for my group of friends. The shop served several dishes that became the standard by which I measure all other restaurant versions. One was a double-decker burger named "The Chubby," with a special sauce smeared on each piece of beef. I have finally recreated that sauce, not only in flavor but in a leaner version. Spread some on your next 95 percent lean beef burger.

⅓ cup nonfat French dressing
1 cup nonfat whipped salad dressing, such as Kraft Miracle Whip
¼ cup sweet pickle relish
1 scant teaspoon grated onion
2 teaspoons granulated sugar
¼ teaspoon fresh-ground black pepper

1. In a small glass or ceramic bowl, whisk together all the ingredients until combined.

2. Pour into a pint glass bottle, cover and chill. Covered and chilled, this sauce keeps well for at least 3 weeks.

NUTRITIONAL INFORMATION PER TABLESPOON: 15.2 CALORIES, 0 FAT, 0 PROTEIN, 3.8 G CARBOHYDRATE, 0 CHO-LESTEROL, 132 MG SODIUM.

LeanTip: This sauce's flavor improves if it is allowed to chill, covered, overnight.

Sauces for Meat

THE FRENCH HAVE ENHANCED THEIR CUISINE with butter for hundreds of years. Americans have been using butter ever since Bessie the Cow wandered onto American soil. For a Lean Guy like me, this is bad news. The fat content of butter is astronomical, and as if that weren't bad enough, it's loaded with cholesterol. Does butter make smooth, silken and lightly thickened sauces? Is the sky blue?

Five years ago, I thought that there must be a way to prepare sauces with less or no fat yet maintain a great flavor and glossy texture. I went to work and made some terrific discoveries. I began by testing cornstarch as a thickener. It worked well, giving my sauces and gravies a beautiful sheen and visual depth. But they had a sticky, gluelike texture. Cornstarch also imparted a flavor that reminded me more of a sweet pudding than of beef.

Continuing my search for just the right thickener, I saw Jacques Pépin, on his television cooking show, using potato starch. I trotted off to my local grocery store and bought a box (it was right next to the cornstarch, in the baking section). Potato starch dissolves in cool liquid, just like cornstarch. What Jacques liked was that it thickens almost on contact and doesn't need to be brought to a simmer to see whether more is needed, making it perfect for Thanksgiving dinner, when the gray is usually made in a rush as other dishes are being readied for the table. However, the finished sauce lacks glossiness. I also found out that potato starch is not readily available in every grocery store.

After that, my brother Chef Tom Mauer introduced me to arrowroot. Like cornstarch and potato starch, it is diluted in a cool liquid before being added to a hot liquid. Arrowroot gives a richer and more refined look than do either cornstarch or potato starch. It produces sauces and gravies with incomparable clarity and sheen. It is easily digestible, is fat-free and never makes sauces and gravies gluelike or gummy.

For traditional meat gravies, a modified roux works best as a thickener. The usual roux is a mixture of fat and flour. The flour is browned in the fat of choice, then added to the sauce. Mixing unbrowned flour with a cool liquid doesn't work because the sauce will have an unappetizing raw flavor.

I found a low-fat solution when I dropped into the healthy cooking class at the Culinary School of Kendall College in Evanston, Illinois. That day, the students were learning how to brown flour using no fat. I took the idea home and went straight into my kitchen. With Browned Roux (page 255), my flour-thickened sauces maintain their nutlike flavor and luminous look.

When used appropriately, these thickeners gave me an ideal lean arsenal. As a result, my sauces and gravies are everything they should be and not the one thing they should not be—fatty.

RECIPES

BROWNED ROUX

MAKES 2 CUPS

THIS IS GREAT STUFF. Browning the flour gives it a nutlike flavor that makes butter unnecessary. If I need to thicken a sauce or gravy, I pull this roux from the freezer, measure out what I need into a cool liquid and return the rest to the freezer for next time. Then I add the liquid with the roux in a stream, whisking, to the hot liquid. Once the sauce returns to a simmer, it thickens beautifully. After the seasonings are adjusted, it is ready to serve.

2   cups all-purpose flour

1. Heat a large cast-iron skillet over medium heat. Add the flour and cook, stirring constantly with a wooden spoon, for 7 to 10 minutes, or until the flour turns a deep gold. Transfer the flour immediately to a plate and cool. (There will be a burnt-toast aroma. Be careful not to let the flour burn; reduce the heat if the flour seems to be browning too quickly.)

Alternatively, preheat the oven to 400 degrees F. Brown the flour on a heavy-duty jelly-roll pan in the oven for 20 minutes. Shake the pan every 5 minutes, until the flour takes on a deep gold appearance.

2. Once the roux is cooled, place it in a glass jar, cover and freeze it. This way it will maintain its fresh taste for 6 months.

NUTRITIONAL INFORMATION PER TABLESPOON: 28 CALORIES, 0.07 G FAT, 0.8 G PROTEIN, 6 G CARBOHYDRATE, 0 CHOLESTEROL, 0 SODIUM.

LeanSuggestion: If you miss the buttery flavor of a true roux-thickened sauce, whisk a teaspoon of dry Butter Buds into your sauce at the end for every tablespoon of butter in the original recipe.

Cider Mustard Sauce

MAKES ABOUT 2 CUPS

PREPARING A WHOLE bone-in ham on Christmas Day is one of my most cherished traditions, even though ham is very high in fat (45 to 63 percent of calories). This sauce is the ideal accompaniment, since it is virtually fat-free. It counterpoints the ham's saltiness.

⅔	cup cider vinegar
½	cup minced shallots
2	tablespoons granulated sugar
2	cups apple cider
1	teaspoon dry mustard
¼	teaspoon crumbled dried thyme
1½	cups defatted low-sodium chicken broth, preferably homemade
1	tablespoon arrowroot
2	tablespoons Dijon-style mustard
	Salt to taste (optional)
	Fresh-ground black pepper to taste

1. In a small heavy-bottomed saucepan, combine the vinegar, shallots and sugar. Bring the mixture to a boil, stirring, until the sugar has dissolved. Boil until the liquid has evaporated and the glaze remaining in the pan is caramelized, being careful not to let it burn.

2. Carefully add the apple cider, dry mustard and thyme. Bring the mixture to a boil, stirring, and boil until it is reduced to about 1 cup.

3. In a separate bowl, set aside 2 tablespoons of the chicken broth. Add the remaining broth to the saucepan and boil the mixture until it is reduced to about 2 cups.

4. Whisk the arrowroot into the reserved chicken broth until combined. Add the arrowroot mixture to the pan, whisking, and return to the boil. Remove the pan from the heat and whisk in the mustard, salt and pepper. Transfer the sauce to a heated serving dish.

NUTRITIONAL INFORMATION PER TABLESPOON (WITHOUT SALT): 8.5 CALORIES, 0.1 G FAT, 0.2 G PROTEIN, 1.7 G CARBOHYDRATE, 0 CHOLESTEROL, 32 MG SODIUM.

LeanNote: Since the kitchen can be hectic with the preparation of other holiday dishes, this sauce may be prepared up to 1 day in advance. Add the chicken broth all at once and omit the arrowroot. When the sauce is complete, cover and chill it. Just before you are ready to serve it, set aside 2 tablespoons of the sauce and add the remainder of the sauce to a small saucepan. Whisk the arrowroot into the reserved 2 tablespoons of sauce and whisk that into the hot sauce. Reheat until thickened. If necessary, thin the sauce with additional cider or broth when reheating.

Not-Your-Usual Ham Sauce

MAKES ABOUT 1½ CUPS

THIS TASTY SAUCE goes together in a flash and is ideal with ham. Even though the ham does have fat, this sauce contains none. It's also tremendous served over extra-lean smoked pork chops.

¼	cup firmly packed light brown sugar
1	tablespoon arrowroot
2	teaspoons dry mustard
¼	teaspoon salt
1	cup beer
⅓	cup golden raisins, chopped
2	teaspoons cider vinegar
1	teaspoon Butter Buds

1. In a small saucepan, combine the brown sugar, arrowroot, mustard and salt. Stir in 2 tablespoons of the beer until the mixture forms a smooth paste. Whisk in the remaining beer.

2. Place the pan over high heat, add the raisins and bring the mixture to a boil, stirring. Lower the heat and simmer, stirring, for 2 minutes. Stir in the vinegar and Butter Buds. Serve hot.

NUTRITIONAL INFORMATION PER TABLESPOON: 18 CALORIES, 0.1 G FAT, TRACE PROTEIN, 3.9 G CARBOHYDRATE, 0 CHOLESTEROL, 26 MG SODIUM.

Fat-Free Cream-Style Chicken Mushroom Gravy

MAKES 2¼ CUPS

AFTER I MOVED TO NORTH CAROLINA, I saw how many local folks loved to pour cream gravy on everything from biscuits to sausage. Most people made the roux with chicken fat and flour. Then, for a really smooth gravy, they added half-and-half. Those gravies were indeed luxurious but not exactly healthful.

I immediately set to work in my kitchen. This gravy looks and tastes just like those high-fat country gravies everyone loves, yet it has no added fat.

1½	cups defatted low-sodium chicken broth, preferably homemade*
½	teaspoon salt
¼	teaspoon fresh-ground black pepper
4	large white button mushrooms, sliced thin and lightly sautéed
2	tablespoons Browned Roux (page 255) or arrowroot
½	cup skim milk

1. In a medium saucepan, over medium-high heat, bring the chicken stock, salt and pepper to a boil. Add the mushrooms and lower the heat to a simmer.

2. In a small bowl, whisk together the roux and the skim milk; whisk into the simmering chicken broth. Cook, whisking constantly, until thickened, about 1 minute. Remove from heat. Serve hot.

NUTRITIONAL INFORMATION PER 2 TABLESPOONS: 4 CALORIES, TRACE FAT, 0.3 G PROTEIN, 0.6 G CARBOHYDRATE, TRACE CHOLESTEROL, 35 MG SODIUM.

If you use a good-quality canned broth, remember that canned broths are frequently high in sodium, so omit the salt called for in the recipe, and taste and adjust the seasonings at the end.

LeanStyle Chicken Gravy

MAKES ABOUT 2 CUPS

Nonfat roux gives this gravy the texture and flavor of a butter-thickened one. I use this recipe as the foundation for my turkey gravy as well.

2 cups plus 2 tablespoons defatted low-sodium
   chicken broth, preferably homemade
½ teaspoon salt
¼ teaspoon fresh-ground black pepper
2 teaspoons Butter Buds
4 tablespoons Browned Roux (page 255)

1. In a medium saucepan, over medium-high heat, bring 2 cups of the chicken broth, seasoned with the salt and pepper, to a boil. Whisk in the Butter Buds and lower the heat to a simmer.

2. In a small bowl, whisk the browned roux with the remaining 2 tablespoons unheated chicken broth until dissolved. In a stream, whisk the roux mixture into the simmering chicken broth. Cook, whisking constantly, until thickened, about 1 minute. Remove from the heat and serve hot.

NUTRITIONAL INFORMATION PER 2 TABLESPOONS: 18 CALORIES, TRACE FAT, 1.1 G PROTEIN, 3.3 G CARBOHYDRATE, 0 CHOLESTEROL, 160 MG SODIUM.

BEEF AND MUSHROOM GRAVY

MAKES 2 CUPS

MY FAVORITE POTATOES had butter, sour cream, heavy cream and egg yolks whipped into them. Then I'd gild the lily with a beef gravy made with fat from the beef I'd been cooking. Today, I still love to make a big pile of Decadent Fat-Free Whipped Potatoes (page 368) and pour my beef and mushroom gravy all over them. But there are three huge differences from the past: Neither the potatoes nor the gravy has any fat, and I'm not fat either.

½   cup diced white button mushrooms

½   teaspoon gravy seasoning, such as Gravy Master

2   cups plus 2 tablespoons defatted low-sodium beef broth,
     preferably homemade*

½   teaspoon salt

¼   teaspoon fresh-ground black pepper
     Pinch crumbled dried thyme

4   tablespoons Browned Roux (page 255)

1. Place a medium nonstick saucepan over medium heat. Lightly spray it with vegetable oil. Add the mushrooms and sauté briefly until they begin to soften, about 4 minutes. Add the gravy seasoning, 2 cups of the beef broth, salt, pepper and thyme and bring to a boil. Lower the heat to a simmer.

2. In a small bowl, whisk the roux into the remaining 2 tablespoons unheated beef broth. Whisk the roux mixture into the simmering beef broth. Cook, whisking constantly, until thickened. Remove from the heat. Serve hot.

NUTRITIONAL INFORMATION PER 2 TABLESPOONS: 18 CALORIES, 0.1 G FAT, 0.5 G PROTEIN, 3.7 G CARBOHYDRATE, 0 CHOLESTEROL, 119 MG SODIUM.

Omit the salt called for in the recipe if you are using canned broth, and taste and adjust the seasoning at the end.

FISH AND SEAFOOD

MY MOM, BLESS HER, dislikes all fish and most seafood. Recently, I tried to get her to try a broiled sea scallop. It was buttery and sweet-tasting, very much like one of the very few seafoods she'd allow past her lips—lobster. "No, thank you," she said pointedly.

"Come on, Mom, this tastes like lobster; give it a small try."

"No, thank you—really," she said with a little more warmth, realizing I meant what I said.

My mom did not take even a small bite of my succulent scallop. In the end, it left more for me, but I felt bad that she would never know how incredible they can be.

After my childhood, it's amazing that I would have anything to do with seafood. It was my wife, Susan, who dragged me kicking and screaming into that wonderful world. Once

I discovered how tasty seafood is, I began to look for recipes I could prepare at home. After I began accumulating those, I started hunting for fish markets in my area that could provide reasonably priced fish that was also impeccably fresh.

Generally, I prepare seafood as simply as possible. I choose to barbecue or broil most fish. Once in a while, I'll bake a fish fillet or steak, and less frequently, I'll poach a fish. If a special Saturday night get-together is happening in my dining room, I'll make my version of cioppino or fish stew.

Not the least of the advantages of seafood is how low in fat it is. The scallop I offered my mother was one of the leanest creatures to exit saltwater. It gets only 7.6 percent of its calories from fat. Shrimp, too, are perfect for lean eaters like me, since they get only 14.6 percent of their calories from fat.

All of the following recipes are easy to prepare and call for fish that is already cut into either steaks or fillets.

RECIPES

HERB-CRUSTED HALIBUT STEAKS

SERVES 6

I AM ALWAYS ON THE LOOKOUT for great ways to prepare fish that are high in taste and low in fat. This recipe takes halibut, which is rather bland but lean, and uses a mixture of basil, thyme, oregano, rosemary and white pepper to heighten the flavor. When the fish is baked in a high-heat oven, the herb-and-flour mixture forms a thin but tasty crust, which becomes a barrier against moisture loss.

1	tablespoon dried basil
1	tablespoon dried thyme
1	tablespoon dried oregano
1	teaspoon dried rosemary
2	teaspoons whole white peppercorns
1	teaspoon salt
¼	cup all-purpose flour
6	halibut steaks (about 6 ounces each)

1. Preheat the oven to 450 degrees F, with a rack in the upper third.

2. Add the herbs and peppercorns to a spice grinder, grinding the mixture until it is fine. Transfer the spices to a bowl. Add the salt and flour to the bowl and stir to combine. Lightly spray both sides of each steak with the olive oil. Dredge each steak in the herb mixture, coating well and shake off any excess.

3. Lightly spray a jelly-roll pan with olive oil (approximately 3 seconds), and arrange the steaks on the pan so they do not touch.

4. Roast for 10 to 12 minutes, or until the steaks offer resistance when pressed. Serve immediately.

NUTRITIONAL INFORMATION PER SERVING: 265 CALORIES, 5.3 G FAT, 46.5 G PROTEIN, 5.7 G CARBOHYDRATE, 70 MG CHOLESTEROL, 474 MG SODIUM.

Baked Red Snapper

SERVES 4

I F YOU ARE GOING TO HAVE some close friends over for dinner, this is the dish to bring to the table. The aromas of the garlic, onion, oregano and anise are superb. The snapper flesh flakes easily, and the rich cheese topping is sublime. The ingredient list is longer than most, but that's why I reserve it for an occasion. What makes this special is the delightfully light yet richly flavored sauce, simmered for a mere 10 minutes. The rest of the dish is made in the same oven-safe skillet.

Red snapper has to be one of the finest eating fish around. My wife began preparing this dish many years ago. The original dish was high in fat, owing to large amounts of olive oil and cheese. Since it was so good, I spent extra effort making certain it could comfortably return to our dinner table.

1	tablespoon extra-virgin olive oil
¼	cup finely chopped onion
2	small garlic cloves, minced
1	16-ounce can plum tomatoes, coarsely chopped
2	teaspoons tomato paste
¼	cup plus 2 tablespoons chopped fresh parsley
2	tablespoons drained capers
1	tablespoon chopped fresh oregano (or 1 teaspoon crumbled dried)
¼	teaspoon hot red pepper flakes
¼	teaspoon fresh-ground black pepper
4	red snapper fillets (about 6 ounces each), rinsed and patted dry
1	cup 1% cottage cheese, drained well
1	tablespoon ouzo (Greek anise-flavored liqueur)

1. Preheat the oven to 425 degrees F.

2. Add 2 teaspoons of the olive oil to a small saucepan and, over medium heat, cook the onion and garlic, stirring, until the onion is soft, about 5 minutes. Add the tomatoes with their juice, tomato paste, parsley, capers, oregano, red pepper flakes and pepper and bring to a boil. Reduce the heat to low and gently simmer for 10 minutes.

3. Coat the bottom of an oven-safe nonstick skillet with the remaining 1 teaspoon olive oil. Lay the red snapper fillets skin side down in the bottom and pour the tomato sauce over all. Place the skillet on the stovetop over medium-high heat and bring the sauce to a boil.

4. Immediately place the skillet in the oven and bake for 15 minutes. Sprinkle the snapper with the cottage cheese and bake for 5 minutes more. Sprinkle with the ouzo and remaining 2 tablespoons parsley and serve.

NUTRITIONAL INFORMATION PER SERVING: 285 CALORIES, 6.4 G FAT, 42 G PROTEIN, 10 G CARBOHYDRATE, 65 MG CHOLESTEROL, 783 MG SODIUM.

Broiled Cod with Fennel and Dill Sauce

SERVES 4

Fennel is an odd-looking vegetable. There is nothing quite like it in the produce case. It's got the crunch of celery with a hint of licorice. This recipe happens to be one of my wife's favorite ways to prepare a fish dinner. She regularly scribbles "fennel?" onto my weekly shopping list, just so we might have this dish.

2	small fennel bulbs
1	teaspoon extra-virgin olive oil
4	tablespoons chopped shallots
2	tablespoons dry white wine (or defatted low-sodium chicken broth)
1	teaspoon salt
1	teaspoon fresh-ground black pepper
4	6-to-8-ounce cod fillets, rinsed and patted dry
2	teaspoons Butter Buds, mixed with
	2 tablespoons hot water
2	tablespoons fresh-squeezed lemon juice
2	tablespoons chopped fresh dill plus 4 sprigs

1. Slice the top pieces (fronds and stems) off the fennel bulbs so only the bulb remains. Trim the bottoms and take the bulbs apart (similar to the layers of an onion) and cut the layers into ⅛-inch-thick slices. (The slicing can also be conveniently and quickly done in a food processor.)

2. Heat the oil in a medium nonstick saucepan over medium heat, and sauté the fennel and shallots for 1 to 2 minutes, or until the shallots begin to soften. Add the wine, ½ teaspoon salt and ¾ teaspoon pepper. Cover and cook for 5 to 6 minutes. Set aside in a warm place.

3. Set the broiler rack 6 inches from the heat source. Preheat the broiler.

4. Lightly spray the broiler pan with vegetable oil. Place the fillets on the pan and spray them with vegetable oil. Sprinkle the fillets with the remaining ½ teaspoon salt and the remaining ¼ teaspoon pepper. Broil for 6 to 7 minutes, depending on the thickness of the fish (10 minutes per inch, figured proportionately), or until the fish is opaque and offers some resistance when pressed.

5. Meanwhile, heat the prepared Butter Buds in a small saucepan, stirring in the lemon juice and 2 tablespoons chopped dill. Keep warm.

6. Place the cooked fillets on 4 plates and spoon the portions of fennel on the side. Spoon the sauce over the fillets, place a sprig of dill on each and serve.

NUTRITIONAL INFORMATION PER SERVING: 186 CALORIES, 2.5 G FAT, 32 G PROTEIN, 7.2 G CARBOHYDRATE, 124 MG CHOLESTEROL, 525 MG SODIUM.

BROILED SEA SCALLOPS

SERVES 2

THIS HAS GOT TO BE one of the easiest ways to prepare seafood. If they are fresh and not overcooked, scallops are buttery in flavor and texture. They come close to melting in your mouth. Lime juice is the perfect astringent foil, and the fructose in the juice caramelizes quickly, lightly browning the edges of each scallop. Fresh-ground black pepper adds a fitting finish. This dish is effortless and excellent.

1   pound sea scallops, small muscle removed, rinsed and patted dry
2   limes
    Fresh-ground black pepper

1. Preheat the broiler, with a rack 4 inches from the heat.

2. Cover a small broiler pan with aluminum foil and lightly spray with vegetable oil. Place the scallops on the pan in a single layer, without touching. With a citrus reamer, squeeze the lime juice from one lime over all the scallops.

3. Broil the scallops for 5 minutes. Remove the pan, turn the scallops over, squeeze on the lime juice from the remaining lime, and return the pan to the broiler. Broil for 5 minutes more, or until they offer resistance when pressed.

4. Remove the pan from the broiler and divide the scallops between 2 dinner plates. Drizzle whatever accumulated juice remains from the pan over the scallops. Grind some black pepper over each serving to taste.

NUTRITIONAL INFORMATION PER SERVING: 205 CALORIES, 1.6 G FAT, 37.5 G PROTEIN, 8.8 G CARBOHYDRATE, 75 MG CHOLESTEROL, 361 MG SODIUM.

Broiled Flounder with Mustard

SERVES 4

IF YOU'RE IN A HURRY some evening and you want to make something quick and delicious yet low in fat, this is it. All you have to do is pick up some flounder fillets, mustard and a lime. You'll be dining like royalty in short order.

In fact, that's how this recipe came about. I was in a big hurry one evening. My fish man, Paul, had exactly four fillets of flounder left in his showcase ice. The rest of the ingredients just happened to be in my refrigerator.

4   flounder fillets (about 6 ounces each)
2   tablespoons Dijon-style mustard
     Fresh-ground black pepper
2   tablespoons snipped fresh chives
1   lime, quartered

1. Place the broiler rack in the uppermost position and preheat the broiler.

2. Lightly spray a broiler pan with vegetable oil. Place the fillets on the pan. With a pastry brush, spread the mustard over the fish. Grind some pepper on each.

3. Place the pan under the broiler for 5 minutes, or until the mustard bubbles and begins to brown; do not turn. Place each fillet on a separate plate, sprinkle with the chives and serve with a wedge of lime on the side.

NUTRITIONAL INFORMATION PER SERVING: 209 CALORIES, 3.3 G FAT, 42 G PROTEIN, TRACE CARBOHYDRATE, 116 MG CHOLESTEROL, 403 MG SODIUM.

LEAN AND EASY HALIBUT CIOPPINO

SERVES 4

A TRUE CIOPPINO is a mixed fish and seafood stew that originated along Fisherman's Wharf in San Francisco. It picked up its Italian accent from many of the fishermen there who were of Italian origin. I am not a big fan of clams, which are an integral part of the dish, so I began to experiment with a one-fish soup. Also, timing is everything when adding different seafood, and the various kinds made it much too complicated.

This wonderful end to my experimental journey generates an amazing aroma from the fennel, basil and oregano with which it is seasoned. The Italian triumvirate of peppers, onion and garlic add sweetness and flavor to the broth. I love how easily and quickly this dish comes together. I always serve it with fresh, warm, crusty French bread to wipe the bowl clean at the end.

1	teaspoon extra-virgin olive oil
1	medium fennel bulb, trimmed of stems and fronds, coarsely chopped, fronds reserved
1	large green bell pepper, cored and diced
1	medium onion, thinly sliced
2	large garlic cloves, minced
2	teaspoons fennel seeds
1	tablespoon chopped fresh basil (or 1 teaspoon crumbled dried)
1½	teaspoons chopped fresh oregano (or ½ teaspoon crumbled dried)
1	14.5-ounce can stewed tomatoes*
1	8-ounce bottle clam juice
1	pound halibut, boned, skinned and cut into 1-inch pieces

1. Heat the oil in a large nonstick saucepan over medium heat. Add the fennel, green pepper, onion, garlic, fennel seeds, basil and oregano. Cover and cook until the vegetables are softened, about 5 minutes.

2. Add the stewed tomatoes and clam juice and bring to a boil. Lower the heat and simmer gently, covered, for 10 minutes.

3. Add the halibut and continue to simmer, stirring occasionally, about 5 minutes, or until the halibut is just cooked through.

4. While simmering, chop the reserved fennel fronds. Ladle the cioppino into the serving bowls and lightly sprinkle the fennel fronds on top.

NUTRITIONAL INFORMATION PER SERVING: 197 CALORIES, 4 G FAT, 26 G PROTEIN, 13 G CARBOHYDRATE, 36 MG CHOLESTEROL, 561 MG SODIUM.

LeanTip: Monkfish or sea bass fillets can be substituted for the halibut.

Some supermarkets now carry Italian-style stewed tomatoes, which can be substituted for the regular stewed tomatoes. However, in that case, omit the basil and oregano.

OVEN-STEAMED HALIBUT STEAKS

SERVES 4

SEVERAL YEARS AGO, while reading the food section in the newspaper, I noticed an article about oven-steaming, an almost fat-free way to prepare fish and keep it moist in the process. The method is relatively simple. A skillet with boiling water is placed on the lower rack of a heated oven. The water in the skillet produces steam and fills the oven with moisture. Meanwhile, the fish is prepared and placed on the upper rack. The fish is then baked in moist instead of dry heat. While the fish steams, I prepare a full-flavored sweet pepper mélange with which to top the fish. All in all, this is elegant yet easy.

1	quart water, heated to boiling in an ovenproof skillet
4	1-inch-thick halibut steaks, rinsed, patted dry and brought to room temperature
1	teaspoon extra-virgin olive oil

SAUCE

2	teaspoons extra-virgin olive oil
1	large onion, peeled and thinly sliced
1	medium red bell pepper, seeded, sliced into thin strips
1	medium green bell pepper, seeded, sliced into thin strips
2	tablespoons balsamic vinegar
½	teaspoon salt
¼	teaspoon crumbled dried thyme
¼	teaspoon fresh-ground black pepper

1. Place one oven rack in the lower third of the oven and another in the upper third. Preheat the oven to 350 degrees F. Once it is hot, carefully place the skillet of boiling water on the bottom rack. Close the oven door.

2. Arrange the halibut steaks on a nonstick baking sheet and brush lightly with the oil. Place the baking sheet on the upper oven rack. Bake for 10 minutes.

3. Sauce: While the halibut is steaming, heat the oil in a large nonstick skillet over medium heat and add the onion. Sauté for 5 minutes, until soft but not browned. Add the pepper strips and continue sautéing until tender, about 3 more minutes. Stir in the balsamic vinegar, salt, thyme and pepper. Remove from the heat.

4. Open the oven door carefully, since steam will be released. Turn the steaks over and return to the oven for 2 minutes more, or until the fish flakes easily. Place the halibut steaks on 4 dinner plates and garnish with a quarter of the vegetable mixture along with any juices from the skillet.

NUTRITIONAL INFORMATION PER SERVING: 304 CALORIES, 8.4 G FAT, 47 G PROTEIN, 8.5 G CARBOHYDRATE, 70 MG CHOLESTEROL, 385 MG SODIUM.

SPICY SHRIMP CREOLE

SERVES 4

CINDY WAS AN EARLY READER of my column and wrote to tell me how much she enjoyed it. She also shared several of her favorite recipes with me, including this shrimp creole. Fresh oregano and thyme freshen this dish, and the red pepper makes it spicy.

1	tablespoon extra-virgin olive oil
1	small onion, chopped
1	small green bell pepper, chopped
½	cup chopped celery
2	medium garlic cloves, chopped
1	16-ounce can whole tomatoes
1	8-ounce can tomato sauce
2	teaspoons Worcestershire sauce
¼	teaspoon hot red pepper flakes
1½	teaspoons chopped fresh oregano (or ½ teaspoon crumbled dried)
1½	teaspoons chopped fresh thyme (or ½ teaspoon crumbled dried)
1½	pounds fresh shrimp, peeled and deveined
3	cups hot cooked rice

1. Heat the olive oil in a medium nonstick skillet placed over medium-high heat. Add the onion, green pepper, celery and garlic and sauté until soft but not browned, about 5 minutes.

2. Stir in the tomatoes and their liquid, breaking them up with the spoon. Stir in the tomato sauce, Worcestershire sauce and red pepper flakes. Reduce the heat to low and gently simmer for 15 minutes. Stir in the oregano and thyme, and simmer for 5 minutes more.

3. Stir in the shrimp and simmer for 5 to 7 minutes more, until the shrimp are cooked through. Serve over the rice.

NUTRITIONAL INFORMATION PER SERVING: 410 CALORIES, 6.5 G FAT, 40.6 G PROTEIN, 45.6 G CARBOHYDRATE, 258 MG CHOLESTEROL, 756 MG SODIUM.

LeanTip: If you use dried oregano and thyme, add them at the same time as the hot red pepper flakes. Don't forget to crumble the leaves to release their flavor.

CHILLED SHRIMP WITH RÉMOULADE SAUCE

SERVES 6

RÉMOULADE SAUCE SOUNDS FANCY, but it's really just seasoned mayonnaise. To my palate, low-fat mayonnaise (1 fat gram per tablespoon) tastes so close to the real thing as to be almost indistinguishable. Assembling impeccably fresh ingredients for the sauce further ensures that no one will ever suspect this is low in fat.

RÉMOULADE SAUCE

1   cup low-fat mayonnaise, such as Hellmann's

2   teaspoons very finely chopped fresh tarragon

1   tablespoon very finely chopped fresh parsley

1   tablespoon drained capers

1   teaspoon sweet paprika

1   teaspoon Dijon-style mustard

   Pinch cayenne pepper (or to taste)

1   tablespoon fresh-squeezed lemon juice

1   garlic clove

12   ruby leaf lettuce leaves, washed, spun dry and chilled

2   pounds shelled, deveined and cooked shrimp, chilled

6   sprigs fresh tarragon

1. Rémoulade sauce: In a small glass or ceramic mixing bowl, whisk together the mayonnaise, tarragon, parsley, capers, paprika, mustard, cayenne and lemon juice until thoroughly combined. Insert a wooden toothpick into the garlic clove and stir it around in the sauce, allowing the garlic to remain in the sauce. Cover and refrigerate for 2 hours. Remove the garlic clove.

2. Place the lettuce leaves on each of 6 chilled salad plates. Divide the shrimp equally among the plates. Spoon the sauce over the shrimp. Garnish with the tarragon sprigs.

NUTRITIONAL INFORMATION PER SERVING: 239 CALORIES, 5.8 G FAT, 32.5 G PROTEIN, 14 G CARBOHYDRATE, 233 MG CHOLESTEROL, 633 MG SODIUM.

LeanSuggestion: Pass some warm-from-the-oven sourdough French bread slices. The combination is unbeatable.

Sweet and Sour Shrimp

SERVES 4

I ONCE LOVED GOING to Chinese restaurants to enjoy sweet and sour shrimp. But I never knew how much fat was coming along for the ride. Then I realized that any sweet and sour dish is composed of meat or seafood that has been battered and fried. My much leaner version has all the great essences of that classic dish, but it isn't deep-fat fried.

4	tablespoons tomato ketchup
3	tablespoons light brown sugar
3	tablespoons white-wine vinegar
2	tablespoons sodium-reduced soy sauce
2	tablespoons dry white wine
½	cup water
2	tablespoons cornstarch
1	tablespoon canola oil
1	medium onion, peeled and quartered, quarters cut in half and separated
1	large green bell pepper, cut into ¾-inch squares
4	plum tomatoes, peeled and cut into ¾-inch pieces
¾	pound cleaned and deveined shrimp, cut into ¾-inch pieces
1	8-ounce can juice-packed pineapple chunks, drained

1. In a medium glass or ceramic mixing bowl, whisk together the ketchup, brown sugar, vinegar, soy sauce and white wine. Set aside.

2. In a 1-cup measuring cup, whisk together the water and cornstarch. Set aside.

3. Heat 1 teaspoon of the oil in a large nonstick skillet over high heat. Sauté the onion for 2 minutes, add the green peppers and sauté for 2 minutes more, or until the onion just begins to soften. Transfer the onion and peppers to a clean bowl.

4. Add 1 teaspoon of the oil to the skillet. Add the tomatoes and sauté for 30 seconds. Transfer the tomatoes to the bowl with the onion and peppers.

5. Add the remaining 1 teaspoon oil to the skillet. When it is hot, add the shrimp and quickly sauté for 2 to 3 minutes, until almost cooked through. Transfer the shrimp to the bowl.

6. Add the ketchup mixture to the skillet, stir and add the cornstarch mixture. When the sauce has thickened, return the cooked ingredients to the skillet, along with the pineapple. Gently stir together until hot and combined. Serve immediately.

NUTRITIONAL INFORMATION PER SERVING: 236 CALORIES, 5 G FAT, 19 G PROTEIN, 28 G CARBOHYDRATE, 129 MG CHOLESTEROL, 562 MG SODIUM.

LeanSuggestions

■ As with any Asian dish, cooked rice is the best accompaniment.

■ Pork tenderloin may be substituted for the shrimp without significantly altering the fat content. Shred ¾ pound of pork tenderloin and proceed as for shrimp.

CURRIED SHRIMP

SERVES 6

I LOVE THIS RECIPE for a couple of reasons. First, it has curry powder in it. Second, except for the peeling and deveining of the shrimp (which you can have your fish store do for you), this goes together very quickly. Third, it's very low in fat but has lots of flavor.

2	teaspoons extra-virgin olive oil
1	medium onion, chopped
2	tablespoons hot curry powder
2	large garlic cloves, chopped
1½	pounds fresh shrimp, peeled and deveined
½	teaspoon salt
¼	cup fresh-squeezed lime juice
½	cup nonfat sour cream
1	cup nonfat plain yogurt, at room temperature
⅓	cup chopped fresh cilantro

1. Heat the oil in a large nonstick skillet over high heat. Add the onion and sauté quickly until just softened. Add the curry powder, stir into the onion and cook for 1 minute. Add the garlic, shrimp and salt. Sauté, stirring frequently, for 3 to 4 minutes.

2. Reduce the heat to medium-low and add the lime juice, sour cream and yogurt. Slowly heat the mixture until hot; do not boil, or it will curdle. Sprinkle with the cilantro and remove from the heat. Serve hot.

NUTRITIONAL INFORMATION PER SERVING: 200 CALORIES, 3.9 G FAT, 27 G PROTEIN, 9.7 G CARBOHYDRATE, 177 MG CHOLESTEROL, 404 MG SODIUM.

LeanSuggestion: Aromatic basmati rice is a great accompaniment to soak up all the tasty sauce.

QUICK AND SPICY SCALLOPS AND PEPPERS

SERVES 4

NOT ONLY ARE BAY SCALLOPS truly sweet little morsels, but they are very low in fat. When multicolored peppers are available, I purchase a couple and zip over to my fish store. This quick dish is wonderful served over rice, since the cooking process gives up a tasty liquid and the rice is ideal for soaking it up.

2   teaspoons extra-virgin olive oil
2   large green bell peppers, cored and thinly sliced
2   large yellow bell peppers, cored and thinly sliced
2   large red bell peppers, cored and thinly sliced
2   jalapeño peppers, seeded and thinly sliced
2   tablespoons dry white wine
1   pound bay scallops, rinsed and patted dry
1   tablespoon minced fresh basil
       (or 1 teaspoon crumbled dried)
½   teaspoon salt

1. In a large nonstick skillet, heat the olive oil over medium-high heat. When it is hot, add all the peppers. Cook, stirring, for 3 minutes. Add the wine and continue to cook for 1 minute.

2. Add the scallops, basil and salt, stirring to combine. Reduce the heat to medium, cover and cook for 2 to 3 minutes, or until the scallops are cooked through. Serve hot.

NUTRITIONAL INFORMATION PER SERVING: 169 CALORIES, 3.3 G FAT, 22 G PROTEIN, 12.4 G CARBOHYDRATE, 40 MG CHOLESTEROL, 462 MG SODIUM.

Pasta and Pasta Sauces

FOR MANY OF MY FAT YEARS, I ate richly sauced pasta with abandon. At that time and after much experimentation, I created what I believed was the world's best home-made fettuccine Alfredo. My sauce began with butter and olive oil, in which I lightly sautéed garlic. I added the pasta to the saucepan, tossing to get it well coated. I whisked egg yolks into a cup of heavy cream and then poured it over the pasta. When it began to simmer and thicken, I added handfuls of freshly grated Parmesan and Romano cheeses. As soon as they melted, I dusted it with fresh-ground black pepper and some minced parsley. It was extraordinary. Unfortunately, it was also a heart attack on a plate.

Up until a few years ago, guess what got the blame for being the fattening part of my fettuccine. The sauce? Nope, the pasta. For decades, people would say, "Pasta makes you fat."

But when I turned to my recipes, I knew it was the fat in my sauces that was the culprit. For when consumed in reasonable quantities, pasta itself is ideal for a lean food plan. The problem was not that I used butter and oils but that I added such liberal amounts of them.

Rather than compulsively eliminating the cheese, I went with greatly reduced quantities of the most highly flavored ones I could find, like imported Parmigiano-Reggiano and Pecorino Romano. Both are sharp, and when grated, they can be added a tablespoon at a time. So that it delivers every last bit of flavor, I also grate my cheese fresh, avoiding canned or pregrated.

I now use no butter in my sauces, only olive oil. Butter has both cholesterol and large amounts of saturated fat. Olive oil has no cholesterol and one-quarter the amount of saturated fat. I am stingy with olive oil and usually add it by the teaspoon. Reducing the quantity makes strength of flavor especially important, so I always choose extra-virgin, which has a green color and a great fruity taste. It's a little more expensive than ordinary olive oil, but it makes for exceptional results.

Finally, I refuse to compromise taste by choosing pasta on the basis of price. I prefer pasta that is imported from Italy, and I especially like DeCecco brand, which is richly flavored, smoothly textured and yet offers resistance to the bite. It takes a little longer to cook than some other brands but it is well worth the wait.

Only on rare occasions do I rinse pasta. The starch left on the pasta is sticky, but rinsing removes the starch and the sauce's ability to cling goes right down the drain, too.

Today, I enjoy pasta at least once a week, topping it with lean sauces and dusting it at the end with small quantities of cheese. Do I miss the fat? Not for a single second.

RECIPES

LeanStyle Lasagna

SERVES 10

WHEN DINING OUT in a favorite Italian restaurant, I would inevitably order the lasagna, primarily because I found it a hassle to make at home. Today that's only partly true. This recipe does not need to have the lasagna noodles precooked for assembly, since they soften by absorbing some of the sauce while baking. And 1½ pounds of 1 percent cottage cheese contributes fewer than 8 total fat grams. My lasagna carries all the flavor of the high-fat restaurant versions, but contains only 13 percent calories from fat.

1 recipe Italian Tomato and Meat Sauce (page 304)
1 pound lasagna noodles, preferably imported
3 cups 1% cottage cheese, drained (about 24 ounces)
2 ounces Parmesan cheese, grated (½ cup)

1. Preheat the oven to 375 degrees F.

2. Lightly spray a 13-by-9-inch baking dish or lasagna pan with olive-oil spray. Spread a small amount of sauce evenly on the bottom and arrange the uncooked noodles in a single layer. Spread one-third of the cottage cheese over the noodles, sprinkle with 2 tablespoons of the Parmesan cheese, and top with one-third of the sauce.

3. Repeat, ending with the noodles, sauce and finally with the Parmesan cheese. Cover the pan with aluminum foil sprayed lightly on the contact side with olive oil.

4. Bake for 45 minutes, or until the pasta is soft. Remove the foil and bake for 10 minutes more. Remove from the oven and allow to cool for 10 minutes. Slice and serve.

NUTRITIONAL INFORMATION PER SERVING: 367 CALORIES, 5.4 G FAT, 27.7 G PROTEIN, 51.5 G CARBOHYDRATE, 31.6 MG CHOLESTEROL, 770 MG SODIUM.

LEAN FETTUCCINE ALFREDO

SERVES 4

I ONCE ENDED A COLUMN by writing, "Now, if I could only figure out how to make a lean fettuccine Alfredo, I'd be the happiest man alive." Several of my readers sent in their versions. Among them was this recipe from Beverly. I immediately noticed some smart substitutions. Instead of butter or large quantities of high-fat cheese, Beverly used low-fat cottage cheese. For the heavy cream normally used, she went with low-fat milk. A single egg yolk remained. I knew it delivered a rich flavor and smooth texture to the sauce. With only 5 fat grams, this was a bargain. Finally, Beverly wisely used a small amount of extra-virgin olive oil for flavor and just 2 ounces of real Parmesan cheese. When I prepared it, I had to admit it was very good. It had almost the same flavor and texture of my own homemade, high-fat version, but with only 21 percent of calories from fat versus 60 percent.

8	ounces fettuccine
1	cup 1% cottage cheese
1	cup 1% milk
1	large egg yolk
½	teaspoon fresh-ground black pepper
2	teaspoons extra-virgin olive oil
1	garlic clove, minced
½	cup fresh-grated Parmesan cheese

1. Bring a large pot of salted water to a rolling boil. While stirring, add the fettuccine. Continue stirring until the water returns to a boil. Cook for 7 minutes, or until the fettuccine gives gentle resistance to the bite. Drain and return to the pan.

2. In a blender, combine the cottage cheese, milk, egg yolk and pepper; puree until smooth.

3. In a small saucepan, heat the oil over medium-low heat. Sauté the garlic in the oil until soft but not browned, about 2 minutes. Stir in the cottage cheese mixture and bring to a simmer, stirring occasionally. Stir ¼ cup of the Parmesan cheese into the saucepan.

4. When the cheese has melted, pour the sauce over the pasta, and over low heat, stir until combined. Sprinkle with the remaining ¼ cup Parmesan and serve.

NUTRITIONAL INFORMATION PER SERVING: 382 CALORIES, 9.1 G FAT, 22 G PROTEIN, 49 G CARBOHYDRATE, 80.5 MG CHOLESTEROL, 404 MG SODIUM.

LeanSuggestion: Beverly suggests adding cooked, diced chicken breast or cooked shrimp, cut into bite-size pieces, at the same time the cottage cheese mixture is added.

CHICKEN AND MUSHROOM FETTUCCINE

SERVES 4

THIS DISH BEGAN with a box of fettuccine, in my kitchen cupboard, leftover mushrooms—both button and shiitake—and two leftover broiled chicken breasts. I started by sautéing onions and garlic, put a pot of water on to boil, and in no time at all, assembled this meal.

12	ounces fettuccine
1	teaspoon extra-virgin olive oil
¼	cup finely chopped onion
1	garlic clove, minced
½	pound white button mushrooms, cleaned, trimmed and chopped
¼	pound fresh shiitake mushrooms, cleaned, stems removed, chopped
¼	cup cornstarch
2	cups defatted low-sodium chicken broth
2	cups diced cooked chicken breast
½	teaspoon crumbled dried tarragon
½	teaspoon salt
¼	teaspoon fresh-ground black pepper

1. Bring a large pot of salted water to a rolling boil. Stirring, add the fettuccine. Continue stirring until the water returns to a boil. Cook for 7 minutes, or until the fettuccine gives gentle resistance to the bite. Drain.

2. While the fettuccine is cooking, heat the oil in a large nonstick skillet over medium heat. Add the onion and garlic and cook, stirring, until the onion begins to soften, about 5 minutes. Add the mushrooms and sauté until they begin to give up their liquid, about 5 minutes.

3. Whisk the cornstarch into ½ cup of the chicken broth until combined. Set aside.

4. Add the chicken and the remaining 1½ cups chicken broth to the skillet, stirring. When the mixture begins to simmer, add the cornstarch mixture, along with the tarragon, salt and pepper and return to a simmer. Remove from the heat.

5. Divide the fettuccine among 4 plates and spoon the chicken and mushrooms over each serving.

NUTRITIONAL INFORMATION PER SERVING: 464 CALORIES, 5.7 G FAT, 27 G PROTEIN, 73 G CARBOHYDRATE, 118 MG CHOLESTEROL, 408 MG SODIUM.

LeanTip: A very light dusting (1 tablespoon) of fresh-grated Parmesan cheese will contribute flavor without adding significantly to the fat content.

Spaghetti in a Flash

SERVES 6

I HAVE ALWAYS BELIEVED that a beef-and-tomato-based sauce does not need to simmer for hours on the back of the stove. In fact, I am uncertain whether there is much to gain during the long simmering process. I made the discovery with this sauce.

I was in a big rush one evening to get our dinner to the table. I was hungry, tired and (okay, I'll admit it) a little cranky. I put the sauce together quickly and when it seemed done, in went the pasta. Dinner hit the table in a flash and—it was great. I concede, though, that if this sauce is chilled overnight in the refrigerator, it tastes better the next day.

1	pound spaghetti
1	teaspoon extra-virgin olive oil
¾	pound 95% lean ground beef
½	cup finely chopped onion
¼	cup finely chopped green bell pepper
2	tablespoons finely chopped pimento-stuffed green olives
2	garlic cloves, minced
2	bay leaves
2	cups coarsely chopped fresh tomato (from 2 medium tomatoes)
1	½-ounce packet Butter Buds
1½	tablespoons minced fresh basil (or 1 rounded teaspoon crumbled dried)
1	teaspoon crumbled dried tarragon
½	teaspoon fresh-ground black pepper
¼	cup dry red wine

1. Bring a large pot of salted water to a rolling boil. While stirring, add the spaghetti. Continue stirring until the water returns to a boil. Cook for 10 minutes, or until the spaghetti gives gentle resistance to the bite. Drain.

2. While the spaghetti is cooking, heat the oil in a large nonstick saucepan over medium heat. Add the ground beef and cook, stirring and breaking up the lumps, until the meat is no longer pink, about 5 minutes.

3. Add the onion, bell pepper, olives, garlic and bay leaves and cook for 10 minutes, stirring occasionally, until the vegetables are softened.

4. Stir in the tomato, Butter Buds, basil, tarragon and black pepper and cook for 5 minutes, or until the tomatoes start to soften. Add the wine and simmer for 5 minutes, or until the sauce thickens slightly. Remove and discard the bay leaves.

5. Add the prepared spaghetti to the saucepan; toss and stir with the sauce until combined. Serve hot.

NUTRITIONAL INFORMATION PER SERVING: 400 CALORIES, 5.6 G FAT, 23 G PROTEIN, 64 G CARBOHYDRATE, 31.2 MG CHOLESTEROL, 386 MG SODIUM.

LeanTip: A 1-tablespoon dusting of fresh-grated Parmesan cheese will add only 1.5 grams of fat. Add tossed salad with nonfat Italian dressing and some oven-warmed French bread, and dinner is served.

MACARONI AND CHEDDAR CHEESE

SERVES 8

WHEN I WAS A CHILD, my mother used to make macaroni and cheese by cooking up a box of elbows and then adding milk, butter and Velveeta. Later, when I began to fend for myself in my own kitchen, I started by duplicating my mother's quick and easy method. As time progressed, I became adventurous and started to try different ingredients. My journey took me to various cheese stores, where I had my first taste of a Cheddar aged for more than four years. It seemed sharp enough to cut my tongue, yet there was a beguiling roundness to its flavor.

My crowning achievement was a macaroni and cheese made with seven cheeses. I used American, Cheddar, brick, Swiss, Parmesan, Romano and full-fat cottage cheese. My masterpiece was topped with buttered fresh bread crumbs. When I changed the way I ate, I contemplated giving the dish a special plaque in my Hall of Fat Foods. But I would not give it up.

I began experimenting and immediately met with failure. First, I tried making a sauce with just nonfat cottage cheese and a little skim milk. It melted together fine. But it refused to stick to the macaroni, slowly sliding off and stubbornly pooling in the bottom of the pan.

My brother suggested that I try making it with reduced amounts of highly flavored cheese. I came up with a way of using a small amount of aged Cheddar and a fat-reduced Cheddar. The numbers worked: 20 percent calories from fat as compared to most versions, which are loaded down with at least 50 percent fat calories.

1   pound macaroni
2   cups skim milk
1   teaspoon dry mustard
2   tablespoons cornstarch
¼   pound reduced-fat Cheddar cheese,
      shredded (1 cup loosely packed)

¼   pound aged Cheddar cheese,
       shredded (1½ cups loosely packed)
½   cup nonfat cottage cheese
1   teaspoon salt
½   teaspoon fresh-ground black pepper

1. Bring a large pot of salted water to a rolling boil. While stirring, add the macaroni. Continue stirring until the water returns to a boil. Cook for 8 minutes, or until the macaroni gives gentle resistance to the bite. Drain.

2. While the macaroni is cooking, whisk together the milk, mustard and cornstarch in a large nonstick saucepan. Bring to a simmer, stirring, over medium heat. Add both cheddars, cottage cheese, salt and pepper and stir until the cheese melts and the sauce is thick. Remove from the heat.

3. Add the prepared macaroni to the cheese sauce. Over medium-low heat, stir together until heated through and combined. Serve immediately.

NUTRITIONAL INFORMATION PER SERVING: 345 CALORIES, 8.3 G FAT, 18.4 G PROTEIN, 48 G CARBOHYDRATE, 16 MG CHOLESTEROL, 500 MG SODIUM.

LeanSuggestion: If you prefer baked macaroni and cheese, do the following: Preheat the oven to 350 degrees F. Lightly spray the bottom and sides of a large casserole dish with vegetable oil. Add the prepared macaroni and cheese to the dish, flattening the top with the back of a serving spoon. Evenly distribute 1½ cups fresh bread crumbs over the top. Lightly spray the crumbs with butter-flavored vegetable oil and dust with sweet paprika to taste. Bake, uncovered for 30 minutes, or until the cheese bubbles and the bread crumbs are light brown.

SPAGHETTI ALLA MATRICIANA

SERVES 6

THIS IS A GREAT PASTA DISH, named for Matriciana, a town in Italy. I have seen several recipes for the high-fat version of this sauce. I created my own, a wonderfully onion-scented, basil-flecked sauce that is very low in fat. If you cannot locate prosciutto ham, any lean but highly flavored ham will do.

2	teaspoons extra-virgin olive oil
4	ounces Italian prosciutto, thinly sliced, trimmed of all fat and cut into bite-size pieces
1	large onion, thinly sliced
½	cup defatted low-sodium chicken broth
¼	cup dry white wine
2	cups ripe tomatoes, peeled and chopped (or drained canned tomatoes)
½	teaspoon salt
¼	teaspoon fresh-ground black pepper
2	tablespoons finely chopped fresh basil
¼	cup finely chopped fresh parsley
1	pound spaghetti
6	tablespoons fresh-grated Parmesan cheese

1. Heat the oil in a nonstick skillet over medium heat and add the prosciutto. Stir in the onion and sauté until soft, about 8 minutes.

2. Add the chicken broth and white wine and simmer, uncovered, stirring occasionally, until much of the moisture evaporates.

3. Add the tomatoes, salt and pepper. Reduce the heat to low and simmer, uncovered, for 30 minutes, or until the sauce slightly thickens. Add the basil and parsley and simmer for 5 more minutes.

4. While the sauce simmers, bring a large pot of salted water to a rolling boil. While stirring, add the spaghetti. Continue stirring until the water returns to a boil. Cook for 10 minutes, or until the spaghetti gives gentle resistance to the bite. Drain the spaghetti well.

5. Serve the finished tomato sauce over the spaghetti. Sprinkle each portion with 1 tablespoon of the Parmesan cheese.

NUTRITIONAL INFORMATION PER SERVING: 382 CALORIES, 5.3 G FAT, 15.7 G PROTEIN, 64.5 G CARBOHYDRATE, 13 MG CHOLESTEROL, 530 MG SODIUM.

Spaghetti with Meatless Tomato Sauce

SERVES 6

AFTER I HAD BEEN A NEWSPAPER COLUMNIST for six months, I got a very nice note from a woman asking me if I was the same Don Mauer she knew in high school. I was. I called her and we brought each other up to date on the last 25 years.

I invited her and her husband over for dinner. It turned out that she was a vegetarian. I could have made a simple marinara sauce, but my friend deserved something unique. Olive oil, onions and garlic are the foundation for my creation. Shredded carrots replace the meat for texture. Adding Cognac at the very end brings a perfect finish to the dish and the dinner.

1	tablespoon extra-virgin olive oil
2	cups finely chopped onions
2	large garlic cloves, minced
3	tablespoons tomato paste
2	cups finely shredded carrots
¼	teaspoon salt
¼	teaspoon fresh-ground black pepper
¼	teaspoon cayenne pepper
¾	cup canned vegetable broth*
1	28-ounce can whole plum tomatoes
1	16-ounce can crushed tomatoes
2	tablespoons finely chopped fresh parsley
1	pound spaghetti
2	tablespoons Cognac or brandy

1. Heat the oil in a large nonstick saucepan over medium-high heat. When it is hot, add the onions and garlic and sauté until lightly browned, 6 to 7 minutes.

2. Add the tomato paste, carrots, salt, black pepper and cayenne. Sauté for 2 minutes more. Stir in the vegetable broth, plum tomatoes and crushed tomatoes, breaking up the plum tomatoes with the edge of a spoon.

3. When the sauce begins to boil, reduce the heat to low and gently simmer, uncovered, for 45 minutes, or until thickened. About 5 minutes before the sauce is ready, stir in the parsley.

4. Meanwhile, bring a large pot of salted water to a rolling boil. While stirring, add the spaghetti. Continue stirring until the water returns to a boil. Cook for 10 minutes, or until the spaghetti gives gentle resistance to the bite. Drain.

5. Stir the Cognac or brandy into the sauce. Divide the spaghetti among 6 serving bowls and ladle the sauce over each.

NUTRITIONAL INFORMATION PER SERVING: 403 CALORIES, 3.5 G FAT, 12.6 G PROTEIN, 78 G CARBOHYDRATE, 0 CHOLESTEROL, 575 MG SODIUM.

LeanTip: A tablespoon or two of nonfat sour cream on the side rounds out this dish. A light dusting of fresh-grated Parmesan cheese will add terrific flavor without appreciably changing the fat content.

Vegetable broth can be found in supermarkets. It is located in the soup section.

PENNE WITH VODKA TOMATO SAUCE

SERVES 6

I'M NOT CERTAIN where the original recipe for this sauce came from. I do know that vodka is not as neutral a flavor as some people believe. To me, good-quality vodka has a sweet note and an earthy edge, which do fine things for a sauce. Choose a pasta that is tubular so it will transport as much of the sauce as possible. You will certainly want to have some warm French bread for mopping up any drops remaining on your plate.

SAUCE

1	tablespoon extra-virgin olive oil
1	small onion, finely chopped
1	28-ounce can plum tomatoes, drained and chopped, liquid reserved
1	tablespoon cornstarch
1	cup skim milk
¼	cup vodka
¼	teaspoon hot red pepper flakes
	Salt to taste

1	pound penne or other tubular pasta
¼	cup fresh-grated Parmesan cheese (1 ounce)
2	tablespoons minced fresh chives

1. Sauce: Heat the oil in a large heavy-bottomed saucepan over medium heat. Add the onion and sauté until translucent, about 6 minutes. Add the tomatoes with their liquid and cook until almost no liquid remains in the pan, stirring frequently, for about 25 minutes. Whisk the cornstarch into the milk and add to the sauce along with the vodka and red pepper flakes. Boil until thickened, stirring, about 2 minutes. Season to taste with salt. Remove from the heat.

2. Meanwhile, bring a large pot of salted water to a rolling boil. Stirring, add the pasta. Continue stirring until the water returns to a boil. Cook for about 12 minutes, or until it gives gentle resistance to the bite. Drain the pasta well.

3. Transfer the pasta to a large bowl. Pour the sauce over the pasta, stir and toss well to coat. Sprinkle with the cheese and chives and serve.

NUTRITIONAL INFORMATION PER SERVING (WITHOUT SALT): 391 CALORIES, 4.5 G FAT, 13.2 PROTEIN, 67.9 G CARBOHYDRATE, 3.3 MG CHOLESTEROL, 573 MG SODIUM.

Bolognese-Style Sauce

SERVES 8

ITALIAN BOLOGNESE SAUCE is loaded with flavor and fat. I took it as my personal mission to figure out how to keep the flavor and dump the fat. Instead of Italian bacon, I went with a small amount of closely trimmed prosciutto ham and the leanest ground beef I could find.

2	teaspoons extra-virgin olive oil
¼	cup finely diced lean prosciutto
½	cup finely diced onion
⅓	cup grated carrot
⅓	cup finely diced celery
1	pound 95% lean ground beef
1	cup chopped white button mushroom caps
1½	cups dry red wine
1	tablespoon finely chopped fresh parsley
1	teaspoon crumbled dried marjoram
½	teaspoon salt
½	teaspoon fresh-ground black pepper
¼	teaspoon fresh-grated nutmeg
1½	teaspoons all-purpose flour
1	½-ounce packet Butter Buds
3	cups crushed tomatoes
2	cups defatted low-sodium beef broth, preferably homemade
½	cup nonfat sour cream

1. Heat the oil in a large nonstick saucepan over medium-high heat. Add the prosciutto and sauté, stirring, until browned, 3 to 4 minutes. Add the onion, carrot and celery and sauté for 6 minutes, or until the onion is golden.

2. Add the ground beef and mushrooms and sauté, breaking up the meat with the edge of the spoon, until it loses its pink color, 3 to 4 minutes.

3. Add the wine, parsley, marjoram, salt, pepper and nutmeg. Reduce the heat to medium and simmer, uncovered, stirring occasionally, for 8 minutes, or until slightly reduced.

4. Remove the pan from the heat and stir in the flour. Return the pan to the heat and add the Butter Buds, crushed tomatoes and beef broth. Reduce the heat to low, and simmer the sauce gently, uncovered, for 1 hour, stirring occasionally.

5. Remove the pan from the heat and stir in the sour cream.

NUTRITIONAL INFORMATION PER SERVING: 180 CALORIES, 4.7 G FAT, 16.5 G PROTEIN, 8.2 G CARBOHYDRATE, 40 MG CHOLESTEROL, 769 MG SODIUM.

LeanTip: The ground beef can be browned separately in a nonstick skillet, placed in a fine sieve, drained and rinsed with hot water to remove any additional fat. In step 2, omit the browning of the beef, and sauté only the mushrooms for 3 minutes; add the precooked beef when the mushrooms are cooked. Proceed as directed.

Italian Tomato and Meat Sauce

SERVES 8

Traditionally, Italian-style meat sauces begin with ground beef. Out of 16 ounces of regular ground beef, 4.3 ounces are fat. I switched to 95 percent lean ground beef and waved goodbye to 100 fat grams. Butter Buds made up for the customary use of olive oil. Red wine, fennel and honey give my sauce a delightful aroma and unique flavor.

1	pound 95% lean ground beef
1½	cups sliced white button mushrooms
2	15-ounce cans tomato sauce, preferably low-sodium
7	8-ounce cans no-sodium-added tomatoes, drained and chopped
1	cup finely chopped onion
3	large garlic cloves, minced
¼	cup dry red wine
1	tablespoon chopped fresh parsley
1	teaspoon clover honey
1	teaspoon crumbled dried oregano (or 1 tablespoon chopped fresh)
1	teaspoon whole fennel seeds
1	teaspoon sweet paprika
½	teaspoon crumbled dried basil (or 1½ teaspoons chopped fresh)
½	teaspoon salt
1	large bay leaf
1	½-ounce packet Butter Buds
¼	teaspoon cayenne pepper

1. Spray a large nonstick saucepan with vegetable oil. Cook the ground beef over medium-high heat, breaking it up with the spoon edge, until it loses its pink color, about 5 minutes. Add the mushrooms and sauté briefly until they begin to give up their liquid, about 5 minutes.

2. Reduce heat to medium-low and add the remaining ingredients. Simmer for 30 minutes, or until reduced slightly.

NUTRITIONAL INFORMATION PER SERVING: 159 CALORIES, 3.2 G FAT, 14.6 G PROTEIN, 19.3 G CARBOHYDRATE, 31 MG CHOLESTEROL, 502 MG SODIUM.

RICE

ONCE, WHILE WRITING A SERIES OF ARTICLES FOR A NEWSPAPER, I traveled to
the home of a reader who wished to have her recipes lightened. The first one she
showed me was her family's favorite: green rice. Through the additions of cream soup,
butter, whole milk and cheese, she had taken the fat in her dish to stratospheric
heights. Her rice abuse is not unusual. Many Americans soak rice with high-fat gravy to
add flavor because when cooked in plain water, rice is bland.

But when properly prepared, brown or white rice is ideal for lean dining, substantive and satisfying, bringing complex carbohydrates into play. My solution is simple. I cook rice in a flavored liquid: chicken, beef or vegetable broth. Sometimes I season it with soy sauce or garlic or I add a drop or two of toasted sesame oil. The rice absorbs the flavors of the liquid in which it is cooked and delivers them intact to the dinner plate.

It was my grandmother who taught me how to make brown rice properly. Long before it had gained mainstream acceptance, it could regularly be found on her dinner table. The natural, nutlike flavor shone through the separate, never sticky, grains.

Recently, I discovered aromatic rice. Basmati rice was my jumping-off point. It fills my kitchen with a scent similar to that of popped corn. Next, I sampled jasmine rice imported from the Far East, which is as flavorful as basmati. Pecan rice, a special strain grown in Louisiana (it is only rice and contains no high-fat nuts) is excellent in rice pudding. The rice cooks up puffy and has the distinct, but not overwhelming, aroma of pecans. All three are delicious, with no sauce, no gravy . . . no fat.

RECIPES

EXCEPTIONAL RED RICE

SERVES 6

THE FAMOUS JAZZ MUSICIAN Louis Armstrong used to give his autograph by signing, "Red beans and Ricely yours," since he loved this dish so much. My red rice has no beans but is very red, and the flavor sings to a definite jazz beat.

I tried making it with canola oil and Canadian bacon, but it just did not have the right taste. Two teaspoons of bacon grease contain only 9 grams of fat and the smoky flavor it imparts makes up for that sin.

2	teaspoons bacon grease
1	medium onion, chopped
1	medium green bell pepper, chopped
1½	cups defatted low-sodium chicken broth, preferably homemade
1	cup long-grain white basmati rice
1	cup tomato sauce
2	tablespoons Worcestershire sauce
1	tablespoon chili powder
1	medium bay leaf
½	teaspoon thyme
¼	teaspoon cayenne pepper
4	slices (3 ounces) thick-sliced bacon, baked on a wire rack until crisp, trimmed of all fat, lean parts crumbled

1. Heat a large nonstick skillet over medium-high heat. When hot, add the bacon grease, onion and green pepper. Sauté until the onion is soft, about 4 minutes.

2. Add the remaining ingredients, stirring to combine. Reduce the heat to low, cover and gently simmer for 35 minutes, stirring occasionally. Serve hot.

NUTRITIONAL INFORMATION PER SERVING: 151 CALORIES, 3 G FAT, 5.7 G PROTEIN, 25.3 G CARBOHYDRATE, 8.2 MG CHOLESTEROL, 364 MG SODIUM.

Rice with Artichokes and Roasted Red Peppers

SERVES 4 AS A MAIN COURSE OR 8 AS A SIDE DISH

THIS IS A UNIQUE DISH. Fat used to be added to the rice in the cooking process, then the artichokes were marinated in olive oil. There were many more olives in the original dish, which are very high in fat, too.

Now, I use no fat in the preparation of the rice. I substitute water-packed artichokes for the marinated ones. I add lemon juice for flavor and have reduced the Parmesan cheese. I use imported Parmigiano-Reggiano and grate it fresh just before serving. A half-teaspoon of black pepper may seem like too much, but it's just right.

1	cup long-grain white basmati rice
1½	cups defatted low-sodium chicken broth, preferably homemade
⅓	cup tomato juice
1	teaspoon crumbled dried basil
1	teaspoon crumbled dried oregano
½	teaspoon salt, or to taste
1	14-ounce can water-packed artichoke hearts, drained and quartered
1	7-ounce jar roasted red peppers, drained and chopped
6	jumbo ripe olives, drained and thinly sliced
2	tablespoons chopped fresh parsley
2	tablespoons fresh-squeezed lemon juice
½	teaspoon fresh-ground black pepper
2	tablespoons fresh-grated Parmesan cheese

1. Place the rice in a large bowl. Cover with water. With your hands, swish the water around to remove the starchy coating on the rice grains. Drain the rice and continue this process until the water is no longer milky in color, but clear. Add cool water to cover the rice by at least 1 inch. Soak for 20 minutes. Drain.

2. Bring the chicken broth and tomato juice to a boil in a medium saucepan. Add the basil, oregano, salt and rice. Return to a boil, stirring once or twice. Reduce the heat to low and gently simmer for 15 minutes.

3. Stir in the artichokes, red peppers, olives, parsley, lemon juice and black pepper. Cover and cook 5 minutes more, or until heated through. Dust with the cheese when serving.

NUTRITIONAL INFORMATION PER SIDE-DISH SERVING (WITH SALT): 140 CALORIES, 1.1 G FAT, 4.4 G PROTEIN, 28.1 G CARBOHYDRATE, 1 MG CHOLESTEROL, 466 MG SODIUM.

CUMIN-SCENTED YELLOW RICE

SERVES 4

I HAVE ALWAYS LOVED THE FLAVOR OF CUMIN, and the combination of it with the basmati rice is perfect. Saffron gives this rice a beautiful yellow color. Be careful to measure the saffron accurately; it's expensive, and too much will give a medicinal aroma. Authentic saffron threads are well worth the price. You can use them in Arroz Con Pollo as well (page 204).

1	cup long-grain white basmati rice
1	tablespoon extra-virgin olive oil
1	teaspoon cumin seeds
⅛	teaspoon crumbled saffron threads
1¾	cups defatted low-sodium chicken broth, preferably homemade
¼	teaspoon salt

1. Place the rice in a large bowl. Cover with water. With your hands, swish the water around to remove the starchy coating on the rice grains. Drain the rice and continue this process until the water is no longer milky in color, but clear. Add cool water to cover the rice by at least 1 inch. Soak for 20 minutes. Drain.

2. Add the oil to a small heavy-bottomed saucepan and place over medium-high heat until hot but not smoking. Add the cumin seeds and sauté for 10 seconds, or until they darken and are fragrant.

3. Stir in the saffron and rice and sauté, stirring, for 1 to 2 minutes, until the rice is well coated with the oil. Stir in the chicken broth (be careful; it will boil and sputter at first) and salt.

4. Reduce the heat to medium and boil the rice, uncovered and without stirring, until the surface is covered with steam holes and the grains on top appear dry, 9 minutes. Reduce the heat to as low as possible and cook, covered, for 10 minutes more. Remove the pan from the heat and let the rice stand, covered, for 5 minutes. Fluff the rice with a fork and serve immediately.

NUTRITIONAL INFORMATION PER SERVING: 208 CALORIES, 3.7 G FAT, 4.3 G PROTEIN, 38 G CARBOHYDRATE, 0 CHOLESTEROL, 170 MG SODIUM.

GARLIC SESAME RICE

SERVES 6

THIS RICE, WHICH I SERVE AS A SIDE DISH with Asian main courses, receives just the right flavor from the small amount of sesame oil and the garlic.

1   cup white basmati rice
½   teaspoon toasted sesame oil*
1   large garlic clove, very thinly sliced
1⅔   cups defatted low-sodium chicken broth,
      preferably homemade

1. Place the rice in a large bowl. Cover with water. With your hands, swish the water around to remove the starchy coating on the rice grains. Drain the rice and continue this process until the water is no longer milky in color, but clear. Add cool water to cover the rice by at least 1 inch. Soak for 20 minutes. Drain.

2. Place a medium nonstick saucepan over medium heat and add the sesame oil. When the oil begins to smoke, add the garlic, stirring for 30 seconds. Add the rice and stir for 30 seconds. Carefully add the chicken broth, which will at first sputter and spit. Boil the rice, uncovered and without stirring, until the surface is covered with steam holes and grains on top appear dry, about 8 minutes.

3. Reduce the heat to as low as possible and cook, covered, for 10 minutes more. Turn off the heat and allow the rice to sit, covered, for 5 minutes. Uncover, fluff with a fork and serve.

NUTRITIONAL INFORMATION PER SERVING: 122 CALORIES, 0.5 G FAT, 2.8 G PROTEIN, 25.2 G CARBOHYDRATE, 0 CHOLESTEROL, 23 MG SODIUM.

Toasted sesame oil can be purchased from most large supermarkets (look for it in the Chinese section) and all Asian markets.

GRANDMA MAUER'S BAKED BROWN RICE

SERVES 6

I STILL USE EXACTLY THE SAME IRON SKILLET to caramelize the rice that my grandmother did. It easily stands the heat and also is ideal for making North Carolina Skillet Cornbread (page 388). The best news is that if you don't already own one, they are very inexpensive and last a lifetime.

I have never found a better way to prepare brown rice than this. All of the grains are cooked just right and are separate, not gloppy. Sometimes, when I know I am going to make rice pudding, I omit the salt and bake a batch of rice expressly for that purpose. This is also an excellent way to prepare brown basmati rice.

1   cup long-grain brown rice
      (preferably organically grown)
2   cups very hot water (or defatted low-sodium
      beef or chicken broth)
1   teaspoon salt (omit if using salted broth)
¼   teaspoon olive oil

1. Preheat the oven to 350 degrees F.

2. Add the rice to a mesh strainer and rinse under cold water. Soak the rice in very warm (120 degrees) water for 5 minutes; drain.

3. Pour the hot water or broth into a medium casserole and stir in the salt, if using. Set aside.

4. Add the oil to the bottom of a 9-inch iron skillet. Heat over medium-high heat until it just begins to smoke. Add the drained rice to the skillet and stir constantly until the rice hulls begin to caramelize (brown) and start to move on their own, 4 or 5 minutes. Be careful not to burn the hulls.*

5. Carefully stir the rice into the casserole dish (be careful; the water will boil up when the hot rice is added). Stir, cover and bake for 50 minutes, or until the surface appears dry. Remove from the oven, but do not uncover until ready to serve. It may be held for 20 to 30 minutes. Once cooled, it may be refrigerated.

NUTRITIONAL INFORMATION PER CUP: 173 CALORIES, 1.6 G FAT, 3.5 G PROTEIN, 36 G CARBOHYDRATE, 0 CHOLESTEROL, 536 MG SODIUM.

Don't be surprised if some of the rice actually pops like miniature popcorn during the caramelizing stage. It will puff, but it won't fly out of the skillet.

SPECIAL SPANISH RICE

SERVES 4 AS A MAIN COURSE

THE FIRST TIME MY WIFE, SUSAN, prepared this fabulous main dish, I was out in front of the house mowing the lawn. The aroma of the basmati rice and chili powder drifted out the kitchen window and made its way to me. The scent made me wonder what neighbor of mine was making something that smelled that good. This is like a chili without beans, in which the rice absorbs the red sauce. Spinach deepens and enriches the flavor. Susan thinks otherwise; that's why it's optional.

2	teaspoons extra-virgin olive oil
½	pound 95% lean ground beef
1	medium onion, chopped
1	medium green bell pepper, chopped
1½	cups water
1	cup white basmati rice
1	tablespoon chili powder
2	tablespoons Worcestershire sauce
1	cup sodium-reduced tomato sauce
	(or fresh tomatoes, peeled, seeded and diced)
1	medium bay leaf
½	teaspoon salt
½	teaspoon dried thyme
1	bunch fresh spinach, washed, trimmed
	and thinly sliced (optional)

1. Heat the oil in a large nonstick skillet over medium-high heat. When it is hot, add the ground beef,

onion and green pepper. Sauté until the beef loses its pink color, breaking it up with the spoon edge, about 5 minutes.

2. Add the water, rice, chili powder, Worcestershire sauce, tomato sauce or tomatoes, bay leaf, salt and thyme, stirring to combine. Reduce the heat to low, cover and simmer for 35 minutes, stirring occasionally, or until the rice absorbs the liquid.

3. Add the optional spinach, stir to combine, cover and simmer for 5 minutes more, until the spinach wilts. Remove the bay leaf before serving.

NUTRITIONAL INFORMATION PER SERVING: 294 CALORIES, 5.8 G FAT, 18.4 G PROTEIN, 43.5 G CARBOHYDRATE, 31.2 MG CHOLESTEROL, 696 MG SODIUM.

LeanTip: Want to boost the flavor even more? Substitute 1½ cups of defatted low-sodium beef broth for the water and proceed as directed.

BEANS

ONE OF THE WAYS I MAINTAIN MY WEIGHT LOSS is by alternating meat and meat-less days, sometimes indulging in a slightly less lean cut and making up for it on my lower-fat vegetarian days. On those days, I invariably turn to beans for my protein. The first time I cooked a dried bean was in split pea soup. It was easy, since split peas are one of the few beans that don't need to be soaked overnight to begin the soften-ing process. Adding bones from a ham shank made my soup rich. When I first tried to prepare other beans from scratch, the process was more difficult. They had to be soaked overnight and slowly simmered on my stovetop.

An easier way to make beans a regular part of lean dining is to use the canned kind. Over the last four years, I have sampled many different brands and types from regular super-markets and natural food stores, and I have found most to have a good flavor. Before buying canned beans, check out the label. Sometimes oil or fatty meats have been added for flavoring. The fat content might surprise you. Look for beans without added fat. A small amount (1 to 2 grams per serving) should be all right. You'll quickly learn which brands are good and which aren't. Most supermarket beans cost less than $1 per can.

When time allows, though, nothing beats the flavor of cooked dried beans. I recommend cooking them in bottled spring water, which has a sweet flavor. Good-quality canned chicken or beef broths also enhance dried beans. Or you can toss one or two vegetable bouillon cubes into the water. I refrigerate my cooked beans and use them for dishes later in the week.

In the last year, I've been able to use dried beans exclusively, ordering different, unusual varieties by mail-order and preparing them in a pressure cooker. The pressure cooker reduces the cooking time to 18 minutes or less, making it possible to enjoy home-cooked beans during the week, when time is short.

RECIPES

BASIC BEANS

BEANS ARE EASILY PURCHASED already cooked and canned. But ever since I started using a pressure cooker, I prefer preparing my own. I can select beans from all over the world and not be limited to the few commercial beans found in cans. I can control the quality of the beans, since I prepare only those that are organically grown. I can season my beans exactly the way I want them. Most commercial beans have too much sodium. For example, ½ cup of a commercial brand of dark red kidney beans contains almost 600 milligrams of sodium. Too much for me. I like using a vegetable bouillon cube I purchase from a health food store that contains all sorts of vegetables and flavorings and some salt.

By cooking my own dried beans, I can also control the quality of the water in which my beans are soaked and cooked. I use premium bottled spring water, which imparts a cleaner, sweeter taste to my beans. If you prefer not to cook your own beans, try the ones in health or natural food stores. Many brands are organic and some have no salt added or are low-sodium. Then you add however much salt you want.

12	ounces dried beans
3	quarts water, preferably bottled spring water
2	vegetable bouillon cubes
3	garlic cloves, peeled

1. Spread the beans on a jelly-roll pan and pick through them, removing any pebbles or discolored beans. Rinse in a colander. Soak the beans for at least 4 hours or overnight in enough water to cover them by at least 2 inches.

2. Drain the beans and discard the water. Place the beans in a large saucepan, add the 3 quarts water and bring to a simmer. Add the bouillon cubes and garlic, stirring until the cubes dissolve. Lower the heat and gently simmer according the following guidelines:

PRESOAKED BEANS	REGULAR POT	PRESSURE COOKER
Adzuki beans	1 hour	10-12 minutes
Black beans	1½ hours	8-10 minutes
Black-eyed peas	30-40 minutes	4-6 minutes
Chick-peas	1½-2 hours	10-12 minutes
Fava beans	2-2½ hours	16-18 minutes
Great Northern	1 hour	10-12 minutes
Kidney beans	1-1½ hours	10-12 minutes
Lima beans	1-1½ hours	6-8 minutes
Mung beans	1 hour	10-12 minutes
Navy beans	1½ hours	6-8 minutes
Peas, whole	45 minutes	4-6 minutes
Pink beans	1 hour	10-12 minutes
Pinto beans	1½-2 hours	6-8 minutes
BEANS THAT DO NOT NEED PRESOAKING		
Black-eyed peas, fresh	25 minutes	4-6 minutes
Lentils	20-30 minutes	8 minutes
Peas, fresh	25 minutes	4-6 minutes
Split peas	30 minutes	15 minutes

The above cooking times are approximate. Some beans may be fresher than others and therefore take less time to cook. To tell if a bean is cooked properly, squeeze a cooled one between your thumb and forefinger. It should crush easily and there should be no hard, white core in the center.

To Quick-Soak Dried Beans

IN A LARGE SAUCEPAN, combine the dried beans, picked over and rinsed, with triple their volume of cold water. Bring the water to a boil and cook the beans, uncovered, over medium heat for 2 minutes. Remove the pan from the heat and let the beans soak for 1 hour. Proceed with the cooking as if they had been soaked overnight.

CREAMY AND CRUNCHY SALAD

SERVES 4

I LOVE DEEP RED KIDNEY BEANS—not just for their color but also for the way their skin resists, for just a moment, being bitten through. Then the beans give up their creamy center. At lunchtime one day, I opened a can of kidney beans, whisked chili sauce into some nonfat mayonnaise, quickly chopped some celery, sweet pickles, green olives and a touch of onion and combined them all in a bowl. After a quick stir, my lunch was ready.

¼	cup nonfat mayonnaise
3	tablespoons chili sauce
2	cups cooked kidney beans (or a 15-ounce can no-salt-added kidney beans, drained)
½	cup chopped celery
⅓	cup chopped sweet pickles (sweet gherkins or bread-and-butter)
⅓	cup sliced pimiento-stuffed green olives
2	tablespoons chopped onion

1. In a small bowl, whisk together the mayonnaise and chili sauce until combined. Set aside.

2. Put the kidney beans, celery, pickles, olives and onion in a medium glass bowl. Add the reserved mayonnaise dressing and, with a rubber spatula, stir and fold until the vegetables are completely coated with the dressing. Cover and refrigerate for 1 hour. Taste and adjust the seasonings and serve.

NUTRITIONAL INFORMATION PER SERVING: 170 CALORIES, 1.6 G FAT, 8.3 G PROTEIN, 32 G CARBOHYDRATE, 0 CHOLESTEROL, 644 MG SODIUM.

LeanTip: This is wonderful piled up on some Bibb lettuce leaves or stuffed in a fresh, ripe tomato.

Bacon, Baby Lima and White Corn Salad

SERVES 8

THE BEGINNING OF THIS SALAD is Southern in origin. I first tried it with fresh lima beans and corn. But those are not available year-round, so I make it with frozen when I can't get fresh.

1	pound frozen baby lima beans
1	pound frozen white (shoepeg) corn (or yellow corn)
8	ounces bacon, thickly sliced
¾	cup nonfat mayonnaise
¼	cup white-wine vinegar
3	tablespoons chopped fresh dill, plus 8 small sprigs for garnish
½	teaspoon salt
½	teaspoon fresh-ground black pepper
1	bunch green onions (white and green parts), chopped
16	Bibb lettuce leaves, washed, spun dry and chilled

1. Place the oven rack in the highest position and preheat the oven to 425 degrees F.

2. Add the lima beans to a medium saucepan and cover with water to a depth of ½ inch. Bring the water to a boil over high heat. Reduce the heat to low and simmer for 15 minutes, or until the beans pierce easily with a knife point. Drain, rinse under cold water and chill.

3. Add the corn to a medium saucepan and cover with water to a depth of ½ inch. Bring to a boil over high heat. Reduce the heat to low and simmer for 1 minute, or until the corn is just cooked. Drain, rinse under cold water and chill.

4. Line a jelly-roll pan with foil and place a wire rack on the pan. Lay the bacon slices on the rack. Bake for 20 minutes, turning once after 10 minutes, until the bacon is brown and crisp. Remove from the oven and

drain on paper towels. Discard any accumulated fat in the bottom of the pan. Trim the bacon of all fat and crumble the remaining lean parts. Set aside.

5. In a large mixing bowl, whisk together the mayonnaise, vinegar, chopped dill, salt and pepper. Add the bacon, lima beans, corn and green onions. With a rubber spatula, stir and fold the ingredients until they are well coated with the dressing. Cover and chill for at least 3 to 4 hours to allow the flavors to blend. Serve on chilled lettuce leaves, garnished with a sprig of fresh dill.

NUTRITIONAL INFORMATION PER SERVING: 160 CALORIES, 1.5 G FAT, 7.8 PROTEIN, 31 G CARBOHYDRATE, 3.4 MG CHOLESTEROL, 537 MG SODIUM.

Kidney Bean, Corn and Tomato Salad

SERVES 6

THE FRESH CORN IN THIS SALAD makes it special. If you can get the super-sweet corn now available widely, use it. At one time, the dressing for this salad had 4 tablespoons of olive oil, which contributed over 50 grams of fat. I gave 3 of those tablespoons the boot and replaced them with chicken broth thickened with some arrowroot. I left in the remaining tablespoon, since the salad just wasn't the same without it.

3	tablespoons defatted low-sodium chicken broth
¾	teaspoon arrowroot
6	tablespoons fresh-squeezed lemon juice
1	tablespoon extra-virgin olive oil
½	teaspoon salt
¼	teaspoon fresh-ground black pepper
⅛	teaspoon cayenne pepper
4	cups cooked kidney beans (or two 15-ounce cans no-salt-added red kidney beans, drained)
2	cups fresh corn kernels, cooked and cooled (about 3 ears; frozen may be substituted)
2	plum tomatoes, seeded and chopped
2	green onions (white and green parts), minced
4	tablespoons minced fresh parsley, plus sprigs for garnish
12	Bibb lettuce leaves, rinsed, spun dry and chilled

1. Place the broth and arrowroot in a small saucepan and place the pan over medium-high heat. While stirring, bring the broth to a boil. Boil for 30 seconds, or until it has thickened slightly. Remove from the heat and cool.

2. In a medium bowl, whisk together the lemon juice, oil, thickened chicken broth, salt, pepper and cayenne.

3. With a rubber spatula, stir and fold in the kidney beans, corn, tomatoes, green onions and minced parsley. Let the salad stand, stirring twice, for at least 15 minutes to allow flavors to blend.

4. Line 6 salad plates with the lettuce leaves and divide the salad among them. Garnish with parsley sprigs.

NUTRITIONAL INFORMATION PER SERVING: 190 CALORIES, 3.3 G FAT, 8.6 G PROTEIN, 16.6 G CARBOHYDRATE, 0 CHOLESTEROL, 196 MG SODIUM.

WHITE BEAN SALAD

SERVES 6

ORIGINALLY, THIS DELICIOUS SUMMER SALAD contained 3 tablespoons of high-fat mayonnaise, which supplied 33 grams of fat. The debut of nonfat mayonnaise salad dressing returned many of my favorite salads to my table, including this one. Fresh rosemary, good-quality red-wine vinegar and sweet, ripe cherry tomatoes make this bean salad sparkle. I have a plastic slicer that makes short work of julienne slicing. If you don't have one, just cut the zucchini into small dice.

DRESSING

3   tablespoons nonfat whipped salad dressing,
      such as Kraft Miracle Whip

6   tablespoons red-wine vinegar

4   garlic cloves, minced

1   tablespoon minced fresh rosemary*
      (or 1 teaspoon crumbled dried)

½   teaspoon salt

½   teaspoon fresh-ground white pepper

SALAD

4   cups cooked navy or other white beans
      (or two 15-ounce cans navy or other white beans, drained)

6   medium zucchini, washed, trimmed and cut into julienne strips

1   pint basket cherry tomatoes, washed, stemmed and halved

1   cup chopped red onion

1   head Bibb or Boston lettuce, washed, spun dry and chilled

1. **Dressing:** In a large glass or ceramic bowl, whisk together all the dressing ingredients until well combined.

2. **Salad:** Add the beans, zucchini, cherry tomatoes and onion to the bowl. With a rubber spatula, gently stir and fold until the salad is coated with the dressing.

3. Place 2 leaves of lettuce on each of 6 plates. Divide the salad evenly among the plates and serve.

NUTRITIONAL INFORMATION PER SERVING: 200 CALORIES, 0.9 G FAT, 11.5 G PROTEIN, 38 G CARBOHYDRATE, 0 CHOLESTEROL, 736 MG SODIUM.

LeanTip: Since I love garlic, this salad has a lot. If you don't appreciate the flavor as much as I do, cut it way back. Or, if you are taking this for lunch and no one else is having any, omit it or use a dash of garlic powder.

LeanSuggestion: This salad is a perfect accompaniment to Mustard-Coated Roast Pork Tenderloin (page 167).

Fresh rosemary is now found in most supermarket produce sections.

Luscious Black Bean Soup

SERVES 6

THIS SOUP IS CREAMY, yet it has no cream. A woman who tried it after seeing it in my column came up to me and said that she and I must be on the same wavelength. She said she had prepared this soup the previous evening and said, "Luscious may be an understatement."

The olive oil used to sauté the onions and sweet peppers adds such a wonderful flavor that my soup would not be the same if it were omitted. Since 2 teaspoons of olive oil contain only 9 fat grams, the taste is worth it.

2	teaspoons extra-virgin olive oil
2	cups chopped onions
1	large green bell pepper, chopped
1	large red bell pepper, chopped
½	cup coarsely chopped fresh cilantro
1	teaspoon dried oregano
1	bay leaf
1	cup defatted low-sodium chicken broth, preferably homemade
1	teaspoon salt (omit if beans are salted)
4½	cups cooked black beans, plus 1½ cups cooking liquid
	(or three 15-ounce cans no-salt-added black beans,
	including the liquid)
¼	cup cider vinegar
1	teaspoon clover honey

1. Add the oil to a large saucepan and place over medium heat. When the oil is hot, add the onions and peppers. Cook, stirring, for 4 to 5 minutes, until the onion is softened but not browned. Add the cilantro, oregano and bay leaf and sauté for 1 minute. Add the chicken broth and salt, if using; bring to a simmer.

   2. Add the black beans with their liquid, turn the heat to low, cover and simmer for 5 minutes, or until heated through. Remove from the heat, stir in the vinegar and honey and serve.

NUTRITIONAL INFORMATION PER SERVING: 277 CALORIES, 2.6 G FAT, 16 G PROTEIN, 49.7 G CARBOHYDRATE, TRACE CHOLESTEROL, 611 MG SODIUM.

LeanTip: A dollop of nonfat sour cream sprinkled with some snipped chives is a tasty, guiltless addition.

Pasta e Fagioli

(MACARONI AND BEANS)

SERVES 8

THIS IS A LEAN VERSION of a terrific and tasty soup. I had often enjoyed it at the beginning of meals in Italian restaurants. There can be quite a bit of hidden fat (olive oil and beef fat) in the restaurant version, but there is very little here.

When it comes to tasty fat-free carbos, this delicious, easy-to-prepare soup fills the bill.

1	teaspoon extra-virgin olive oil
4	garlic cloves, minced
4	cups defatted low-sodium beef broth, preferably homemade
1	16-ounce can diced tomatoes
1½	tablespoons chopped fresh basil
2	teaspoons salt
¼	teaspoon fresh-ground black pepper
¼	teaspoon fresh-ground white pepper
1	pound dried macaroni
2	16-ounce cans white kidney beans
2	tablespoons minced fresh parsley

1. Add the oil to a large nonstick saucepan. Over medium heat, sauté the garlic until soft but not browned, about 2 minutes. Add the beef broth, tomatoes, basil, salt, black pepper and white pepper and bring to a simmer.

2. Add the macaroni and return to a simmer, cooking for 7 to 10 minutes, or until tender. Add the white kidney beans and simmer until just heated through. Serve with parsley sprinkled on top.

NUTRITIONAL INFORMATION PER SERVING: 253 CALORIES, 2.1 G FAT, 12 G PROTEIN, 52.7 G CARBOHYDRATE, 0 CHOLESTEROL, 745 MG SODIUM.

LeanTip: Sprinkle a little freshly grated imported Parmesan cheese over the top. You'll get the flavor and keep the fat to a minimum.

LeanSuggestion: If you can't find white kidney beans, substitute Great Northern or navy beans.

LENTIL AND TOMATO STEW

SERVES 6

MY BROTHER THE CHEF sent me this recipe via fax. He wrote, "This is terrific." Right he was. This always seems like too much onion until it has finished cooking, then it's perfect.

1	tablespoon extra-virgin olive oil
2	large onions, chopped
2	large carrots, chopped
½	teaspoon crumbled dried thyme
½	teaspoon crumbled dried marjoram
3	cups defatted low-sodium chicken or vegetable broth
1	cup lentils
	Salt to taste (optional)
¼	cup chopped fresh parsley
1	16-ounce can diced tomatoes
¼	cup dry sherry (not cooking sherry)
1½	cups shredded nonfat Swiss cheese

1. Add the oil to a large nonstick saucepan and place over medium heat. When the oil is hot but not smoking, add the onions and carrots and cook, stirring, for 5 to 6 minutes, or until the onions are soft but not browned. Add the thyme and marjoram and cook for 1 minute more, or until fragrant.

2. Add the broth, lentils, salt, parsley and tomatoes. Cook, covered, until the lentils are tender, about 30 minutes.

3. Just before serving, stir in the sherry. Top each serving with ¼ cup of the Swiss cheese.

NUTRITIONAL INFORMATION PER SERVING (WITHOUT SALT): 278 CALORIES, 2.6 G FAT, 19 G PROTEIN, 40 G CARBO-HYDRATE, 0 CHOLESTEROL, 761 MG SODIUM.

GREAT GREAT NORTHERN BEANS WITH TOMATOES

SERVES 6

I KNOW IT LOOKS LIKE I STUTTERED when I named this recipe, but it *is* great, and I didn't want to be shy about it. I love the flavor of sage, which really shines in this dish. The prosciutto adds just the right spicy, smoky flavor. If you cannot locate any, substitute any lean smoked ham.

1   tablespoon extra-virgin olive oil
1   leek (white part only), rinsed well and chopped
4   ounces prosciutto, trimmed of all visible fat and chopped
2   teaspoons crumbled dried sage
1   28-ounce can Italian plum tomatoes, drained and chopped
4   cups cooked Great Northern beans, from about 1½ cups dried
        plus 1½ cups cooking liquid (or two 15-ounce cans
        low-sodium Great Northern beans, liquid included)
1   tablespoon balsamic vinegar
½   teaspoon fresh-ground black pepper

1. Heat the oil in a large saucepan over medium heat. When it is hot, add the leek and cook until slightly softened, stirring. Add the prosciutto and sage and cook for 1 minute.

2. Add the tomatoes and the beans with their liquid, and bring to a boil. Reduce the heat to low and simmer for 20 minutes.

3. Remove from the heat and stir in the vinegar and pepper. Serve immediately.

NUTRITIONAL INFORMATION PER SERVING: 270 CALORIES, 3.9 G FAT, 18.2 G PROTEIN, 43 G CARBOHYDRATE, 9 MG CHOLESTEROL, 726 MG SODIUM.

Tricolor Bean Stew

SERVES 8

SHALLOTS ADD JUST THE RIGHT TOUCH to this stew. Each of the beans contributes a completely different texture. Cooked garbanzo beans have starchy centers, navy beans almost melt in your mouth, and kidney beans have resistant skin and soft insides. This stew is not nearly as good without fresh herbs. Use a strong, newly purchased hot curry powder.

1	tablespoon extra-virgin olive oil
2	large garlic cloves, minced
2	teaspoons shallots, minced
2	celery stalks, finely diced
1	medium carrot, finely diced
¾	cup finely chopped onion
1	medium vine-ripened tomato, peeled, seeded and finely diced
2	teaspoons hot curry powder
1	teaspoon ground cumin
1	15-ounce can garbanzo beans (chick-peas), drained
1	15-ounce can kidney beans, drained
1	15-ounce can navy beans, drained
1	cup vegetable broth,* preferably homemade
1	tablespoon arrowroot, whisked into 2 tablespoons vegetable broth
1	teaspoon fresh-ground black pepper
1	tablespoon minced fresh parsley
1	tablespoon minced fresh cilantro
1	tablespoon minced fresh mint

1. In a large saucepan, heat the oil over medium heat until hot. Add the garlic, shallots, celery, carrot and onion. Sauté until the onion is light golden, 6 to 7 minutes.

2. Add the tomato and sauté for 30 seconds. Add the curry powder and cumin and sauté for 2 minutes more, or until very fragrant.

3. Add the beans and vegetable broth, cover, reduce the heat to low and simmer gently for 20 minutes, or until the onion is translucent.

4. Stirring gently, add the arrowroot mixture, pepper, parsley, cilantro and mint. When the stew is slightly thickened, about 1 minute, remove it from the heat and serve.

NUTRITIONAL INFORMATION PER SERVING: 224 CALORIES, 2.9 G FAT, 14 G PROTEIN, 40 G CARBOHYDRATE, 0 CHO-LESTEROL, 562 MG SODIUM.

Canned vegetable broth can be found in supermarkets and is usually located with the canned chicken and beef broths.

Casseroles

I PREPARE MY CASSEROLES ON SUNDAY because that's when I have the most time available. On some Sundays, I start a pot of soup broth simmering in the morning and then in the late afternoon, assemble a casserole. That evening we have part of the casserole for dinner, and the remainder lands in the refrigerator for future lean meals.

After dinner, I bottle up the newly made broth and park it in the refrigerator, too. At that point, I have many meals for the following week under control. Some of the broth will end up as a soup-based dinner. The casserole will reappear at the most needed moment for a quick dinner.

Casseroles are substance food for me, particularly during the winter. Most traditional casseroles, however, come with a load of fat. Take a look in your recipe box for one of your favorite covered dishes. Pull it out and scan the ingredient list. I'll bet you spot the high-fat elements immediately. Luckily, most of them can be lightened or removed by using several easy techniques. For example, if your recipe requires a cream-based sauce and a cream-based soup, substitute a fat-reduced soup. Campbell's Healthy Request soups have reduced fat, low sodium and no MSG.

When I have time, I make my own soup. In a nonstick saucepan, I sauté a pound of sliced mushrooms (sliced in a food processor, for speed) in a small amount of olive oil. I add defatted chicken broth and skim milk, to which I have added cornstarch or arrowroot. I season my soup with some salt, fresh-ground pepper, nutmeg and a touch of sherry. The result is a better-tasting, lower-fat cream of mushroom soup than any commercial company can make. I use this soup as the basis for a casserole.

When your casserole recipe calls for a whole chicken, substitute 2 whole chicken breasts. You'll need to skin the chicken breasts, since that's where their fat resides. If a recipe calls for sautéing onions, green peppers or garlic in ¼ cup of oil, reduce the oil to 1 teaspoon and use a nonstick pan. You will not only have cut the fat by 50 grams but reduced the total calories by 450.

What if your casserole sauce is thickened with butter and flour? Simply substitute a tablespoon of cornstarch or arrowroot for the flour called for. You'll have to whisk it into some cool liquid, but your sauce will thicken just as nicely, and for every tablespoon of butter not used, you'll save over 11 grams of fat and 100 calories.

Many casserole recipes often require ¾ pound of regular cheese. Switch to nonfat, and for every ounce save 9 fat grams and 80 calories. Not crazy about nonfat cheese? Okay, substitute fat-reduced cheese and save an average of 4 fat grams per ounce and 36 calories. My palate cannot tell the difference between a reduced-fat cheese and a full-fat one when it's used in a casserole.

Does your casserole use sour cream? Today, there are at least four major brands of nonfat sour cream on the market. Most are great and work even better than high-fat sour cream because they don't curdle if the liquid to which they are added comes to the boil. By switching from high-fat to nonfat, you save almost 50 grams of fat and cut almost 250 calories for every cup.

Of the following recipes, only two border on 10 fat grams per serving. The remaining eight have 6 fat grams or fewer, with a couple having fewer than 3 fat grams.

RECIPES

South-of-the-Border Casserole

SERVES 6

DURING THE BLUSTERY WINTER MONTHS I spent in northern Illinois, I loved making real stick-to-your-ribs meals. My wife created this skillet pasta casserole featuring penne in a sweet and spicy sour-cream-based sauce. Because the pasta goes in uncooked, it absorbs all the flavors.

1	pound 95% lean ground beef
¾	cup diced onion
¾	cup diced green bell pepper
2	fresh jalapeño peppers, seeded and minced
1	28-ounce can whole tomatoes
2	cups nonfat sour cream
1	tablespoon clover honey
1	tablespoon chili powder
½	teaspoon salt
8	ounces uncooked penne or macaroni

1. Lightly spray a large nonstick skillet with vegetable oil. Add the beef and cook over medium-high heat, breaking it up with the edge of a spatula, until it has lost its pink color, about 5 minutes. Drain any fat from the pan. Add the onion and green pepper, cooking until softened, about 5 minutes more.

2. Stir in the jalapeño peppers, tomatoes, sour cream, honey, chili powder and salt.

3. Add the pasta, stir, cover and simmer until the pasta is tender, about 25 minutes. Stir every 5 minutes, to keep the pasta from sticking to the skillet bottom. Serve hot.

NUTRITIONAL INFORMATION PER SERVING: 373 CALORIES, 4.8 G FAT, 24.8 G PROTEIN, 42 G CARBOHYDRATE, 52 MG CHOLESTEROL, 845 MG SODIUM.

LEAN AND LAYERED SPAGHETTI CASSEROLE

SERVES 8

LONG BEFORE MY WIFE AND I lost more than 175 pounds together, she made a much higher-fat version of this casserole for dinner. Susan used regular ground beef (184 fat grams), full-fat cottage cheese (10 fat grams), sour cream (24 fat grams) and cream cheese (80 fat grams). Grand fat total: 298 grams. Zounds!

By simply switching to 95 percent lean ground beef, I removed 150 fat grams—over half of it. By using 1 percent cottage cheese, nonfat sour cream and nonfat cream cheese, I took out another 106 fat grams. The flavor, though, remains beefy.

12	ounces spaghetti
1½	pounds 95% lean ground beef
½	teaspoon fresh-ground black pepper
1	28-ounce can tomato sauce
1	6-ounce can tomato paste
1	cup small-curd 1% cottage cheese
¼	cup nonfat sour cream
1	8-ounce package nonfat cream cheese, at room temperature
⅓	cup chopped green onions, (white parts only)
2	tablespoons minced green bell pepper

1. Bring a large pot of salted water to a rolling boil. While stirring, add the spaghetti. Continue stirring until the water returns to a boil. Cook for 10 minutes, or until the spaghetti gives gentle resistance to the bite. Drain.

2. Meanwhile, sauté the ground beef with the pepper in a large nonstick skillet over medium heat, breaking up the meat with a spatula edge, until it loses its pink color. Drain off any fat. Return the skillet to the heat and add the tomato sauce and tomato paste. Stir until the paste has dissolved and is evenly distributed. Remove from the heat and set aside.

3. Preheat the oven to 350 degrees F.

4. In a large bowl, mix the cottage cheese, sour cream and cream cheese with an electric mixer set on medium speed until well combined. (The mixture won't be smooth.) By hand, stir in the green onions and green pepper.

5. Lightly spray the bottom and sides of a medium casserole dish with vegetable oil. Put half of the cooked spaghetti evenly in the bottom. Spread the cheese mixture evenly over the spaghetti. Add the remaining spaghetti over the cheese mixture. Pour the meat sauce over the spaghetti. Bake, covered, for 35 minutes. Uncover and bake for 10 minutes more, or until the sauce loses its sheen and looks dull.

NUTRITIONAL INFORMATION PER SERVING: 377 CALORIES, 5.7 G FAT, 33.5 G PROTEIN, 45.3 G CARBOHYDRATE, 53 MG CHOLESTEROL, 1,141 MG SODIUM.

MACARONI PIE

SERVES 4

AFTER I MOVED TO NORTH CAROLINA, I discovered a terrific Southern dish called macaroni pie, a casserole perfect for what Southerners called "covered dish dinners." Up North, these occasions are known as potluck suppers. But whatever they are called, they are great fun, and the feeling of community and good food abounds.

At its foundation, this is macaroni and cheese, and who doesn't like that? Further investigation revealed that this casserole originally had eggs, butter, whole milk and full-fat cheese. It should have been called "Macaroni Floating in Fat Pie."

I tossed out the eggs and replaced them with nonfat egg substitute. I gave the heave-ho to the butter and whole milk and exchanged a larger amount of 1 percent milk and some Butter Buds. Finally, I zapped the whole-milk cheese and used reduced-fat Cheddar. The end result is richly flavored and low in fat.

1½	cups macaroni
½	cup nonfat egg substitute, such as Egg Beaters
2	teaspoons all-purpose flour
½	teaspoon salt*
4	teaspoons Butter Buds, mixed with ¼ cup hot water
1	cup 1% milk
1½	cups shredded reduced-fat Cheddar cheese
	Fresh-ground black pepper
	Sweet paprika

1. Bring a pot of salted water to a rolling boil. While stirring, add the macaroni. Continue stirring until the water returns to a boil. Cook for 8 minutes, or until the macaroni is tender. Drain well. Set aside.

2. Preheat the oven to 325 degrees F. Lightly spray the bottom and sides of a medium casserole dish with vegetable oil. Set aside.

3. In a medium mixing bowl, whisk together the egg substitute, flour, salt, Butter Buds mixture and milk until combined. Stir in 1 cup of the Cheddar cheese and the cooked macaroni. Turn out into the casserole dish. Top with the remaining ½ cup cheese. Grind on the black pepper to taste and dust with the paprika.

4. Bake for 40 minutes, or until firm and lightly browned. Serve immediately.

NUTRITIONAL INFORMATION PER SERVING: 319 CALORIES, 9 G FAT, 22 G PROTEIN, 36 G CARBOHYDRATE, 32.5 MG CHOLESTEROL, 740 MG SODIUM.

LeanTip: The quantities can easily be doubled or tripled for large gatherings.

By omitting the salt, the sodium content will be reduced to 474 mg per serving.

GREEN BEAN CASSEROLE

SERVES 10

FROM THE TIME I was a child, the high-fat version of this casserole always made an appearance as part of Thanksgiving dinner. Originally, it had real Swiss cheese, which tasted wonderful and brought along 8 grams of fat with every ounce. The casserole was topped with sliced almonds—certainly tasty but very high in fat, too.

I went straight to nonfat Swiss cheese and saved almost 130 fat grams. Skim milk and nonfat sour cream stood in admirably for the whole milk and real sour cream—adios to another 100 plus fat grams. Corn flakes happily replaced the high-fat almonds (71 grams per cup).

The Mauer family has been preparing this casserole for the last five years as the replacement for the high-fat version, and I believe everyone has forgotten that the older one even existed.

2	pounds frozen French-cut green beans
2	tablespoons unsalted butter
¼	cup grated onion
2	tablespoons all-purpose flour
½	cup skim milk
16	ounces nonfat Swiss cheese, torn into strips or shredded
1	pint nonfat sour cream
2	teaspoons granulated sugar
½	teaspoon fresh-ground white pepper
3	cups corn flakes

1. Preheat the oven to 350 degrees F.

2. Immerse the frozen beans in a pot of boiling water. When the water returns to a boil, remove the pot from the heat, pour off the water and add cold tap water to stop the cooking. Drain well and set aside.

3. Add the butter to a large nonstick saucepan and place over medium heat. Add the onion to the pan and sauté for 2 minutes, until softened. Add the flour, stir and cook for 2 minutes. Whisk in the skim milk and the Swiss cheese. When the cheese melts, add the sour cream, sugar and pepper; stir until smooth. Remove from the heat. Add the green beans. Stir and fold until coated.

4. Lightly spray the bottom and sides of a large glass casserole dish with vegetable oil. Spread the bean mixture evenly in the casserole and distribute the corn flakes evenly over the top.

5. Bake for 30 to 35 minutes, or until the casserole bubbles and the corn flakes are browned slightly. Serve immediately.

NUTRITIONAL INFORMATION PER SERVING: 204 CALORIES, 2.7 G FAT, 14.6 G PROTEIN, 29 G CARBOHYDRATE, 12.8 MG CHOLESTEROL, 738 MG SODIUM.

Quick Turkey and Vegetables with Noodles

SERVES 6

WHEN I PUT TOGETHER A CASSEROLE, I do not want it to take long. Elaborate casseroles have their place, certainly, but not when I want a quick meal. This is a casserole I created for just such a purpose.

When Thanksgiving Day is history, this dish comes into being. Into it goes at least a pound of beautifully roasted turkey breast I have left over. Cutting the carrots in julienne strips adds a colorful and fancy look. I chop the mushrooms and celery in my food processor. The whole thing is bound together with a creamy chicken-flavored, sherry-enriched sauce.

Any leftover casserole can be chilled for another meal. If I am really in a hurry, a serving of the chilled casserole, popped in the microwave, is ready in 6 minutes flat.

12   ounces medium noodles made without egg yolks
1   teaspoon canola oil
1   pound white button mushrooms, cleaned and coarsely chopped
2   celery stalks, chopped
1   large carrot, peeled and cut into julienne strips
¼   cup arrowroot
3   cups defatted low-sodium chicken broth, preferably homemade
1   pound cooked all-white-meat turkey, cut into ½-inch cubes
1   cup skim milk
1   tablespoon dry sherry
1   teaspoon celery salt
½   teaspoon fresh-ground black pepper
2   tablespoons chopped fresh parsley

1. Cook the noodles according to their package directions, about 8 minutes. Drain, rinse and set aside.

2. While the noodles are cooking, heat the oil in a large nonstick saucepan over medium-high heat. When hot, add the mushrooms and stir until they begin to give up their liquid and soften, about 4 minutes. Add the celery and carrot; stir and cook for 2 minutes, or until the celery turns bright green.

3. In a medium bowl, whisk the arrowroot into the chicken broth. Add the broth mixture, turkey, milk, sherry, celery salt and pepper to the saucepan with the mushrooms. Bring to a simmer, reduce the heat to low and simmer for 5 minutes, stirring occasionally, until the turkey is heated and the celery and carrot are cooked. Add the prepared noodles and stir to combine. Garnish each serving with some of the fresh parsley.

NUTRITIONAL INFORMATION PER SERVING: 414 CALORIES, 4.6 G FAT, 34 G PROTEIN, 55 G CARBOHYDRATE, 118 MG CHOLESTEROL, 400 MG SODIUM.

New-Fashioned Macaroni and Cheese with Ham

SERVES 8

The Daily Herald, where my column runs, ran a picture and recipe for Old-Fashioned Macaroni and Cheese with Ham. It was virtually an ocean of fat. First, 7 ounces of macaroni. No problem so far. Then one pound of cooked ham. Uh-oh. Next problem, one pound of Cheddar cheese. Final ingredient: evaporated milk.

I whipped out my nutritional analysis book and started calculating. The total fat content of the original casserole was 224 grams. Turn those 224 grams into liquid oil and pour it into a measuring cup, and the fat would exceed 1 cup by almost a tablespoon.

I made this nightmare into a dream by more than doubling the pasta. I reduced the ham by half. Next, I substituted reduced-fat cheese for the high-fat stuff and cut back the quantity of that to three-quarters. Finally, I used evaporated skim milk: it tastes virtually identical to regular evaporated milk but is fat-free.

I never missed a single one of the 11 tablespoons of fat I removed.

- 1   pound elbow macaroni
- ½   pound leanest possible cooked ham, diced
- 12   ounces fat-reduced Cheddar cheese, shredded
- 1   12-ounce can evaporated skim milk
       Sweet paprika

1. Bring a pot of salted water to a rolling boil. While stirring, add the macaroni. Continue stirring until the water returns to a boil. Cook for 8 minutes, or until the macaroni is tender. Drain well. Set aside.

2. Preheat the oven to 375 degrees F.

3. Lightly spray the bottom and sides of a 13-by-9-inch glass baking dish with vegetable oil. Set aside.

4. In a large bowl, mix the macaroni, ham and cheese until well blended. Spoon the macaroni mixture into the baking dish. Evenly pour the evaporated milk over the macaroni mixture. Dust the top with the paprika to taste.

5. Bake for 55 minutes, or until the top is crispy brown and bubbling. Let stand for 5 minutes before serving.

NUTRITIONAL INFORMATION PER SERVING: 404 CALORIES, 9.9 G FAT, 29 G PROTEIN, 48 G CARBOHYDRATE, 15 MG CHOLESTEROL, 750 MG SODIUM.

Speedy Scallop Casserole

SERVES 4

Not only do scallops have superb flavor and texture, but they are about the leanest thing to come from the ocean. Good-quality scallops are certainly not cheap. But they cook at the speed of light. I used to make this dish with white wine. However, one evening I was all set to put this casserole together and discovered I was completely out of the wine. I didn't have any white vermouth and didn't have time to go to the store. So, I decided to use red wine from an already opened bottle. It became the standard ingredient, and a new casserole was created.

1	tablespoon extra-virgin olive oil
1	pound sea scallops, small muscles removed, rinsed, patted dry and cut in half
2	medium onions, chopped
1	medium green bell pepper, seeded and chopped
½	cup chopped celery
½	pound white button mushrooms, cleaned and sliced
1	28-ounce can crushed plum tomatoes
¼	teaspoon crumbled dried oregano
¼	teaspoon crumbled dried basil
¼	teaspoon fresh-ground black pepper
¼	cup dry red wine
4	cups cooked white rice (1¼ cups uncooked)

1. Heat the oil in a large nonstick skillet over medium heat until hot. Add the scallops and sauté for 4 minutes, or until they are opaque. Transfer the scallops to a warm plate and set aside.

2. Preheat the oven to 350 degrees F.

3. Return the skillet to the heat and add the onions, green pepper, celery and mushrooms. Cook for 5 minutes, stirring occasionally, until softened.

4. Add the tomatoes, oregano, basil, pepper and wine. Bring to a boil, turn the heat to low and simmer, uncovered, for 15 minutes. Remove the skillet from the heat and gently stir in the scallops.

5. Spray a medium casserole with olive oil. Add the rice to the bottom of the casserole and spoon the scallop mixture over the rice. Bake, covered, for 20 minutes, or until bubbling and hot. Serve immediately.

NUTRITIONAL INFORMATION PER SERVING: 433 CALORIES, 5.3 G FAT, 27 G PROTEIN, 66 G CARBOHYDRATE, 38 MG CHOLESTEROL, 721 MG SODIUM.

Beefy Potato and Corn Casserole

SERVES 6

I T HAD BEEN AN UNUSUALLY COLD AND SNOWY DAY, and going to the supermarket was not on either my wife's or my "to do" list. As it began to get dark outside, Susan wanted something for dinner that would be easy to prepare, substantial and warming. She found some already cooked potatoes, nonfat Cheddar cheese, lean ground beef and a green pepper in the refrigerator. Our pantry provided onions, cream-style corn and a can of tomato paste. The freezer offered corn kernels. She created this layered and hearty casserole, which turned out wonderfully.

2	russet potatoes
2	teaspoons extra-virgin olive oil
2	medium onions, chopped
1	medium green bell pepper, chopped
1	pound 95% lean ground beef
½	teaspoon fresh-ground black pepper
1	6-ounce can tomato paste
1	16-ounce can cream-style corn
1	cup frozen corn kernels, defrosted
½	pound shredded nonfat sharp or Cheddar cheese

1. Place the unpeeled potatoes in a medium saucepan and cover with cold water to a depth of 1 inch. Over high heat, bring the water to a boil. Turn the heat to medium-low and simmer for 20 minutes, or until the potatoes pierce easily with a sharp knife. Drain, cool and slice ¾ inch thick.

2. Preheat the oven to 350 degrees F.

3. Heat the oil in a large nonstick skillet over medium-high heat. When it is hot, add the onions and sauté for 3 minutes, or until they wilt. Add the green pepper and sauté for 2 minutes, or until it begins to soften. Add the ground beef and black pepper and sauté until the beef loses its pink color, 4 to 5 minutes. Stir in the tomato paste and remove the skillet from the heat.

4. In a small bowl, stir together the cream-style corn and corn kernels. Set aside.

5. Lightly spray the bottom and sides of a large casserole dish with vegetable oil. Cover the bottom of the casserole with one-half of the sliced potatoes. Cover the potatoes with one-half of the ground-beef mixture. Spoon one-half of the corn mixture over the ground beef. Sprinkle half of the Cheddar cheese over all. Repeat the layers, ending with the cheese.

6. Cover and bake for 45 minutes, or until the cheese melts and the casserole is bubbling. Serve hot.

NUTRITIONAL INFORMATION PER SERVING: 351 CALORIES, 6.1 G FAT, 29 G PROTEIN, 48 G CARBOHYDRATE, 41 MG CHOLESTEROL, 856 MG SODIUM.

Vegetables

"EAT YOUR VEGETABLES." That phrase echoes through my mind. I was brought up in a family that did not allow me to leave the dinner table until I had finished what was on my plate. This was a problem because my Mom loved beets but I hated them. She served them regularly, and I would spend the remainder of the evening in my seat, staring down forlornly at my serving of cooked beets. My parents would pass through the dining room at regular intervals intoning, "Eat your vegetables." Once bedtime arrived, I was allowed to leave the table. Fortunately, there was no rule about saving the uneaten beets for the next meal. If that had been true, I would never have gotten out of the dining room.

Beets are, however, the only vegetable I don't eat. I love vegetables that many people turn up their noses at. For example, I love Brussels sprouts. I love to go to the farmer's market the first Saturday after the first frost in the fall to buy fresh Brussels sprouts. Brussels sprouts don't fully develop their exquisite flavor until they have gone through one frost. I rush my treasure trove of sprouts home and prepare them that night for dinner. I peel back the leaves of each sprout until I reach unblemished, beautifully green ones. Then I slice them in half through their stems and drop them in a small amount of boiling spring water. When they turn an even brighter green and resist a knife point only slightly when pierced, they are done. I drain them, drizzle on some prepared Butter Buds and grind on some fresh black pepper.

In the spring, I love to buy a bag or two of fresh-picked spinach leaves and ready them to be cooked. Julia Child, via my television, taught me how to hold a spinach leaf in my left hand while stripping the stem and its strings with my right, leaving a tender leaf. I then heat a large pot over medium heat. I rinse the spinach leaves well until no sand remains in their intricate folds and put them into the hot, dry pot. The water on the leaves is sufficient for cooking them. I use a chopstick to stir everything and turn the uncooked leaves to the bottom, where they cook instantly. Moments later, the enormous pile of leaves has cooked down to a half-inch layer. I squeeze out the water and serve with Butter Buds, a sprinkle of fresh-ground salt and black pepper.

In many ways, vegetables are at their best when left relatively unsullied by elaborate preparation. An acorn squash, split, seeds removed and baked in the oven, with Butter Buds and brown sugar in the hollowed-out center, is a delight. Spring peas, cooked briefly in boiling spring water, become sweet morsels.

These recipes are, for the most part, simple. A few are a touch more complex, but the effort expended will be well worth it.

RECIPES

CHICKEN-AND-SPINACH-STUFFED ACORN SQUASH

SERVES 4 AS A MAIN COURSE

THIS IS A MEAL IN ITSELF. I use frozen spinach to keep the preparation time to a minimum, but fresh spinach leaves, briefly cooked, make the dish even better. This contains almost everything I love: squash, spinach, chicken and Parmesan cheese. When it's brought to the table, it looks absolutely beautiful.

2	medium acorn squash
1	10-ounce package frozen chopped spinach, thawed, water squeezed out
¾	cup grated Parmesan cheese
4	large hard-cooked eggs, whites only, finely chopped
4	teaspoons Butter Buds, mixed with ¼ cup hot water
1	cup diced cooked skinless chicken breast meat
2	tablespoons chopped green onion, white parts only
¼	teaspoon cayenne pepper
¼	cup fresh bread crumbs

1. Preheat the oven to 350 degrees F.

2. Halve each squash. Scrape out the seeds and discard. Lightly spray the bottom of a large baking pan with vegetable oil and place the squash in it, cut side down. Cover and bake for 45 to 60 minutes, or until tender. Remove from the oven and let cool slightly until the squash can be handled.

3. Remove the squash pulp, leaving a ¼-inch shell. In a large mixing bowl, combine the squash pulp, spinach, ½ cup of the cheese, egg whites, Butter Buds, chicken, green onion and cayenne. Fill the squash shells with the squash mixture, mounding it attractively. Combine the remaining ¼ cup cheese and bread crumbs; sprinkle 2 tablespoons of the mixture on top of each squash.

4. Return the squash to the baking pan and bake for 25 to 30 minutes, or until heated through. Serve immediately.

NUTRITIONAL INFORMATION PER SERVING: 208 CALORIES, 5.1 G FAT, 20.5 G PROTEIN, 23.3 G CARBOHYDRATE, 29 MG CHOLESTEROL, 485 MG SODIUM.

CELERY WITH DILL AND SOUR CREAM

SERVES 6

INEVER HEARD OF ANYONE ELSE cooking celery as a dinner vegetable except for me. When it is sauced with dill, sour cream and honey, it is exquisite and can be readied quickly. Since this dish is almost fat-free, it makes a wonderful accompaniment to just about anything, but is great with chicken or fish.

- 1 bunch celery, separated, cleaned, strings removed,
     cut crosswise at a 45-degree angle into ½-inch slices
- 2 tablespoons nonfat sour cream
- 2 tablespoons finely chopped fresh dill
- 1 teaspoon clover honey

1. Add the sliced celery to a saucepan and cover with water. Place the pan over high heat and bring to a boil. Cover, lower the heat and simmer for 2 minutes. Drain the water and leave the celery in the pan.

2. While the celery is cooking, whisk together the sour cream, dill and honey in a small bowl until combined. Pour the sour-cream mixture over the celery and toss until coated. Serve immediately.

NUTRITIONAL INFORMATION PER SERVING: 21 CALORIES, 0.1 G FAT, 1.6 G PROTEIN, 3.5 G CARBOHYDRATE, 0.6 MG CHOLESTEROL, 66 MG SODIUM.

Broccoli with Black Olives

SERVES 4

THIS IS MY WIFE's favorite recipe for broccoli. Normally, we serve this with baked potatoes dressed with Butter Buds and nonfat sour cream as part of a meatless meal. While the potatoes are baking, this is quickly prepared on the stovetop.

1	bunch fresh broccoli (about 1½ pounds)
1	teaspoon extra-virgin olive oil
1-2	garlic cloves, finely chopped
½	teaspoon salt
¼	teaspoon fresh-ground black pepper
¼	cup chopped small pitted black olives
3	tablespoons fresh-grated Parmesan cheese

1. Trim the stem ends of the broccoli and cut off the stems to just beneath the florets. Peel the tough outer skin and cut the stems on the diagonal into 1½-inch sections. Separate the larger florets so they are approximately the same size as the stem pieces. Set aside.

2. Add 3 quarts of water to a large pot and bring to a boil over high heat. Add the broccoli and return to the boil. Lower the heat to medium-high and cook for 2 minutes, or just until the broccoli is crisp-tender. Drain the broccoli in a colander (reserve a little of the water) and refresh it under cold running water; drain.

3. In a large nonstick skillet, heat the oil over medium heat. When hot, add the garlic and sauté until it just starts to brown, about 30 seconds. Add the broccoli, salt and pepper. Reduce the heat to low, cover and cook for 6 minutes, adding some of the reserved water if the pan becomes too dry, shaking the pan from time to time. Add the olives and heat for an additional 2 minutes. Serve, sprinkled with the cheese.

NUTRITIONAL INFORMATION PER SERVING: 70 CALORIES, 3.5 G FAT, 4 G PROTEIN, 7 G CARBOHYDRATE, 3 MG CHOLESTEROL, 438 MG SODIUM.

CABBAGE WITH TOMATOES AND CORN

SERVES 6

I F I DON'T TURN a head of cabbage into a cabbage slaw, then I'll cook it up in this dish. It mixes the flavors and colors of cabbage, corn, tomatoes, celery and red pepper so beautifully that it's worth the slightly longer preparation time. This cooks quickly in a single skillet and is great served with broiled lean pork chops.

2	teaspoons extra-virgin olive oil
2	garlic cloves, finely chopped
3	cups shredded green cabbage
2	medium tomatoes, peeled and cut into cubes
1	medium onion, thinly sliced
1	cup thinly sliced celery
1	cup corn kernels
½	cup chopped red bell pepper
1	teaspoon sugar
1	teaspoon salt
1	teaspoon dried dill
¼	teaspoon fresh-ground black pepper

1. Heat the oil in a large nonstick skillet over medium heat. Add the garlic and cook for 30 seconds. Stir in the cabbage, tomatoes, onion, celery, corn and red pepper. Season with the sugar, salt, dill and pepper.

2. Cover and cook for 6 to 8 minutes, stirring occasionally, until the cabbage has wilted. Serve hot.

NUTRITIONAL INFORMATION PER SERVING: 70 CALORIES, 2 G FAT, 2.8 G PROTEIN, 12 G CARBOHYDRATE, 0 CHO-LESTEROL, 388 MG SODIUM.

Sweet and Sour Cabbage

SERVES 6

THE COMBINATION OF SWEET AND SOUR has always intrigued my palate. I am crazy for Asian sweet, sour and hot sauces, and I love cabbage in a sweet and sour soup. Wedges of cabbage, cooked until just tender but still light green, are incredible. One evening, while my cabbage wedges were simmering away, I devised a new sauce. I whisked honey instead of sugar into the vinegar. Then I stirred in a touch of onion, some celery seeds and fresh ginger.

1	small head green cabbage, cut into 6 wedges
3	tablespoons distilled white vinegar
1	tablespoon clover honey
1	teaspoon Butter Buds, mixed with 1 tablespoon hot water
1	teaspoon grated onion
½	teaspoon salt
¼	teaspoon celery seeds
¼	teaspoon grated fresh gingerroot

1. In a large skillet over medium-high heat, bring 1 inch of salted water to a boil. Add the cabbage wedges, cover and return to the boil. Reduce the heat to low and simmer until tender, 15 to 20 minutes. Remove the cabbage to a serving platter with a slotted spoon, draining any excess water.

2. Meanwhile, in a small saucepan, bring the vinegar, honey, Butter Buds, onion, salt, celery seeds and ginger to a boil, stirring occasionally. Remove the pan from the heat, pour the sauce over the cooked cabbage wedges and serve.

NUTRITIONAL INFORMATION PER SERVING: 43 CALORIES, 0.4 G FAT, 3.3 G PROTEIN, 10 G CARBOHYDRATE, 0 CHOLESTEROL, 210 MG SODIUM.

ROASTED ONIONS

SERVES 4

ROASTED VEGETABLES cook in their own juices, increasing in flavor. Onions roast particularly well because the heat releases their natural sugar. The combination of fresh herbs and sweet onions is unbeatable.

2 pounds sweet onions, such as Vidalia
2 tablespoons defatted low-sodium chicken broth
1 tablespoon balsamic vinegar
1 teaspoon extra-virgin olive oil
12 fresh sage leaves (or 1 teaspoon crumbled dried)
1 teaspoon salt
1 teaspoon coarse-ground black pepper
2 tablespoons finely chopped fresh parsley

1. Preheat the oven to 375 degrees F.

2. Peel the onions and slice into ½-inch rounds. In a large glass or ceramic mixing bowl, whisk together the chicken broth, vinegar, oil, sage, salt and pepper. Separate the sliced onions into rings and add to the bowl, stirring and tossing until coated.

3. Lightly spray the bottom and sides of a medium casserole dish with vegetable oil. Add the onions, cover and bake for 30 minutes, or until the onions collapse and the liquid simmers. Carefully uncover the casserole (steam will billow out), stir, cover and return to the oven for 15 minutes.

4. Remove from the oven, carefully uncover, stir again and return to the oven, uncovered, for 15 minutes more, or until the juices have reduced to a syrup and the onions are done. Serve, uncovered, in the casserole with the chopped parsley sprinkled over all.

NUTRITIONAL INFORMATION PER SERVING: 105 CALORIES, 1.2 G FAT, TRACE PROTEIN, 21 G CARBOHYDRATE, 0 CHOLESTEROL, 539 MG SODIUM.

FENNEL WITH MUSHROOMS AND ONIONS

SERVES 4

FENNEL, SOMETIMES MISTAKENLY CALLED ANISE, is certainly an odd-looking vegetable, resembling white, squat celery. The fronds, if left on, are frilly and lacy. For all its strange appearance, fennel tastes wonderful. It has a clean anise flavor, a crisp texture and is very low in calories. I like to serve it with a piece of broiled fish.

2   medium fennel bulbs
1   teaspoon extra-virgin olive oil
2   garlic cloves, minced
1   large red onion, thinly sliced
4   shallots, thinly sliced
12   ounces brown cremini mushrooms
      (or white button mushrooms), cleaned,
      trimmed and sliced ¼ inch thick
2   tablespoons balsamic vinegar
½   teaspoon salt
¼   teaspoon fresh-ground black pepper

1. Trim the fronds and green stems from the tops of the fennel bulbs. Remove the outer layer from the bulbs and discard. Trim the root ends. Slice the bulbs crosswise as thin as possible. Set aside.

2. Heat a large nonstick skillet over medium heat. When it is hot, add the oil. Add the garlic and sauté for about 30 seconds, without allowing the garlic to brown. Add the onion and shallots. Sauté for 2 to 3 minutes, until they begin to soften.

3. Add the mushrooms and sauté for 2 minutes.

4. Add the fennel and sauté for 2 minutes. Cover, reduce the heat to medium-low and cook for 4 minutes, or until the fennel pierces easily with a knife point. Uncover, and stirring, add the vinegar, salt and pepper. Cover and cook for 1 minute more. Serve immediately, drizzled with the pan liquid.

NUTRITIONAL INFORMATION PER SERVING: 90 CALORIES, 1.7 G FAT, 1.5 G PROTEIN, 16 G CARBOHYDRATE, 0 CHOLESTEROL, 400 MG SODIUM.

LeanNote: Fennel is great grilled over hot coals on a barbecue. Trim the leaves and the stems to about 1½ inches from the bulb. Then split the bulb crosswise into 2 pieces. Brush lightly with a little olive oil and grill for 5 to 6 minutes per side.

Zucchini and Mushrooms with Basil and Garlic

SERVES 4

THERE ARE SEVERAL TIMES during the year when small zucchini are available. I have never enjoyed anything prepared from those monstrously overgrown zucchinis that appear in local markets late in the growing season. What I prize are the small, young yellow summer squash or zucchini. They have a light, almost sweet flavor and are virtually seedless. When I discover these special squash, I cook them briefly with fresh mushrooms and season them with garlic and fresh basil.

2	garlic cloves, finely chopped
8	small zucchini (about 1 pound), cut into quarters lengthwise
½	pound white button mushrooms, cleaned and quartered
1	tablespoon chopped fresh basil (or 1 teaspoon dried)
½	teaspoon salt
½	teaspoon fresh-ground black pepper
2	tablespoons chopped fresh parsley

1. Spray a nonstick skillet with vegetable oil. Add the garlic and zucchini and sauté over medium-high heat, turning the zucchini once or twice, for 2 minutes.

2. Add the mushrooms and sauté for 1 minute more.

3. Stir in the basil and salt; cover the pan, reduce the heat and simmer for 2 minutes. Add the pepper and serve, topped with the parsley.

NUTRITIONAL INFORMATION PER SERVING: 31 CALORIES, 0.5 G FAT, 1.8 G PROTEIN, 6.1 G CARBOHYDRATE, 0 CHO-LESTEROL, 272 MG SODIUM.

DECADENT FAT-FREE WHIPPED POTATOES

SERVES 6

I USED TO MAKE TRULY DECADENT and decidedly unhealthy whipped potatoes. I used butter, high-fat sour cream, whipping cream and several egg yolks. I would often be invited to dinner and asked to prepare my whipped potatoes for everyone. They had a definite following.

After I lost weight, I went back to my lean kitchen and created these excellent potatoes. Butter Buds replaced the flavor lost when I took out the real butter. Skim milk replaced the cream, and nonfat sour cream supplanted its high-fat brother. I decided the egg yolks should remain just a memory. The potatoes are now light, creamy and rich-tasting. But they have less than ½ gram of fat per serving. Try them with one of my lean gravies over the top.

2½	pounds red potatoes, peeled (if large, cut into quarters)
¼	cup warm skim milk
2	teaspoons Butter Buds, mixed with 2 tablespoons hot water
2	tablespoons nonfat sour cream
½	teaspoon salt
¼	teaspoon fresh-ground black pepper
	Sweet paprika
1	tablespoon minced fresh parsley

1. Place the potatoes in a large pot. Add cold water to 1 inch above the potatoes. Place the pan over high heat and bring the water to a boil. Reduce the heat to medium and simmer for about 20 minutes. When the potatoes can be pierced easily with a fork, remove the pan from the stove and drain.

2. Place the drained potatoes in a large bowl. With an electric mixer on low speed, begin to break up the potatoes. As they break up, slowly raise the speed of the mixer to medium. Add the milk, Butter Buds, sour cream, salt and pepper and mix until smooth. Spoon the whipped potatoes into a warmed serving bowl and dust with the paprika and parsley.

NUTRITIONAL INFORMATION PER SERVING: 158 CALORIES, 0.3 G FAT, 5.5 G PROTEIN, 35 G CARBOHYDRATE, 0.8 MG CHOLESTEROL, 225 MG SODIUM.

LeanTip: Drizzle a couple tablespoons more liquid Butter Buds over the whipped potatoes before dusting with the paprika and parsley.

LeanSuggestion: Use Yukon Gold potatoes instead of red potatoes. They have a golden, buttery look.

Light and Tasty Scalloped Potatoes

SERVES 4

HOLIDAY DINNERS OF THE PAST always seemed to include scalloped potatoes. I loved them. But they had lots of butter and cream and sometimes cheese. Instead, I use homemade fat-free chicken broth to replace the butter and substitute 1 percent milk for the cream, since it has a slightly richer flavor than skim. Instead of using cheese, I let the taste of the potatoes shine through. Fresh-grated nutmeg adds a buttery note. Now I can enjoy this delicious holiday delight anytime I want.

1	large red onion
2	tablespoons water
3	russet (baking) potatoes (about 1¼ pounds)
1¼	cups 1% milk
¾	cup defatted low-sodium chicken broth, preferably homemade
1½	tablespoons all-purpose flour
½	teaspoon salt
¼	teaspoon fresh-ground black pepper
	Pinch grated nutmeg, preferably fresh-grated

1. Halve the onion lengthwise and cut crosswise into ¼-inch-thick slices. Put the onion slices and the water in a large nonstick saucepan and place over medium heat. Cook, covered, stirring occasionally, for 5 minutes, or until softened. Uncover and cook the onion until the liquid in the saucepan just evaporates. Remove the pan from the heat.

2. Place a rack in the lower third of the oven and preheat the oven to 425 degrees F.

3. Peel the potatoes and cut crosswise into ¼-inch-thick slices. In a small bowl, whisk together the milk, broth and flour until well combined. Add the milk mixture to the onion with the potatoes, salt, pepper and

nutmeg. Return the saucepan to the heat and bring to a simmer, stirring frequently. Simmer for 1 minute, or until the mixture slightly thickens.

4. Carefully pour the potato mixture into a shallow medium baking dish and bake for 45 minutes, or until the top is golden and the potatoes are tender when pierced with a knife. Serve hot.

NUTRITIONAL INFORMATION PER SERVING: 223 CALORIES, 1 G FAT, 6.8 G PROTEIN, 47 G CARBOHYDRATE, 3 MG CHOLESTEROL, 400 MG SODIUM.

LeanSuggestions

■ For a flavorful variation, reduce the amount of potatoes to ¾ pound and add 2 parsnips (about ½ pound), peeled and grated, with the potatoes to the saucepan. Proceed as directed.

■ Or for a colorful variation, reduce the amount of potatoes to ¾ pound and add ½ to ¾ pound peeled sweet potatoes cut crosswise into ¼-inch-thick slices. Add the sweet potatoes with the white potatoes to the saucepan. Proceed as directed.

Oven-Browned Potatoes

SERVES 6

I USED TO LOVE EATING French fries, especially those that came sailing across the counter in the restaurant with golden arches out front. But those landed on my "Nope, can't-have-it" list more than six years ago. However, I really get a hankering for dipping crisp potatoes into ketchup and firing them into my mouth.

I asked myself, "Where do the more than 21 grams of fat come from in a large order of French fries?" Certainly not from the potato. They come from the oil in a deep-fat fryer. I realized that I could create beautifully browned and relatively crisp potatoes by first tossing them in a touch of olive oil and then browning them in an oven as hot as a fryer. Now an equivalent serving of my potatoes has only 2.4 grams of fat, and they taste great dragged through ketchup.

1½	tablespoons extra-virgin olive oil
2	large garlic cloves, minced
1½	teaspoons crumbled dried oregano
1½	teaspoons crumbled dried rosemary
1	teaspoon salt
¼	teaspoon fresh-ground black pepper
10	medium red or white potatoes (about 2½ pounds)
	Sweet paprika

1. In a large mixing bowl, combine the oil, garlic, oregano, rosemary, salt and pepper. Stir to combine and set aside.

2. Preheat the oven to 425 degrees F, with a rack in the middle.

3. Scrub and quarter the potatoes. Pat dry the surfaces of the potatoes with a paper towel. Add the potatoes to the mixing bowl and, with a rubber spatula, stir and toss the potatoes to coat them with the oil mixture.

4. Line a jelly-roll pan with aluminum foil. Spread the potatoes evenly in the pan, cut sides up. Sprinkle the paprika on the potatoes to taste.

5. Bake until potatoes are browned, 40 to 45 minutes. Serve immediately.

NUTRITIONAL INFORMATION PER SERVING: 216 CALORIES, 3.6 G FAT, 4.2 G PROTEIN, 43 G CARBOHYDRATE, 0 CHOLESTEROL, 369 MG SODIUM.

LeanSuggestions

■ If you like a little more heat, as I do, add ¼ to ½ teaspoon hot red pepper flakes to the oil mixture, and continue as directed.

■ Another flavorful touch is to add 1 teaspoon hot curry powder to the oil mixture.

Sweet Potato Puddin'

SERVES 6

THIS IS AN ABSOLUTELY CLASSIC Southern dish. It is versatile and can be served as a vegetable course to accompany a ham, or for dessert. The first time I tasted sweet potato pudding, it was served for dessert. It was very rich, almost too rich for my palate, but it had a delightful pumpkin pie flavor. I couldn't wait to figure out a way to make this remain as rich but without all the fat. The first thing I did was trade 1 percent milk for whole milk, saving 11 fat grams. Nonfat egg substitute removed another 10 fat grams and all the cholesterol yet still gave this a custardlike texture. Using Butter Buds cut out a final 23 fat grams.

2	cups 1% milk
½	cup nonfat egg substitute, such as Egg Beaters
½	cup light brown sugar, or to taste
2	teaspoons Butter Buds, mixed with 2 tablespoons hot water
1	teaspoon ground allspice
1	teaspoon ground cinnamon
½	teaspoon fresh-grated nutmeg
1½	teaspoons grated fresh gingerroot
	Pinch salt (optional)
3	cups finely shredded peeled sweet potatoes

1. Preheat the oven to 325 degrees F. Lightly spray the bottom and sides of a medium casserole dish with vegetable oil. Set aside.

2. In a large mixing bowl, whisk together the milk, egg substitute, brown sugar, Butter Buds mixture, allspice, cinnamon, nutmeg, ginger and optional salt until thoroughly combined. Stir in the sweet potatoes.

3. Pour into the prepared casserole and bake for 1 hour, or until set. Serve warm.

NUTRITIONAL INFORMATION PER SERVING (WITHOUT SALT): 157 CALORIES, 1.1 G FAT, 5.3 G PROTEIN, 28 G CARBOHYDRATE, 3.3 MG CHOLESTEROL, 130 MG SODIUM.

LeanTip: If you are serving this for dessert, reduce the brown sugar to ¼ cup and serve it warm with a scoop of nonfat vanilla frozen yogurt.

Spiced Sweet Potatoes

SERVES 8

Is there anything more tasty than a bright orange sweet potato? Not for me. Sweet potatoes retain their sweetness best when baked like a regular potato. However, it is possible to take an excellent baked sweet potato and turn it into an even more flavorful dish. This one has almost no added fat but a terrific flavor.

Originally, this recipe had almost 50 grams of fat and 400 calories coming from butter. Through the useful magic of Butter Buds, it now has less than 1 gram of fat per serving. These sweet potatoes are absolutely stupendous with slices of lean roasted ham.

6	medium-size sweet potatoes, scrubbed and pierced in several places with a sharp knife
½	teaspoon ground cinnamon
½	teaspoon ground ginger
½	teaspoon fresh-grated nutmeg
½	teaspoon ground cloves
½	teaspoon salt
¼	cup Butter Buds, mixed with ¾ cup hot water
3	tablespoons clover honey

1. Preheat the oven to 425 degrees F.

2. Bake the sweet potatoes for 40 minutes. Cool until they can be handled easily. Peel them and cut into ½-inch-thick slices. Set aside.

3. Reduce the oven temperature to 375 degrees.

4. Lightly spray the bottom and sides of a deep medium baking dish with vegetable oil.

5. In a small bowl, stir together the cinnamon, ginger, nutmeg, cloves and salt.

6. Place one-third of the potatoes in the bottom of the baking dish. Drizzle ¼ cup of the Butter Buds mixture and 1 tablespoon of the honey on top and sprinkle with one-third of the spice mixture. Distribute another layer of potatoes on top of the first and top as before. Distribute the final layer of potatoes and top as before.

7. Bake, uncovered, for 20 minutes, or until heated through. Serve with some of the liquid from the casserole drizzled over the top.

NUTRITIONAL INFORMATION PER SERVING: 131 CALORIES, 0.5 G FAT, 1.5 G PROTEIN, 31 G CARBOHYDRATE, 0 CHOLESTEROL, 50 MG SODIUM.

Veggie Kebabs

SERVES 2

WHEN SUMMER ARRIVES and fresh corn, eggplant and sweet red peppers are spilling off the tables at my local farmer's market, this is what I make. I love cooking both the kebabs and chicken breasts out on the grill. I start them simultaneously, since they take about the same time to cook. The corn kernel tips will caramelize during the cooking, and that adds a wonderful flavor.

BASTING SAUCE

½	cup hot defatted low-sodium chicken broth
1	½-ounce packet Butter Buds
½	teaspoon salt
¼	teaspoon fresh-ground black pepper

KEBABS

2	ears fresh corn, shucked, silk removed, cut in half
6	large white button mushrooms, stems trimmed close to the cap, peeled
1	small eggplant, washed and cut crosswise into 4 pieces
1	medium red bell pepper, washed, stem and core removed, cut into 4 pieces

1. Prepare a charcoal or gas grill.

2. **Basting sauce:** In a small bowl, whisk together the chicken broth, Butter Buds, salt and pepper. Set aside.

3. Kebabs: On 12- or 16-inch metal shish kebab skewers, thread the vegetables in the following order: corn, mushroom, eggplant, red pepper, mushroom, eggplant, red pepper, mushroom, corn.

4. Grill the kebabs for 8 to 10 minutes over medium-hot coals, turning every 2 minutes, basting frequently with the sauce. Serve immediately.

NUTRITIONAL INFORMATION PER SERVING: **166** CALORIES, **1.5** G FAT, **4** G PROTEIN, **19** G CARBOHYDRATE, **0** CHOLESTEROL, **421** MG SODIUM.

LeanSuggestions

■ You can make the basting sauce with vegetable broth instead of chicken broth.

■ Prepare basmati or jasmine rice to serve alongside.

Quick Breads and Muffins

F OR LIFESTYLES THAT ARE MOVING FASTER EVERY DAY, quick breads are a god-
send. Most go together—just as their name suggests—quickly. Quick breads are
flavored with fresh or dried fruits or spices or both. They generally take an hour or less
to bake, in a loaf pan. Good ones are always moist, dense and keep very well. They
freeze well, too.

Many of my quick breads are terrific sliced and crowned with a scoop of nonfat frozen
yogurt. A slice can also be popped in a toaster oven and eaten for breakfast.

Quick breads of the past were always made in some high-fat way. A pound cake, which
is essentially a quick bread, was originally named because it had one pound of butter. It's
hard to imagine that it was okay to add 368 fat grams and almost 3,300 fat calories and

not be concerned. I used to smear a tablespoon or more of butter on my slice of pound cake. Gilding an already weighty lily, perhaps?

About three years ago, people attending my classes started asking me if I had ever used applesauce as a part or total substitute for the shortening in quick breads. At the time I had not. I asked if they had tried it. "Love it!" they responded.

I headed to my kitchen and started to experiment. The first thing I learned was to use the unsweetened kind. Many commercial applesauces contain high-fructose corn syrup, but since quick breads already have sugar, I didn't need the extra sweetening. I always use "natural" or unsweetened applesauce.

I began my tests by substituting half the shortening with applesauce. I could not tell the difference in flavor or texture. This meant that in a single recipe, I was often cutting out almost 800 calories and nearly 100 fat grams.

I started thinking about applesauce and realized that apple juice is a component of applesauce. The other component is apple fiber. I continued to ponder. A baking quick bread is subjected to high heat. What happens to water under high heat? It turns to steam, rises and escapes. Therefore, the water in the apple juice was leaving the bread and, in fact, causing a slightly drier end result. Because the fat in shortening does not turn to steam when subjected to high temperatures, it remains in the bread, keeping it moist.

Back to my lean kitchen. If I didn't want my quick bread to dry out during baking, I'd have to keep as much moisture inside as possible. I got out a bowl and a mesh strainer, added a couple cups of applesauce to the strainer and let it sit while I went about preparing all the ingredients for my next quick bread. From prior baking experiments, I had learned to whisk all the wet ingredients together with the sugar, just as butter is creamed together with sugar in most recipes.

When I measured the cup of applesauce that I was about to substitute for the cup of butter, I was amazed to find almost ½ cup of the liquid in the bottom of the bowl. I scooped up the applesauce remaining in the strainer and proceeded with my recipe. When the bread was done, I cut a slice. It was moist, had a beautiful texture and wasn't rubbery at all.

Eureka! When I did the math, it was astounding. My cup of drained applesauce eliminated not only 184 fat grams but over 1,400 fat calories.

I have shared my applesauce exchange in several columns and on television and radio shows. It works perfectly every time. Take one of your favorite quick bread recipes and make two easy substitutions. First, replace every egg except one with two egg whites. Drain some unsweetened applesauce and substitute it in equal measures for all the shortening in your recipe. Sift or stir together all the dry ingredients except for the sugar. Whisk together all the wet ingredients plus the sugar. Stir in whatever fruit is called for. Add the dry ingredients and stir until they are just moistened. Bake in the usual manner.

This technique will make you a successful quick-bread baker from the very first time.

RECIPES

APRICOT QUICK BREAD

MAKES 1 LOAF, 12 SLICES

A WOMAN FROM LOUISIANA sent me this wonderful recipe. She wrote that it was already low in fat except for the ½ cup of pecans (40 grams of fat). I reduced the pecans to 2 tablespoons, since this wonderful bread wasn't the same when they were entirely eliminated. The flavor was tremendous, and a slice now contains only 1.4 fat grams with a meager 7.2 percent of the calories coming from fat.

This recipe calls for a unique technique during preparation. The batter is poured into the loaf pan and then allowed to stand for 30 minutes. This step seems to allow the flour to absorb moisture, thereby losing less steam when baked and resulting in a bread with a luxurious texture. So don't think that's a misprint; it's absolutely necessary.

1	cup dried apricots
2	cups all-purpose flour (not self-rising)
2	teaspoons baking powder
¼	teaspoon baking soda
1	cup granulated sugar
2	tablespoons drained unsweetened applesauce
1	large whole egg
¼	cup unsweetened pineapple juice
½	cup fresh-squeezed orange juice
2	tablespoons finely chopped pecans

1. Soak the apricots in warm water to cover for 30 minutes.

2. Lightly spray the bottom and sides of a 9-by-5-by-3-inch loaf pan with vegetable oil. Dust with flour, knocking out the excess. Set aside.

3. In a medium bowl, sift or stir together the flour, baking powder and baking soda. Set aside.

4. In a large mixing bowl, whisk together the sugar, drained applesauce and egg until thoroughly combined. Whisk in the fruit juices. Drain and chop the apricots and stir them in. Add the flour mixture and stir until the dry ingredients are just moistened. Pour the batter into the prepared pan and sprinkle the pecans evenly over the batter. Let stand for 30 minutes.

5. Set the oven rack in the middle and preheat the oven to 350 degrees F.

6. Bake the bread for 55 minutes, or until a toothpick inserted into the center comes out clean. Place the pan on a wire cooling rack and cool for 5 minutes. Run a knife around the pan edge to loosen the bread and lift it out. Return the bread to the rack to cool completely before serving.

NUTRITIONAL INFORMATION PER SLICE: 177 CALORIES, 1.4 G FAT, 2.9 G PROTEIN, 43 G CARBOHYDRATE, 18 MG CHOLESTEROL, 84 MG SODIUM.

Easy Buttermilk Gingerbread

MAKES 1 LOAF, 16 SQUARES

Gingersnap cookies have always been one of my favorites. In order for a gingersnap to truly snap, it has to be made with high-fat shortening that is solid at room temperature. Butter gives a better flavor but never the same snap.

When I decided gingersnap cookies were forbidden territory, I turned to gingerbread. Nothing compares to a gingerbread prepared from the freshest possible ingredients. It's hard to believe how little fat this gingerbread contains because the flavor explodes with ginger. This is a light snack cake.

2	cups all-purpose flour (not self-rising)
2	teaspoons baking powder
¼	teaspoon baking soda
¾	cup buttermilk
⅓	cup drained unsweetened applesauce
1	large whole egg
¾	cup dark molasses
½	cup granulated sugar
2	teaspoons ground ginger
1	teaspoon ground cinnamon
¼	teaspoon ground cloves
	Powdered sugar for sprinkling on top

1. Set the oven rack in the middle and preheat the oven to 350 degrees F. Lightly spray the bottom and sides of a 8-by-8-by-2-inch pan with butter-flavored vegetable oil. Set aside.

2. In a medium bowl, sift or stir together the flour, baking powder and baking soda. Set aside.

3. In a large mixing bowl, whisk together the buttermilk, drained applesauce, egg, molasses, sugar, ginger, cinnamon and cloves until well combined, about 45 seconds. Add the flour mixture and whisk until the dry ingredients are just moistened, about 25 seconds.

4. Pour the batter into the prepared pan and bake for 45 minutes, or until a toothpick inserted into the center comes out clean.

5. Set the pan on a wire rack until the bread is completely cooled. Dust the top with sifted powdered sugar before cutting into squares.

NUTRITIONAL INFORMATION PER SQUARE: 134 CALORIES, 0.7 G FAT, 2.3 G PROTEIN, 30.3 G CARBOHYDRATE, 14 MG CHOLESTEROL, 80 MG SODIUM.

LeanTip: This is wonderful with applesauce or a scoop of nonfat frozen vanilla yogurt.

North Carolina Skillet Cornbread

SERVES 6

In North Carolina, cornbread is just not cornbread unless it's prepared in a skillet. Bacon fat is normally used to grease the skillet. I started with a wonderful recipe shared with me by a generous North Carolina friend. I substituted drained unsweetened applesauce for the fat within the bread. However, the bread, if made properly, has a slightly crunchy crust from the greased skillet. Applesauce did not produce the authentic effect.

Consequently, for this part of the process, I substitute canola oil, the least saturated of all vegetable oils. It has no cholesterol. Was mine as good as the high-fat version? Almost. It came even closer when I drizzled on some North Carolina honey that came from the blossoms of a tulip poplar tree.

2	large egg whites
1	cup buttermilk
3	tablespoons drained unsweetened applesauce
2	teaspoons canola oil
1¼	cups yellow cornmeal, preferably stone-ground
½	cup all-purpose flour (not self-rising)
2	tablespoons granulated sugar
1½	teaspoons baking powder
½	teaspoon baking soda

1. Set the oven rack in the middle and preheat the oven to 425 degrees F.

2. In a medium mixing bowl, whisk the egg whites until bubbles appear. Whisk in the buttermilk and drained applesauce until well combined. Set aside.

3. Add the oil to an 8-inch cast-iron skillet and place in the heated oven for 4 minutes, until hot but not smoking.

4. Meanwhile, in a large mixing bowl, stir together the cornmeal, flour, sugar, baking powder and baking soda. Add the buttermilk mixture to the bowl and stir until the dry ingredients are just moistened.

5. Carefully remove the hot skillet from the oven. Tip and rock the skillet to distribute the oil across the bottom and slightly up the sides and set on a heat-safe surface. Spoon the batter into the skillet and smooth the top with the back of the spoon. Bake for 20 minutes, or until the cornbread is lightly browned and a toothpick inserted into the center comes out clean. Serve immediately, cut into wedges.

NUTRITIONAL INFORMATION PER SERVING: 198 CALORIES, 2.5 G FAT, 6.2 G PROTEIN, 38 G CARBOHYDRATE, 1.5 MG CHOLESTEROL, 222 MG SODIUM.

LeanSuggestions

■ ½ cup fresh or frozen corn kernels and/or 1 seeded, minced jalapeño pepper can be added to the batter at the same time the dry ingredients are added.

■ I love serving my cornbread with a strong-flavored honey or high-quality strawberry preserves. Neither has any fat and both enhance the flavor of the cornbread.

Fresh Strawberry Bread

MAKES 2 LOAVES, EACH WITH 12 SLICES

THIS RECIPE CAME FROM a reader about two years ago. She wrote, "I have a makeover request. It's a great strawberry bread—but so full of fat!" How full? Almost half (47 percent) of the calories came from fat. A single serving had over 15 fat grams and 284 calories. Zounds! I headed straight for my lean kitchen and began wringing the fat from her recipe.

For the first high-fat ingredient—three eggs—I substituted one whole egg and four egg whites, sending 10 fat grams packing. Next, for the 1 cup of vegetable oil, which contained 218 grams of fat and almost 2,000 fat calories, I substituted drained applesauce and gave hundreds of fat grams the boot, vaporizing 1,800 calories.

The bread was finished with 2 cups of chopped walnuts. Those 2 cups contained over 140 grams of fat, so I slashed the amount to ½ cup and finely chopped them. I made up for the lost flavor by adding black walnut flavoring, found in the baking section of every supermarket. So long to more than 100 fat grams.

Finally, I added a new twist. I added a packet of Butter Buds to the batter, and it worked like a charm. The reader had used frozen strawberries; I went with fresh.

Shortly, the loaves were out of my oven and sufficiently cool for tasting. My lean version was incredible. Even more amazing, a slice now contains only 1.7 fat grams (9.4 percent of calories) and 165 calories.

3	cups all-purpose flour (not self-rising)
1	tablespoon ground cinnamon
1	teaspoon baking soda
½	teaspoon salt
1	large whole egg
4	large egg whites
1	teaspoon vanilla extract

1½   teaspoons black walnut flavoring*
1   ½-ounce packet Butter Buds
1   cup drained unsweetened applesauce
2¼   cups granulated sugar
2½   cups thickly sliced fresh strawberries
½   cup finely chopped walnuts

1. Set the oven rack in the middle and preheat the oven to 350 degrees F. Lightly spray the bottom and sides of two 9-by-5-by-3-inch loaf pans with vegetable oil. Dust with flour, knocking out the excess. Set aside.

2. In a medium mixing bowl, whisk or stir the flour, cinnamon, baking soda and salt together. Set aside.

3. In a large mixing bowl, with an electric mixer, beat the egg and egg whites on medium speed until frothy, 30 to 45 seconds. Stop the mixer. Add the vanilla, black walnut flavoring, Butter Buds, applesauce and sugar, and mix on medium speed until the sugar seems to dissolve. By hand, stir in the strawberries. Add the dry ingredients, stirring just until moistened, about 20 seconds. The batter will appear slightly lumpy.

4. Divide the batter equally between the prepared loaf pans. Dust the top of each with ¼ cup of the walnuts. Bake for 60 minutes, or until a toothpick inserted in the center comes out clean.

5. Cool in the pans on wire racks for 5 minutes. Lift the breads out onto the rack and cool completely before serving.

NUTRITIONAL INFORMATION PER SLICE: 165 CALORIES, 1.7 G FAT, 3.3 G PROTEIN, 35.2 G CARBOHYDRATE, 9 MG CHOLESTEROL, 120 MG SODIUM.

LeanSuggestion: Substitute a heaping 2 cups fresh blueberries or a heaping 2 cups fresh, ripe peaches, cut into bite-size chunks.

Black walnut flavoring (not artificial) is found in most supermarkets in the section where vanilla extract is located.

Banana-Nut-Raisin Bread

MAKES 1 LOAF, 18 SLICES

My cousin Kathryn Mauer started making healthy changes to her food plan more than three years ago. She lost some weight and tells me that she's never felt better. A terrific cook who loves to bake, she created this recipe. The aroma drifting from a fresh-cut slice is cinnamon, but the flavor is bananas and walnuts all the way.

For breakfast, I toast a slice in a toaster oven and smear on some whipped nonfat cream cheese. Served with a generous slice of ripe cantaloupe, this is indeed a treat.

1	½-ounce packet Butter Buds
1	cup mashed very ripe bananas (about 2 medium)
2	cups sifted all-purpose flour (not self-rising)
⅔	cup granulated sugar
1¼	teaspoons baking powder
½	teaspoon baking soda
½	teaspoon ground cinnamon
½	cup drained unsweetened applesauce
½	cup nonfat egg substitute, such as Egg Beaters
½	cup chopped raisins
¼	cup chopped walnuts

1. Set the oven rack in the middle and preheat the oven to 350 degrees F. Lightly spray the bottom and sides of a 9-by-5-by-3-inch loaf pan with vegetable oil. Set aside.

2. In a small bowl, mix the Butter Buds into the mashed bananas with a fork. Set aside.

3. In a large mixing bowl, whisk or stir together the flour, sugar, baking powder, baking soda and cinnamon until well combined. With a pastry blender, cut in the applesauce until the mixture appears crumbly. With a rubber spatula, stir and fold the banana mixture and egg substitute into the dry ingredients until incorporated. Stir in the raisins and walnuts.

3. Pour the batter into the prepared loaf pan. Bake for 1 hour, or until a toothpick inserted into the center comes out clean.

4. Cool the bread in the pan on a wire rack for 10 minutes. Lift out the bread and return it to the rack to continue cooling. The bread is at its best when served warm. To store, cool completely, wrap in foil and store in a cool place or refrigerate.

NUTRITIONAL INFORMATION PER SLICE: 121 CALORIES, 1.2 G FAT, 2.7 G PROTEIN, 26 G CARBOHYDRATE, 0 CHOLESTEROL, 98 MG SODIUM.

Glazed Pumpkin Bread

MAKES 1 LOAF, 18 SLICES

Pumpkin is the foundation for this sensational quick bread. My cousin Kathryn Mauer created it using nutmeg, cloves, cinnamon and allspice—all spices normally found in a pumpkin pie. The crowning touch is a fresh lemon glaze.

2	cups sifted all-purpose flour (not self-rising)
1	teaspoon baking soda
½	teaspoon baking powder
½	teaspoon fresh-grated nutmeg
½	teaspoon ground cloves
½	teaspoon ground cinnamon
¼	teaspoon ground allspice
¼	teaspoon salt
1½	cups granulated sugar
1¼	cups canned solid-pack pumpkin
½	cup nonfat egg substitute, such as Egg Beaters
½	cup fresh-squeezed orange juice
¼	cup nonfat plain yogurt
1	½-ounce packet Butter Buds

GLAZE

¼	cup powdered sugar
2	teaspoons warm water
½	teaspoon fresh-squeezed lemon juice

1. Set the oven rack in the middle of the oven and preheat the oven to 350 degrees F. Lightly spray the bottom and sides of a 9-by-5-by-3-inch loaf pan with vegetable oil. Set aside.

2. Sift together the flour, baking soda, baking powder, nutmeg, cloves, cinnamon, allspice and salt. Set aside.

3. In a large bowl, whisk together the sugar, pumpkin, egg substitute, orange juice, yogurt and Butter Buds until well combined and the sugar seems to have dissolved, about 45 seconds to 1 minute. Add the dry ingredients to the bowl and, with a rubber spatula, stir and fold until just moistened, 30 to 40 seconds.

4. Pour the batter into the prepared pan and bake for 1 hour and 25 minutes, or until a toothpick inserted in the center comes out clean.

5. Cool the bread in the pan on a wire rack for 15 minutes. Lift the bread from the pan and return to the rack. Cool for 1 hour, or until thoroughly cooled.

6. **Glaze:** In a small bowl, whisk together the powdered sugar, water and lemon juice until combined. Brush the glaze evenly over the cooled bread and serve. To store, when the glaze is set and dry, wrap the bread in aluminum foil and refrigerate.

NUTRITIONAL INFORMATION PER SLICE: 132 CALORIES, 0.21 G FAT, 2.4 G PROTEIN, 31.3 G CARBOHYDRATE, TRACE CHOLESTEROL, 129 MG SODIUM.

LeanSuggestion: One cup seedless golden raisins added to the batter makes this tasty bread even better.

Zucchini Bread

MAKES 2 LOAVES, EACH WITH 12 SLICES

A READER from Des Plaines, Illinois, sent me the original for this recipe in response to a request in my column. She wrote, "I have made it many times and we really enjoy it, but with the eggs and oil, I can see that it is not very healthy."

Her original contained over 310 grams of fat. I took this delicious-sounding bread to my kitchen and then shared the new recipe in my newspaper column. A reader wrote, "My daughter in Birmingham, Alabama, has a garden so I sent her the Zucchini Bread recipe. Her response was 'fantastic,' and she liked the pineapple in it."

3	cups all-purpose flour
2	teaspoons baking soda
¼	teaspoon baking powder
1½	teaspoons ground cinnamon
¾	teaspoon fresh-grated nutmeg
1	teaspoon salt
1	large whole egg
4	large egg whites
1	cup drained unsweetened applesauce
2	cups granulated sugar
2	teaspoons vanilla extract
2	cups shredded unpeeled zucchini
1	8¼-ounce can crushed pineapple, well drained
1	cup chopped pitted dates
1	cup Grape-Nuts cereal

1. Set the oven rack in the middle and preheat the oven to 350 degrees F. Lightly spray the bottom and sides of two 9-by-5-by-3-inch loaf pans with vegetable oil.

2. In a medium bowl, stir or whisk together the flour, baking soda, baking powder, cinnamon, nutmeg and salt until well combined. Set aside.

3. In a large bowl, with an electric mixer, beat the egg, egg whites, applesauce, sugar and vanilla until the sugar has dissolved. On low speed, add the flour mixture and mix until the dry ingredients are just moistened. (The batter will appear lumpy.) By hand, fold in the zucchini, pineapple and dates.

4. Divide the batter equally between the loaf pans. Sprinkle ½ cup of the Grape-Nuts over the top of each and lightly press them into the batter.

5. Bake for 1 hour, or until a toothpick inserted in the center comes out clean. Remove the pans from the oven and set on a wire cooling rack. Cool completely before serving.

NUTRITIONAL INFORMATION PER SLICE: 177 CALORIES, 0.5 G FAT, 3.3 G PROTEIN, 41.6 G CARBOHYDRATE, 8.9 MG CHOLESTEROL, 211 MG SODIUM.

LeanTip: A slice of this bread, warmed in the microwave, and a cup of hot coffee makes an almost unbeatable start to the day. Served with a scoop of pineapple sorbet, this becomes a delightful dessert.

FRESH BLUEBERRY YOGURT MUFFINS

MAKES 12 MUFFINS

B Y COMBINING, adjusting and experimenting with two recipes, I created these wonderful muffins. They literally burst with the fresh flavor of this terrific berry. Using beaten egg white lightened them without adding any fat. Nonfat yogurt enriched them and made up for the vegetable oil found in most recipes.

2	cups all-purpose flour (not self-rising)
1	tablespoon baking powder
½	teaspoon salt
1	cup fresh blueberries, rinsed and picked over (or frozen), plus 12 whole blueberries for topping
4	large egg whites, at room temperature
½	cup plus 3 teaspoons granulated sugar
1	teaspoon vanilla extract
1½	cups plain nonfat yogurt, at room temperature

1. Set the oven rack in the middle of the oven and preheat the oven to 400 degrees F.

2. In a medium mixing bowl, stir together the flour, baking powder and salt. Add the blueberries and stir to lightly coat the berries with the flour. Set aside.

3. In a large bowl, with an electric mixer, beat the egg whites at high speed until they reach the soft-peak stage. Add the sugar, vanilla and yogurt. Mix for 15 seconds until combined. Turn off the mixer. Add the dry ingredients and the blueberries. With a rubber spatula, stir and fold together only until the flour is moistened. The batter is not meant to be smooth. Do not overmix.

4. Divide the batter evenly among the cups of a nonstick 12-cup muffin pan.* Place a blueberry in the center of each muffin. Sprinkle ¼ teaspoon of sugar evenly over each muffin.

5. Bake for 20 minutes or until golden. Remove from the tins immediately and let cool before serving.

NUTRITIONAL INFORMATION PER MUFFIN: 141 CALORIES, 0.3 G FAT, 4.9 G PROTEIN, 30 G CARBOHYDRATE, TRACE CHOLESTEROL, 221 MG SODIUM.

A standard muffin pan can be substituted. Spray each cup with vegetable oil before adding the batter.

LeanSuggestions

■ **Cinnamon-Raisin Muffins:** In a microwave-safe container, place 1 cup of raisins in 2 tablespoons of brandy or Cognac. Cover. Place in a microwave oven and microwave on high for 1 minute. Remove, uncover and set aside. Prepare muffins as directed, but omit the blueberries. Instead, drain the excess liquor and add the raisins to the flour mixture. Continue as directed. Combine the 3 teaspoons sugar with 2 teaspoons of ground cinnamon. Sprinkle about ¼ teaspoon of the mixture over each muffin. Bake as directed.

■ **Cinnamon-Green Apple Muffins:** Prepare the recipe as directed, but omit the blueberries. Instead, add 1 cup chopped green apples that have been sprinkled with a little lemon juice and drained to the flour mixture. Prepare according to directions. Prepare the cinnamon-sugar mixture as for Cinnamon-Raisin Muffins. Sprinkle about ¼ teaspoon of the mixture over each muffin. Bake as directed.

■ **Cherry Muffins:** Prepare the recipe as directed, but omit the blueberries. Instead, add 1 cup fresh sweet or tart cherries (or 1 cup dried cherries, soaked in warm white wine or water) to the flour mixture.

■ **Cherry-Nut Muffins:** Prepare the recipe as directed, but omit the blueberries. Instead add 1 cup fresh sweet or tart cherries (or dried cherries soaked in warm white wine or water) to the flour mixture. Finely chop 3 tablespoons of whole pecans or walnuts. (If using tart cherries, combine the nuts with the 3 tablespoons sugar.) Omit the 3 tablespoons of sugar from the topping and sprinkle ¼ teaspoon of the nuts over each muffin. (This will increase the fat content of each muffin to 10 percent of calories.)

■ **Apricot Muffins:** Prepare the recipe as directed, but add 1 tablespoon baby-food strained apricots with the sugar, vanilla and yogurt. Omit the blueberries and instead add 1 cup chopped fresh apricots (or 1 cup chopped dried apricots) to the flour mixture.

■ **Dried Cranberry and Orange Muffins:** Prepare as directed, but increase the sugar to ¾ cup and add 1 teaspoon pure orange extract (not imitation). Omit the blueberries and instead add 1 cup dried cranberries (available at some specialty food shops and supermarkets) soaked in hot water for 5 minutes, drained and patted dry. Sprinkle the top of each muffin with a couple thin strips of fresh orange zest and some granulated sugar. These are best served warm.

LEMON POPPY SEED MUFFINS

MAKES 15 LARGE MUFFINS

A COLUMN READER from Island Lake, Illinois, wrote me about her favorite muffin recipe: "As you can see, it is loaded with fat. Could you please try to adjust so it would be lower?" Taking a close look, I saw that a single large muffin contained almost 500 calories and 19 grams of fat (35 percent of calories). I identified the four problem ingredients and made substitutions. First, her recipe called for three eggs. I substituted four egg whites and left one whole egg. Goodbye to 10 fat grams. Second, her recipe called for 1 cup of vegetable oil. I am sure that it made her original muffins tender and moist, but it contains a whopping 218 grams of fat. I substituted a cup of drained unsweetened applesauce, kicked out 218 grams of fat and cut 1,734 fat calories, too. Third, her recipe contained 2 cups of whole milk. Simple substitution here: the same volume of skim milk. Adios to 17 fat grams. Finally, her recipe called for ½ cup of whole poppy seeds. Although those tiny blue seeds have fat—½ cup contains 31 grams of it, equal to 7 teaspoons of vegetable oil—I knew they had to stay.

Each of these dandy-tasting muffins contains 354 calories, 3 grams of fat (7.6 percent of calories).

5¾	cups all-purpose flour (not self-rising)
3	tablespoons baking powder
4	large egg whites
1	large whole egg
1	cup drained unsweetened applesauce
2	cups skim milk
2½	cups granulated sugar
⅓	cup fresh-squeezed lemon juice
2½	teaspoons lemon extract
½	cup whole poppy seeds

1. Set the oven rack in the middle and preheat the oven to 350 degrees F. Lightly spray oversize (also called Texas-size) muffin tins with vegetable oil.*

2. In large mixing bowl, stir or whisk the flour and baking powder together until the baking powder is well distributed. Set aside.

3. In a large mixing bowl, whisk or stir together the egg whites, whole egg, applesauce, milk and sugar until the sugar dissolves and the mixture is well combined, about 1½ minutes. Add the flour mixture and whisk or stir until the flour is just moistened, about 60 seconds. Add the lemon juice, lemon extract and poppy seeds and whisk until incorporated, 20 to 30 seconds.

4. Fill each cup three-fourths full with batter. Bake for 22 to 25 minutes, or until a toothpick inserted in the center comes out clean.

NUTRITIONAL INFORMATION PER MUFFIN: 354 CALORIES, 3 G FAT, 8.8 G PROTEIN, 78 G CARBOHYDRATE, 14.7 MG CHOLESTEROL, 334 MG SODIUM.

If you use regular-size muffin tins, you'll need 2 pans. Reduce the baking time to 17 minutes. If a toothpick inserted into the center does not come out clean, bake for 2 more minutes and test again.

Desserts

THERE WOULD NEVER HAVE BEEN any way for me to maintain my weight loss, even with a tastily altered food plan, without dessert. When I weighed over 300 pounds, an entire package of Oreos was dessert. Today, there are reduced-fat Oreos, but a whole package is never going to be considered a single serving.

When a commercial bakery introduced the first fat-free chocolate cake, I swooped down on my local grocery store and purchased one. I could barely contain my excitement when I got home. I burst into the house exclaiming, "Susan, you won't believe what I found. A fat-free chocolate cake."

We quickly proceeded to the kitchen table and sat down. I zipped open the cake box and cut two generous slices. I noticed there was no frosting. I placed the slices on the plates and handed one, with a fork, to Susan. We each eagerly took a bite. I looked at her and said one word, "Disappointing." The cake had a chocolate flavor, but it was flat. The cake's texture was slightly spongy and dry. We poured some skim milk on the cake, vainly in search of more moisture.

That moment began my search for great-tasting, rich, moist desserts that were also as low in fat as possible. I focused my efforts on creating chocolate desserts because those were the ones I loved the most. I could not stay on my lean path forever if the foods I was eating felt like deprivation dining. My new desserts had to scream chocolate. Above all, they had to have a good texture.

Most desserts are built on a platform of fat. Many use butter, which gives a great flavor and texture. You can slightly overbake a butter-based cake and still have it be moist because fat does not evaporate. A low-fat cake, overbaked for even a minute or two, will be drier than if it had been removed from the oven at the proper moment, so watch carefully.

Gumminess is another typical problem with ordinary homemade low-fat desserts. It usually results from overmixing. Food scientists go into long and tedious discussions about proteins, elasticity and mixing times. The bottom line is that mixing any lean batter for the least amount of time possible usually results in a decent texture.

Over the past four years, I have spent hundreds of hours testing dessert recipes and techniques. I used every imaginable substitution for fat, including prune puree and nonfat mayonnaise. Some recipes I made over and over again, changing my mixing times and blending techniques until I felt the texture was right. My neighbors, friends and my wife's co-workers have all been willing samplers (except for the prune brownies) and harsh critics, since many of them didn't give a flying fig for low-fat. When everyone, including me, was pleased, I knew I had finally achieved my goal. The desserts on the following pages are light, flavorful, moist, delicious and seemingly sinful. You'll swear you are indulging in something that must be bad for you.

I am not suggesting that my desserts can be eaten with abandon. They cannot. I eat desserts in normal portions and then stop. Those desserts intended for 12 people can be refrigerated, so they keep long enough to be consumed at a normal pace.

RECIPES

APPLE OATMEAL CRUMBLE

SERVES 6

ONE NIGHT MY WIFE surprised me with this recipe. Her original used to have ¼ cup of butter, which supplied 46 very saturated fat grams. Now, it has only 5.5 percent calories from fat but tastes as if there are many more.

- 4 cups thinly sliced tart apples (such as Gala, Jonagold or Winesap)
- 1 tablespoon fresh-squeezed lemon juice
- ¼ cup granulated sugar
- 1 cup quick-cooking oats
- ½ cup dark brown sugar
- ⅓ cup all-purpose flour (not self-rising)
- ¼ teaspoon ground cinnamon
  Pinch salt (optional)
- 4 teaspoons Butter Buds, mixed with ¼ cup hot water

1. Set the oven rack in the middle and preheat the oven to 375 degrees F. Lightly spray the bottom and sides of a shallow medium baking dish with vegetable oil and spread the sliced apples in it evenly. Sprinkle them with the lemon juice and granulated sugar. Set aside.

2. In a small bowl, combine the oats, brown sugar, flour, cinnamon and optional salt, stirring to combine. Sprinkle the oat mixture evenly over the apples. Drizzle the Butter Buds liquid over the top.

3. Bake for 30 minutes, or until apples are tender but not mushy. Allow to cool slightly. Serve warm.

NUTRITIONAL INFORMATION PER SERVING: 181 CALORIES, 1.6 G FAT, 2.7 G PROTEIN, 42 G CARBOHYDRATE, 0 CHOLESTEROL, 76 MG SODIUM.

LeanTip: *Frozen nonfat vanilla yogurt makes an excellent topping for this dessert.*

Black Bottom Cupcakes

MAKES 20 CUPCAKES

THIS WONDERFULLY RICH and moist dessert came from my friend Kalon Sloan of North Carolina. However, her recipe contained ⅓ cup vegetable oil, a whole egg, 6 ounces of chocolate chips and many more pecans. These ingredients vastly exceeded my lean restrictions. Hating to give up this cupcake, I switched to nonfat cream cheese and removed 80 fat grams. Using nonfat plain yogurt instead of vegetable oil saved another 72 fat grams. Adding a single ounce of mini-morsel chocolate chips meant every cupcake would still have little bits of chocolate in the filling but eliminated 40 fat grams. Finally, dusting the top with a small amount of ground pecans removed an additional 32 fat grams.

CHOCOLATE CHIP FILLING

- 2 large egg whites, at room temperature
- 8 ounces nonfat cream cheese, softened
- ⅓ cup granulated sugar
- ½ teaspoon vanilla extract
- 2 tablespoons mini-morsel semisweet chocolate chips

CUPCAKE BATTER

- 1½ cups all-purpose flour (not self-rising)
- ¼ cup unsweetened cocoa powder
- 1 teaspoon baking soda
- 1 teaspoon baking powder
- ½ teaspoon salt
- 1 cup water
- ½ cup plain nonfat yogurt
- 1 teaspoon vanilla extract

1   cup granulated sugar
2   tablespoons ground pecans

1. Set the oven rack in the middle and preheat the oven to 350 degrees F. Lightly spray the inside of 20 foil cupcake cups with vegetable oil.

2. Chocolate chip filling: In a small bowl, with an electric mixer, beat the egg whites until foamy. Add the cream cheese, sugar and vanilla and blend until smooth. By hand, stir in the chocolate chips. Set aside.

3. Cupcake batter: In a medium mixing bowl, whisk or stir together the flour, cocoa, baking soda, baking powder and salt until well combined, about 20 seconds. Set aside.

4. In a large mixing bowl, whisk together the water, yogurt and vanilla until combined, about 30 seconds. Add the sugar and whisk until dissolved, about 30 seconds. Add the flour mixture, and whisk until dry ingredients are just moistened, about 15 seconds. Do not overmix.

5. Fill each cupcake cup half full with batter. Top each with 1 tablespoon of the filling. Dust each cupcake top with about ¼ teaspoon of the pecans. Bake for 25 to 28 minutes, or until the tops spring back when gently pressed. Cool before serving.

NUTRITIONAL INFORMATION PER CUPCAKE: 113 CALORIES, 1.1 G FAT, 3.5 G PROTEIN, 76 G CARBOHYDRATE, 1.6 MG CHOLESTEROL, 177 MG SODIUM.

CREAM CHEESE FRUIT SQUARES

MAKES 24 SQUARES

T HESE REALLY GOT MY KNICKERS in a twist. A couple years ago, a magazine ran an ad displaying a richly colored picture of "easy cream cheese fruit squares" that was so appealing I wanted to take a bite right out of the page. Although it seemed smugly healthy, this dastardly goodie contained almost 1 stick of butter, three 8-ounce packages of cream cheese and 4 eggs. My trusty calculator showed me the dessert had 329 fat grams (almost 14 fat grams per serving), with almost 60 percent of the total calories coming from fat.

Guess what? The company could have created just as terrific a recipe with 3 percent of calories from fat by making a better crust with no butter. Use 1 whole egg and 6 egg whites, and say sayonara to the cholesterol-laden saturated fat of 3 egg yolks. Finally, wave a joyous farewell to the 240 fat grams from full-fat cream cheese by switching to nonfat cream cheese.

1	8-ounce package pitted dates
1½	cups graham cracker crumbs
2	tablespoons hot water
1	21-ounce can blueberry filling or topping
3	8-ounce packages nonfat cream cheese, at room temperature
¾	cup granulated sugar
1	large whole egg
6	large egg whites
1	teaspoon vanilla extract

1. Set the oven rack in the middle and preheat the oven to 325 degrees F. Lightly spray the bottom and sides of a 13-by-9-inch baking pan with vegetable oil.

2. In a food processor fitted with the steel blade, pulse the dates and graham cracker crumbs to begin chopping the dates, then process continuously for 20 to 25 seconds, or until small, pea-size lumps appear. Add the hot water and process for 5 to 10 seconds, or until it has a doughlike consistency.

3. Place the graham-cracker mixture in the bottom of the baking pan, shaking the pan to distribute evenly. Wet your fingertips and press the mixture firmly and evenly to the edge of the pan, wetting your fingertips as you go. Spoon the blueberry filling over the crust. Set aside.

4. In a large bowl, with an electric mixer, beat the cream cheese until smooth. Gradually beat in the sugar. Add the egg, egg whites and vanilla and beat until well blended. Pour the cream cheese mixture over the blueberries, spreading evenly with a spatula to the edge. Bake until set, about 45 minutes. Remove the pan from the oven and set on a wire rack to cool. Chill until cold, at least 2 hours, before serving.

NUTRITIONAL INFORMATION PER SQUARE: 132 CALORIES, 0.4 G FAT, 7.9 G PROTEIN, 24 G CARBOHYDRATE, 5.8 MG CHOLESTEROL, 247 MG SODIUM.

Soft Oatmeal Raisin Cookies

MAKES 3 DOZEN COOKIES

I HAVE LOVED GOOD COOKIES since even before I could speak. Grandmother Mauer was the "Queen of Cookies" in my family. When I gave up eating high-fat foods, cookies instantly hit my list of forbidden foods. I was not crazy about store-bought nonfat ones, so I set out to make my own. These have the terrific flavor and chewy texture of high-fat oatmeal raisin cookies but are completely guilt-free.

My recipe is based on the best oatmeal cookie I ever tasted, my grandmother's; she started making them more than 50 years ago. Her oatmeal cookies had ground pecans in them and were very crisp. These no longer contain the pecans, so they are soft and rich. It's very difficult to eat just one.

1	scant cup all-purpose flour (not self-rising)
½	teaspoon salt
1	teaspoon baking soda
½	cup nonfat plain yogurt
1	tablespoon Butter Buds
½	cup firmly packed light brown sugar
½	cup granulated sugar
2	large egg whites
1½	teaspoons vanilla extract
1	cup seedless raisins
1½	cups quick-cooking oats

1. Set the oven rack in the middle and preheat the oven to 375 degrees F.
2. In a medium bowl, stir or whisk together the flour, salt and baking soda. Set aside.

3. In a large bowl, with an electric mixer at medium speed, mix the yogurt, Butter Buds, brown sugar and granulated sugar together until combined, 30 to 45 seconds. Add the egg whites and vanilla, and mix for 10 seconds, until just combined. Add raisins and oats, and mix for 15 seconds. Add the sifted flour mixture and mix at low speed until just moistened. Do not overmix.

4. Drop the dough, by level tablespoons, onto cookie sheets lightly sprayed with vegetable oil. Bake for 8 minutes. Carefully press the center of a cookie; if it springs back, it is done.

5. Transfer the cookies to a wire rack and let cool completely. Store in an airtight container.

NUTRITIONAL INFORMATION PER COOKIE: 58 CALORIES, 0.3 G FAT, 1.4 G PROTEIN, 13.2 G CARBOHYDRATE, TRACE CHOLESTEROL, 61 MG SODIUM.

LeanNote: These cookies do not keep well at room temperature; refrigerate to store.

LeanSuggestion: For chocolate chip oatmeal cookies, omit the raisins and add 6 tablespoons mini-morsel semisweet chocolate chips to the batter. Mix and bake as above. This will increase the fat to 13.4 percent of calories.

Better-Than-"Hershey's Best" Brownies

MAKES 24 BROWNIES

ONE DAY, I was scanning the back of my favorite cocoa container and spied a brownie recipe. I love brownies big time and would have baked this version if it had contained fewer than 212 grams of fat in a batch. So I worked on the recipe and created what I believe to be better brownies. The flavor and texture are superb, yet the brownies have had over 199 grams of fat removed. I deep-sixed 15 fat grams by substituting egg whites. Hershey's original recipe called for 2 sticks (½ pound) of butter. Drained applesauce made 184 fat grams and over 1,400 calories vanish. Mine contain only 1.5 grams of fat per serving, thereby making the best better.

1½	cups unsweetened applesauce
1	cup all-purpose flour (not self-rising)
¾	cup unsweetened cocoa powder
½	teaspoon baking powder
¼	teaspoon salt
1	large whole egg
3	large egg whites
2	cups granulated sugar
2	teaspoons vanilla extract
3	tablespoons finely chopped pecans

1. Set the oven rack in the middle and preheat the oven to 350 degrees F. Lightly spray the sides and bottom of a 13-by-9-inch baking pan with vegetable oil. Set aside.

2. Place 1½ cups unsweetened applesauce in a mesh strainer placed over a bowl. Allow the applesauce to drain until needed.

3. In a medium bowl, whisk or stir together the flour, cocoa powder, baking powder and salt until combined, about 30 seconds. Set aside.

4. In a medium mixing bowl, whisk the egg and egg whites until bubbles appear and they are slightly foamy. Measure 1 cup of the drained applesauce and add it, along with the sugar and vanilla, to the egg mixture. Whisk until the sugar dissolves and the egg mixture is lighter, 20 to 30 seconds. Add the dry ingredients and whisk until just moistened, 20 to 25 seconds. Do not overmix, as this will make the brownies tough and rubbery.

5. Pour the batter into the prepared pan, sprinkle the chopped nuts evenly over the top and bake for 35 minutes. Check the brownies; if they have pulled away from the pan sides, they are done. Cool. Cut into 24 brownies, each 2 by 2 inches.

NUTRITIONAL INFORMATION PER BROWNIE: 108 CALORIES, 1.5 G FAT, 3 G PROTEIN, 23.5 G CARBOHYDRATE, 9 MG CHOLESTEROL, 50 MG SODIUM.

LeanTip: These brownies keep beautifully when covered and refrigerated.

Sensational Cream Cheese Brownies

MAKES 24 BROWNIES

THESE ARE THE ULTIMATE BROWNIES. Once, they had over 220 fat grams, with slightly fewer than 10 fat grams per brownie. Nasty stuff. Thanks to nonfat cream cheese, cocoa powder and fewer egg yolks, they now have less than a gram of fat per brownie.

2   8-ounce packages nonfat cream cheese, softened
2   medium whole eggs*
5   medium egg whites*
2   teaspoons vanilla extract
1   cup all-purpose flour (not self-rising)
⅔   cup unsweetened cocoa powder
½   teaspoon salt
2   cups granulated sugar
½   cup drained unsweetened applesauce
    (from about ¾ cup undrained)

1. Set the oven rack in the middle and preheat to 350 degrees F. Lightly spray a 9-by-13-inch pan with vegetable oil. Set aside.

2. In a large bowl, with an electric mixer, beat the cream cheese, 1 of the eggs, 2 of the egg whites and 1 teaspoon of the vanilla on medium speed until light and fluffy. Set aside.

3. In a medium bowl, whisk or stir together the flour, cocoa powder and salt. Set aside.

4. In a large mixing bowl, whisk the remaining 1 egg and remaining 3 egg whites until foamy, about 20 seconds. Add the sugar and whisk until dissolved and the eggs are light in color, about 30 seconds. Add the drained applesauce and the remaining 1 teaspoon vanilla and whisk for 10 seconds, until combined. Add the cocoa mixture and stir and whisk until the dry ingredients are just moistened, about 25 seconds.

5. Pour half the brownie batter into the prepared pan. Spoon the cream cheese mixture on top. Pour the remainder of the brownie mixture on top of the cream cheese layer. With a butter knife aimed toward the pan bottom, make swirls through the batter to produce a marbled effect.

6. Bake for 38 minutes (the center should be set). Place the pan on a wire cooling rack until the brownies are completely cool. Cut into 24 brownies, each 2 by 2 inches.

NUTRITIONAL INFORMATION PER BROWNIE: 118 CALORIES, 0.7 G FAT, 6.3 G PROTEIN, 22.7 G CARBOHYDRATE, 21 MG CHOLESTEROL, 152 MG SODIUM.

Medium eggs are necessary, since large eggs make the brownies too wet in the center.

Fresh Gingerbread Skillet Cake

MAKES 12 WEDGES

I HAVE LOVED GINGERBREAD ever since Nana, my maternal grandmother, made it. She used a box mix from Dromedary. Once it was baked and cooled, she dusted the top with powdered sugar and served it with butter. I would slather all four cut sides with the butter and take my first bite. The ginger would sing on my tongue, and the butter made it very rich.

Not only does from-scratch gingerbread taste better than anything from a box, but this version uses fresh ginger for a ginger bite like no other. It is a minor pain to get the fresh ginger in the right condition to make this bread, but the small effort produces a flavor beyond description.

8	ounces fresh gingerroot
3	cups cake flour (not self-rising)
¾	teaspoon baking soda
½	teaspoon salt
½	cup drained unsweetened applesauce
1	cup granulated sugar
1	large whole egg
2	large egg whites
1	cup molasses
	Powdered sugar for sprinkling on top

1. Set the oven rack in the middle and preheat the oven to 350 degrees F. Lightly spray the bottom and sides of a 12-inch cast-iron skillet with butter-flavored vegetable oil. Set aside.

2. Peel the ginger and coarsely chop. Process the chopped ginger in a food processor until pureed very fine. Rub the pureed ginger through a mesh strainer, pushing with the back of a wooden spoon, until it measures ⅓ cup. Discard the remaining ginger.

3. In a medium mixing bowl, stir or whisk together the flour, baking soda and salt. Set aside.

4. In a large mixing bowl, whisk together the ginger puree, applesauce, sugar, egg, egg whites and molasses until the sugar dissolves and the ingredients are combined, about 30 seconds. Add the flour mixture and whisk until the dry ingredients are just moistened, about 20 seconds.

5. Pour the batter into the prepared skillet. Bake for 20 minutes, or until the batter appears set. Lower the oven temperature to 325 degrees and continue baking for 20 minutes more, or until a toothpick inserted in the center comes out clean.

6. Remove from the oven and cool completely on a wire rack. Dust the top with sifted powdered sugar before serving.

NUTRITIONAL INFORMATION PER WEDGE: 161 CALORIES, 0.6 G FAT, 1.2 G PROTEIN, 39.3 G CARBOHYDRATE, 18 MG CHOLESTEROL, 166 MG SODIUM.

LeanSuggestion: 1½ tablespoons of ground ginger can be substituted for the fresh ginger.

Celebration Carrot Cake

MAKES A 10-INCH BUNDT CAKE, SERVES 12

THIS IS A RICH, MOIST CAKE. My friend David says the original version of this delicious cake has concluded his family's Thanksgiving dinner for as long as he can remember. Drained applesauce substituted for 1 cup of butter and egg whites for whole eggs now make this a perfect ending to any dinner, Thanksgiving or not.

2	cups all-purpose flour (not self-rising)
2	teaspoons baking powder
1	teaspoon baking soda
¼	teaspoon salt
½	teaspoon ground nutmeg
½	teaspoon ground cinnamon
1	cup drained unsweetened applesauce (from 1½ cups undrained)
1½	cups dark brown sugar
2	teaspoons fresh-squeezed lemon juice
1	large whole egg
3	large egg whites
4	cups finely grated carrots (about 1 pound)

1. Set the oven rack in the lower third and preheat the oven to 325 degrees F. Lightly spray a 10-inch Bundt pan with vegetable oil. Set aside.

2. In a large bowl, sift together the flour, baking powder, baking soda, salt, nutmeg and cinnamon. Sift twice more. Set aside.

3. In a large bowl, with an electric mixer, beat the applesauce, brown sugar, lemon juice, egg and egg whites at medium-high speed until smooth. Add the carrots and continue mixing until combined. Turn off the mixer. Add all the dry ingredients to the bowl at once. Mix on low speed until the dry ingredients are moist but not smooth, about 20 seconds.

4. Pour the batter into the prepared pan. Bake for 30 minutes. Increase the oven heat to 375 degrees and continue baking for 20 minutes more. A toothpick inserted into the center of the cake should come out clean.

5. Remove the pan from the oven. Cool for 5 minutes and invert onto a wire cooling rack. Cool completely. Decorate with Cream Cheese Frosting (page 432).

NUTRITIONAL INFORMATION PER SERVING (WITHOUT FROSTING): 182 CALORIES, 0.8 G FAT, 4 G PROTEIN, 40 G CARBOHYDRATE, 18 MG CHOLESTEROL, 217 MG SODIUM.

LeanSuggestion: One cup dried currants, added with the carrots, makes this cake even better.

Chocolate Upside-Down Cake

MAKES 1 RECTANGULAR CAKE, SERVES 16

My great-grandmother "Nama" Matthews was known far and wide for this incredible cake. She took the much higher-fat version to church meetings. I am certain the members could barely wait for business to be concluded so this luscious cake could be served.

Since it is eggless, the texture of the cake is similar to a very rich brownie. The chocolate sauce sinks to the bottom during baking and is spooned over the cake for serving.

CAKE

2	cups all-purpose flour (not self-rising)
¼	cup unsweetened cocoa powder
4	teaspoons baking powder
1⅔	cups granulated sugar
1	cup skim milk, at room temperature
¼	cup nonfat plain yogurt
2	teaspoons vanilla extract
1	ounce unsweetened chocolate, melted and cooled slightly

SAUCE

1	cup granulated sugar
1	cup firmly packed dark brown sugar
½	cup plus 2 tablespoons unsweetened cocoa powder
1¾	cups hot water

1. Set the oven rack in the middle and preheat the oven to 325 degrees F. Lightly spray the bottom and sides of a 9-by-13-inch glass baking dish with butter-flavored vegetable oil. Set aside.

2. Cake: In a medium mixing bowl, whisk or stir together the flour, cocoa powder and baking powder, about 30 seconds. Set aside.

3. In a large mixing bowl, whisk together the sugar, milk, yogurt, vanilla and melted chocolate until combined, about 1 minute. Add the dry ingredients to the bowl and whisk until they are just moistened, 30 to 40 seconds. Pour the batter into the prepared dish; smooth the top. Set aside while preparing sauce.

4. Sauce: In a medium bowl, whisk together the sugars and cocoa. Gradually add the hot water and whisk until the sugar is dissolved and the sauce is smooth, about 30 seconds. Gently drizzle the sauce over the back of a spoon or rubber spatula onto the cake batter, covering completely. (Some of the batter may float up from the bottom; do not be concerned.)

5. Bake until the cake is firm to the touch, about 50 minutes. Allow the cake to cool slightly, about 30 minutes. Run a knife around the edge of the dish to release the sides. Cut the warm cake into 16 squares. Transfer the squares to serving plates. Spoon the fudge sauce from the bottom of the baking dish over each piece and serve.

NUTRITIONAL INFORMATION PER SERVING: 242 CALORIES, 1.6 G FAT 3.3 G PROTEIN, 58 G CARBOHYDRATE, 0.3 MG CHOLESTEROL, 108 MG SODIUM.

LeanSuggestion: This cake can be cooled completely and then covered. The cake squares can be removed as needed and drizzled with some sauce; cover the remaining cake. The cake will keep well in this manner for about 2 days.

Too-Tasty-to-Be-No-Fat Chocolate Cake

SERVES 12

THIS RECIPE WAS THE VERY FIRST ONE I created that satisfied my chocolate tooth. It remains high on my "favorite" list. Not only does it taste like a devil's food cake but if prepared properly, it is also very close in texture to high-fat cakes. It is about as foolproof as a cake gets, too. If you use a high-sided pan, you'll be a successful baker the first time you try this. This cake is definitely a winner.

1	cup all-purpose flour (not self-rising)
⅓	cup plus 1 tablespoon Dutch-process unsweetened cocoa powder, plus more for dusting pan
1	teaspoon baking powder
1	teaspoon baking soda
6	large egg whites, at room temperature
1⅓	cups firmly packed dark brown sugar
1	cup nonfat plain yogurt
1	teaspoon vanilla extract

TOPPING

1	tablespoon Dutch-process unsweetened cocoa powder
1	tablespoon powdered sugar

1. Set the oven rack in the middle and preheat the oven to 350 degrees F. Lightly spray the bottom and sides of a 9-inch high-sided springform pan with vegetable oil. Dust the bottom and sides of the pan with cocoa powder; tap out the excess. Set aside.

2. In a medium mixing bowl, whisk or stir the flour, cocoa, baking powder and baking soda together, about 30 seconds. Set aside.

3. In a large bowl, with an electric mixer, beat the egg whites, brown sugar, yogurt and vanilla until blended, 1 to 2 minutes. Turn off the mixer. Add the dry ingredients to the bowl. Set the mixer on low and blend until dry ingredients are just moistened. This will take about 10 seconds and no more than 15 seconds. Do not overmix. This is not a smooth batter like that of normal cakes.

4. Pour the batter into the prepared pan and bake for 35 minutes, or until a toothpick inserted into the center comes out clean.

5. Cool in the pan on a wire rack for 15 minutes. With a knife, loosen the cake from the sides of the pan and release the pan bottom from the outer ring. Remove the outer ring. Cool the cake completely.

6. Topping: Combine the cocoa powder and powdered sugar in a small bowl. Put the cocoa mixture in a fine sieve and dust the top of the cake before serving.

NUTRITIONAL INFORMATION PER SERVING: 128 CALORIES, 0.7 G FAT, 4.8 G PROTEIN, 27.6 G CARBOHYDRATE, TRACE CHOLESTEROL, 148 MG SODIUM.

CHOCOLATE PUDDING

SERVES 4

WHEN I WAS A CHILD, my maternal grandmother, Nana, would pack a picnic lunch and take me for a nice walk down to a park at the edge of Lake Michigan. We would find a comfortable spot, spread out a blanket and listen to the lake. Then we would have lunch. Since she knew I was crazy for chocolate pudding, she always had some hidden in the bottom of the basket ready to bring out "if you're a member of the Clean Plate Club." Well, I was a charter member.

Chocolate pudding is my comfort food. You can make boxed chocolate pudding almost fat-free by using skim, rather than whole, milk. If you would like to make it from scratch, controlling the quality of every ingredient, give this a try.

½	cup granulated sugar
¼	cup cornstarch
3	tablespoons Dutch-process unsweetened cocoa powder
2¾	cups skim milk
2	teaspoons dry Butter Buds
1	teaspoon vanilla extract

1. In a medium nonstick saucepan, stir together the sugar, cornstarch and cocoa. Place the pan over medium heat and add 1 cup of the milk to the saucepan. Whisk until the sugar is dissolved and the cornstarch is evenly dispersed.

2. Whisk in the remaining 1¾ cups milk and the Butter Buds. Bring to a low boil, stirring constantly. Boil for 1 minute, stirring. Remove the pan from the heat.

3. Stir in the vanilla. Pour into 1-cup heatproof bowls or custard cups. Chill for about 3 hours, or until cold.

NUTRITIONAL INFORMATION PER SERVING: 195 CALORIES, 0.7 G FAT, 6.3 G PROTEIN, 44 G CARBOHYDRATE, 2.8 MG CHOLESTEROL, 124 MG SODIUM.

LeanTips

■ Stirring continuously is important because the cocoa can settle to the bottom of the saucepan and scorch, giving the finished pudding a burnt flavor.

■ If you find the "skin" that forms on puddings unappealing, cut squares of plastic wrap slightly larger than the top of the pudding containers, and quickly (and carefully) allow them to settle into the pudding before it sets. Chill. Remove before serving.

LeanSuggestions

■ For vanilla pudding, omit the cocoa and increase the vanilla to 1½ teaspoons.

■ For butterscotch pudding, substitute brown sugar for white, omit the cocoa and increase the dry Butter Buds to 3 teaspoons.

■ For chocolate almond pudding, add 2 to 3 drops of almond extract or 2 teaspoons Amaretto liqueur.

Vanilla Custard with Fresh Blueberry Sauce

SERVES 4

ONE OF MY FAVORITE TREATS when I was young was Grandmother Mauer's wonderful vanilla egg custard. It was heaven in a cup. She always tucked a few of her gingersnap cookies around the edge of the plate on which her custard was served. The combination of those two made my eyes sparkle and lifted my spirits. When I was older, I began experimenting with Grandma's beloved custard recipe. I tried it fifty-fifty: half-and-half and whipping cream.

Today, my custard is as close to fat-free as custard gets, thanks to nonfat egg substitute and skim milk. The small amount of diet margarine adds just enough fat to enrich the flavor. Smooth and creamy-tasting, the custard is crowned with a fresh-fruit topping.

CUSTARD

½ cup nonfat egg substitute, such as Egg Beaters
½ cup granulated sugar
⅔ cup skim milk
2 teaspoons reduced-calorie (not fat-free) margarine, melted
1 teaspoon vanilla extract
¼ cup all-purpose flour (not self-rising)

FRUIT TOPPING

2 tablespoons granulated sugar
2 tablespoons water
2 teaspoons cornstarch
1 teaspoon grated lemon rind
2 teaspoons fresh-squeezed lemon juice
1 pint fresh blueberries

1. **Custard:** Set the oven rack in the lower third and preheat the oven to 325 degrees F.

2. In a small bowl, with an electric mixer, beat the egg substitute on high speed for 1 minute. Add the sugar and beat for 1 more minute. Add the milk, melted margarine and vanilla, beating well. Add the flour, beating until well blended.

3. Pour the mixture into four 6-ounce custard cups sprayed with vegetable oil. Place the cups in a medium baking pan and add water to the pan to a depth of 1 inch. Bake for 30 minutes, or until set. Remove the pan from the oven. Remove the cups from the pan and set aside.

4. **Fruit topping:** In a microwave-safe bowl, whisk together the sugar, water, cornstarch, lemon rind and lemon juice until the sugar dissolves. Add the blueberries, stirring well. Microwave on high for 3 minutes. Stir and then microwave on high for 2 minutes more, or until thickened and bubbly. Divide and spoon evenly over the baked custards. Refrigerate the custards until well chilled before serving.

NUTRITIONAL INFORMATION PER SERVING: 232 CALORIES, 1.6 G FAT, 5.5 G PROTEIN, 51.3 G CARBOHYDRATE, 0.8 MG CHOLESTEROL, 88 MG SODIUM.

LeanSuggestions

■ For a wonderful lemon custard, substitute 1 teaspoon grated lemon rind and ¼ cup fresh-squeezed lemon juice for the vanilla extract and proceed as directed.

■ If red, black or golden raspberries are in season, substitute 1 pint for the blueberries and proceed as directed.

Banana Pudding

SERVES 12

FROM MY FIRST TASTE of true banana pudding, I was hooked. Although its flavor was superb and the texture was wonderfully creamy, it contained a large amount of fat. The pudding was a very rich egg custard, and the vanilla wafers lining the pan and placed in between the layers of pudding were just as full of fat as any cookie.

Keebler unlocked the lean door for me when they debuted their reduced-fat vanilla wafers. I used vanilla pudding mix, knowing I could make it nonfat by preparing it with skim milk. But to give it a creamy rich texture, I pureed a banana into the milk before adding it to the mix.

60	Keebler fat-reduced vanilla wafers
6	large bananas, peeled, cut crosswise into ¼-inch thick slices, plus 1 banana, peeled and cut into chunks
4	cups skim milk
2	3-ounce packages vanilla pudding mix (not instant)

1. Line the bottom of a 3-quart heatproof glass dish with 20 vanilla wafers. Cover the vanilla wafers with a layer of sliced bananas (about 2 whole bananas). Set aside.

2. Place the banana chunks and ½ cup of the skim milk in a blender and puree until smooth, about 10 seconds. Transfer the banana puree to a heavy-bottomed medium saucepan. Add the remaining 3½ cups milk and the pudding mixes. Over medium heat, stirring constantly, cook until the mixture comes to a full boil, about 4 minutes. Remove the pan from the heat.

3. Pour one-third (1½ cups) of the pudding over the bananas and wafers, spreading it to the edge. Place a layer of 20 vanilla wafers and banana slices on the pudding layer and cover with the second third (1½ cups) of the pudding. Place a final layer of wafers and banana slices over the pudding and top with the remaining pudding. Chill for 3 to 4 hours, until set, before serving.

NUTRITIONAL INFORMATION PER SERVING: 225 CALORIES, 2.5 G FAT, 4.5 G PROTEIN, 49 G CARBOHYDRATE, 1.3 MG CHOLESTEROL, 221 MG SODIUM.

LeanTip: If you are concerned about sugar in your diet, there is at least one brand of cook-and-serve vanilla pudding mix sweetened with aspartame (NutraSweet) available in most supermarkets. This product can be substituted for the vanilla pudding mix in this recipe.

Luscious Fat-Free Rice Pudding

SERVES 6

MY COUSIN K took it as a personal mission to create a fat-free rice pudding, taking out the egg yolks and whole milk and using dates to add flavor. It worked like a charm.

- 1½ cups skim milk
- ⅓ cup clover honey
- ½ cup nonfat egg substitute, such as Egg Beaters
- 2 teaspoons vanilla extract
- ½ teaspoon ground cinnamon
- ¼ cup raisins
- ¼ cup dates
- 2 cups cooked short-grain white rice, such as Arborio
  Fresh-grated nutmeg

1. Preheat the oven to 325 degrees F.

2. In a medium mixing bowl, whisk together the milk, honey, egg substitute, vanilla and cinnamon.

3. Put the raisins and dates in a food processor and chop for 20 to 30 seconds. Stir the rice, raisins and dates into the milk mixture.

4. Ladle into six ½-cup custard cups and dust each lightly with the nutmeg. Place the custard cups in a large baking pan and add hot water to the pan to a depth of 1 inch.

5. Bake for about 55 minutes, or until the custards are set in the center and light brown on top. Carefully remove the cups from the baking pan to cool. Serve warm or chilled.

NUTRITIONAL INFORMATION PER SERVING: 194 CALORIES, 0.3 G FAT, 5.7 G PROTEIN, 43 G CARBOHYDRATE, 1 MG CHOLESTEROL, 62 MG SODIUM.

RICH CHOCOLATE FUDGE FROSTING

MAKES ENOUGH TO FILL AND FROST A TWO-LAYER CAKE OR SHEET CAKE, OR TO THICKLY FROST A 13-BY-9-INCH CAKE

MANY PEOPLE who made my Too-Tasty-to-Be-No-Fat Chocolate Cake asked if there were some way to frost it with a chocolate buttercream–like frosting. Since butter was the base, I first believed that it would be impossible. Then Promise brought out a nonfat margarine with an improved flavor. I went to the kitchen and began experimenting. I threw out many failures, mostly because this product does not act like butter. I finally came up with a good buttercream frosting. The small amount of fat here comes from the cocoa, which has 3 grams per ounce, and the nonfat margarine, which actually contains small amounts of fat.

I can't keep from dipping into a bowl of this frosting and licking it off my fingers.

½	cup Promise Ultra Fat Free Margarine
¾	cup Dutch-process unsweetened cocoa powder
2	tablespoons skim milk
1½	teaspoons vanilla extract
3½	cups powdered sugar, sifted

1. In a small bowl, with an electric mixer, beat the margarine and cocoa on medium speed until the mixture is well combined (it will appear dry and crumbly).

2. Turn off the mixer. Add the milk and vanilla to the bowl. Set the mixer on medium-low and mix until combined (the mixture will appear thick, like clay).

3. Add the sugar in three parts. (The first cup of sugar will make the mixture thinner and appear runny. Do not worry, the frosting will thicken and become spreadable as you continue adding the sugar.) Mix until smooth and creamy and spread on cooled cake.

NUTRITIONAL INFORMATION PER TABLESPOON: 62 CALORIES, 0.4 G FAT, 0.5 G PROTEIN, 15.8 G CARBOHYDRATE, TRACE CHOLESTEROL, 23.6 MG SODIUM.

CREAM CHEESE FROSTING

MAKES ABOUT 1 CUP,
ENOUGH TO FROST THE TOP OF A 9-INCH CAKE

To create this frosting, I started with a package of nonfat cream cheese, some powdered sugar and a bottle of vanilla extract. I added the cream cheese to my food processor and started adding small amounts of vanilla and sugar. I'd stop the processor and take a very small taste, then continue adding sugar and vanilla until it was perfect. The consistency is stiff enough to pipe out of a pastry bag, or it can be spread with a frosting spatula. Either way, it is delicious.

- 8   ounces Healthy Choice nonfat cream cheese, at room temperature
- 1   teaspoon vanilla extract
- 6   tablespoons powdered sugar, sifted

1. In a food processor fitted with the steel blade, process the cream cheese, vanilla and sugar for 5 seconds. Scrape down the sides of the bowl and process for 5 seconds more, until the frosting is smooth and combined.

2. Fit a pastry bag with a small round tip. With a rubber spatula, transfer the frosting from the processor to the pastry bag. Use to decorate a cake creatively.

NUTRITIONAL INFORMATION PER TABLESPOON: 36 CALORIES, TRACE FAT, 4 G PROTEIN, 4.3 G CARBOHYDRATE, 3.3 MG CHOLESTEROL, 133 MG SODIUM.

LeanTip: To fill and frost a 9-inch two-layer cake, triple the recipe.

Chocolate Syrup

MAKES 3½ CUPS

YOU CAN MAKE YOUR OWN chocolate syrup at home, and know exactly what is in it. The fat in this recipe comes from the cocoa, which has (if you use Hershey's) 27 percent fat calories. Your reward is only 5.1 percent fat calories.

- 1 cup unsweetened cocoa powder
- 1 cup hot water
- 1 cup clover honey
- ½ cup firmly packed dark brown sugar
- Pinch salt (optional)
- 1 tablespoon vanilla extract

1. Place the cocoa powder, hot water, honey, brown sugar and optional salt in a heavy medium saucepan over medium-low heat. Stir constantly until melted and smooth. With the pan still on the heat, using a portable hand mixer, beat the syrup until it has a satiny texture, 3 to 4 minutes. Stir in the vanilla. Remove the saucepan from the heat and cool completely.

2. Pour into a 1-quart glass jar, seal and refrigerate. This sauce keeps well for 2 weeks and may be frozen.

NUTRITIONAL INFORMATION PER TABLESPOON: 26 CALORIES, 0.2 G FAT, 0.3 G PROTEIN, 6.8 G CARBOHYDRATE, 0 CHOLESTEROL, 4 MG SODIUM.

LeanTip: Serve over frozen nonfat vanilla yogurt for a low-sin treat.

LEAN N' CREAMY TOPPING

MAKES 2½ CUPS

WHIPPED CREAM, the luscious fat-filled substance that puts the sun in a sundae, is a big fat problem. I sailed off to my local supermarket to check out whipped cream substitutes, thinking they might be a decent alternative. What I learned may shock you.

According to my nutritional analysis books, nondairy whipped toppings, such as Cool Whip, contain about 7 percent more fat than pressurized real whipped cream. Not only do products like Cool Whip have more fat, they have more saturated fat: exactly 87 percent more.

The nondairy fats in Cool Whip and other brands are a mixture of hydrogenated coconut and palm kernel oils, two of the most saturated oils there are. In fact, coconut oil and palm kernel oil both contain more than twice as much saturated fat as lard. Coconut oil has no cholesterol, which whipped cream has. But cholesterol consumption doesn't raise LDL ("bad cholesterol") blood levels nearly as much as the consumption of saturated fat. The liquid coconut oil and palm kernel oil contained in Cool Whip have more than three times as much saturated fat, measure for measure, than does heavy cream.

My whipped topping is smooth in texture, creamy on the tongue and has only 0.1 gram of fat and no saturated fat per 2 tablespoons. Hooked on chocolate-flavored nondairy whipped toppings? You can make mine chocolate, too.

6	ounces Kraft Philadelphia Free Fat-Free cream cheese, at room temperature
1	cup nonfat sour cream
½	cup silken extra-firm tofu
2½	teaspoons vanilla extract
7	tablespoons superfine sugar

Add all the ingredients to a food processor fitted with the steel blade. Process until very smooth, scraping down the processor bowl several times, about 3 minutes.

NUTRITIONAL INFORMATION PER 2 TABLESPOONS: 40 CALORIES, 0.1 G FAT, 2.1 G PROTEIN, 4.8 G CARBOHYDRATE, 2.9 MG CHOLESTEROL, 64 MG SODIUM.

LeanSuggestions

■ **Chocolate Whipped Topping:** Increase the sugar by 2 tablespoons and add 2 tablespoons unsweetened cocoa powder. Proceed as directed.

■ **Chocolate-Almond Whipped Topping:** Increase the sugar by 2 tablespoons, add 2 tablespoons unsweetened cocoa powder and ¼ teaspoon almond extract. Proceed as directed.

■ **Chocolate-Coconut Whipped Topping:** Increase the sugar by 2 tablespoons, add 2 tablespoons unsweetened cocoa powder and 1 teaspoon coconut flavoring. Proceed as directed.

■ **Almond Whipped Topping:** Add ¼ teaspoon almond extract or 1 tablespoon Amaretto liqueur. Proceed as directed.

■ **Coconut Whipped Topping:** Add 1 teaspoon coconut flavoring. Proceed as directed.

■ **Lemon Whipped Topping:** Increase the sugar by 2 tablespoons, reduce the sour cream by 2 tablespoons and add 1 tablespoon of fresh-squeezed lemon juice and 1 teaspoon of grated lemon zest. Proceed as directed.

■ **Butterscotch Whipped Topping:** Reduce the sugar by 2 tablespoons and add 2 tablespoons of dark brown sugar. Proceed as directed.

LeanTip: The plain topping is great on any flavor of gelatin dessert or spooned over a low-fat chocolate pudding. Chocolate topping is wonderful spooned over a slice of angel food cake. Spoon lemon topping over a low-fat vanilla custard, coconut topping over mixed fruit salad.

Springtime Fruit Mélange

SERVES 4

Looking for a great way to start a lean and special Sunday brunch? Try bright orange slices, green kiwi and red strawberries sweetened with a light, yet flavorful tangerine syrup.

TANGERINE SYRUP*

1 tablespoon tangerine rind (colored part only, no pith),
   removed with a zester or fine grater
½ cup fresh-squeezed tangerine juice
¼ cup water
2 tablespoons granulated sugar
¼ teaspoon vanilla extract

FRUIT

2 very large or 3 medium navel oranges
4 ripe kiwi fruits
1 pint strawberries, rinsed, drained, dried and hulled
  Mint leaves for garnish

1. Tangerine syrup: Bring the tangerine rind, tangerine juice, water and sugar to a boil in a small non-aluminum saucepan, stirring occasionally. Simmer, uncovered, for 5 minutes, until slightly thickened. Remove from the heat and cool to room temperature. Stir in the vanilla.

2. Fruit: Slice the ends off the navel oranges so they will stand upright on a cutting board. With a sharp, serrated knife, remove the rind down to flesh, cutting downwards. Holding each orange upright in the palm of the hand, cut between the membranes to release the segments so you have whole segments with no transparent membrane covering them. Transfer the segments to a medium glass or ceramic mixing bowl. Peel the kiwi fruits, cut them into sixths lengthwise, and add them to the bowl. Pour the syrup over, stir gently and set aside.

3. Quarter the strawberries, if large, or slice them in half if they are small. Just before serving, add the strawberries to the fruit mixture and gently toss to mix.

NUTRITIONAL INFORMATION PER SERVING: 150 CALORIES, 0.8 G FAT, 2 G PROTEIN, 37 G CARBOHYDRATE, 0 CHOLESTEROL, 7 MG SODIUM.

The syrup can be made in advance and refrigerated.

COLD PEACH SOUP WITH FRESH BLUEBERRIES

SERVES 4

ONE SATURDAY, I bought way too many peaches to eat during the week. They were ripe when we were having some good friends over for dinner. So for dessert, I prepared this peach soup. It glowed in the bottom of the bowl, the blueberries floated around the top and the sprig of fresh mint from my garden made it a picture. When I brought the bowls to the table, topped with a dollop of nonfat sour cream, my guests ooohed and aaahed.

4	cups sliced peeled fresh peaches (or a 1-pound package frozen peaches)
½	cup fresh-squeezed orange juice
½	cup unsweetened pineapple juice
¼	cup fresh-squeezed lime juice
½	cup nonfat plain yogurt
½	cup nonfat sour cream, plus more for topping
4	tablespoons powdered sugar, or to taste
½	teaspoon grated fresh gingerroot
½	cup fresh blueberries, rinsed and picked over
	Fresh mint sprigs

1. Place the peach slices, orange, pineapple and lime juices, yogurt and sour cream in a food processor fitted with the steel blade. Process until smooth, about 45 seconds. Add the sugar and ginger and process until incorporated, 4 to 5 seconds.

2. Transfer the soup to a glass or ceramic bowl, cover and chill until cold, about 1 hour.

3. Before serving, stir in the blueberries and divide among 4 chilled serving bowls. Garnish with the mint sprigs and a dollop of sour cream.

NUTRITIONAL INFORMATION PER SERVING: 160 CALORIES, 0.2 G FAT, 2.8 G PROTEIN, 53 G CARBOHYDRATE, 4.5 MG CHOLESTEROL, 68 MG SODIUM.

INDEX